Little
Theologians

David M. Csinos

Little Theologians

Children, Culture, and the Making of Theological Meaning

McGill-Queen's University Press
Montreal & Kingston • London • Chicago

ISBN 978-0-2280-0382-3 (cloth)
ISBN 978-0-2280-0383-0 (paper)
ISBN 978-0-2280-0439-4 (ePDF)
ISBN 978-0-2280-0440-0 (ePUB)

Legal deposit fourth quarter 2020
Bibliothèque nationale du Québec

This book has been published with the help of a grant from the Canadian Federation for the Humanities and Social Sciences, through the Awards to Scholarly Publications Program, using funds provided by the Social Sciences and Humanities Research Council of Canada.

Funded by the Government of Canada | Financé par le gouvernement du Canada | Canada | Canada Council for the Arts | Conseil des arts du Canada

We acknowledge the support of the Canada Council for the Arts.

Nous remercions le Conseil des arts du Canada de son soutien.

Library and Archives Canada Cataloguing in Publication

Title: Little theologians : children, culture, and the making of theological meaning / David M. Csinos.
Names: Csinos, David M., 1984- author.
Description: Includes bibliographical references and index.
Identifiers: Canadiana (print) 20200289101 | Canadiana (ebook) 20200289276 | ISBN 9780228003823 (cloth) | ISBN 9780228003830 (paper) | ISBN 9780228004394 (ePDF) | ISBN 9780228004400 (ePUB)
Subjects: LCSH: Children—Religious life—Canada. | LCSH: Religion and culture—Canada. | LCSH: United Church of Canada.
Classification: LCC BV4571.3 .C75 2020 | DDC 270.083—dc23

In memory of my grandparents,
George and Elizabeth Csinos
and
Allan and Marceline Masson,
and my great aunt,
Laurette Delorme.

My inheritance from you has infused my life
with an intercultural spirit.

Contents

Table and Figures

Table

Figures

Acknowledgments

This book would not have been possible without the effort, assistance, and support of many people. I'm particularly grateful to the people of the congregations that I have here called Parkdale United Church, Messiah Methodist United Church, Burke Street United Church, and Colkirk United Church. Their willingness to welcome me into their lives and open themselves to me has left me humbled. I'm especially appreciative of the children in these congregations, whose thoughts and practices have left lasting marks on my own.

My gratitude also extends to the many people who provided support and assistance with my research and the process of writing this book. Pamela Couture has been a champion of this project from its conception, cheering me on every step of this marathon. Natalie Wigg-Stevenson graciously offered feedback that pushed me to go deeper in my thinking about the structure and methods of my research. Nam Soon Song, Michael Stoeber, Pamela McCarroll, and Élaine Champagne all provided helpful feedback that improved this manuscript at its various stages. Through the financial support of Pine Hill Divinity Hall, Kate Jones and Sr Gemma MacLeod served as capable research assistants as I completed final drafts. Of course, any limitations of the final product you hold in your hands are mine.

It has been a tremendous joy to work with the team at McGill-Queen's University Press. Beginning in our first conversation at a Congress of the Humanities and Social Sciences, Kyla Madden has been an incredibly helpful and supportive editor from proposal to publication. And it was a joy to work with as skilled a managing editor as Kathleen Fraser and as meticulous a copy editor as Scott Howard. Entrusting this labour of love to this publishing house has been a privilege.

It is difficult to put into words all that my family has poured into this book. Whether meeting my sister for coffee between research sessions or running countless ideas by my parents, by serving as proofreaders and giving me permission to take breaks, my family have written themselves into these pages. Of course, they were not alone. Although she entered my life toward the end of the research process, my wife Lydia has been an unparalleled source of support. I'm eternally grateful for all that she did to push me, pull me, and, most of all, walk next to me on this road.

Little
Theologians

Introduction

Burning Questions and Bustling Congregations

Children are not simply passive consumers of theology; they actively generate theological meaning for themselves. As they do, they take in information and experiences from their contexts as raw material and tools for building theology. For children who participate in the lives of faith communities, their congregations have a hand in providing them with sources and methods used in theological meaning-making. But in what ways is this so? How do children generate theology in line with the particularities of their congregation's culture? And do children make theology their own as they draw from other experiences and ideas?

Drawing from research into the spiritual lives of children, I have written this book as a response to these questions. For over a year, I conducted qualitative research among children within four congregations – each of which subscribes to a cultural self-identification distinct from the other three – in order to better understand children's theological meaning in light of cultural contexts. My interpretation of the data generated through this research demonstrates that culture matters to children's theology; that is, the theological meaning that young people make is significantly related to the culture of the congregation in which they participate. Not only is the content of children's theology consistent with that of their congregation, but the ways that they come to create their theological meaning and the sources that they draw from often parallel the meanings and sources upheld and used by their broader faith community – though not without their own nuances and particularities.

Some Introductory Remarks

For half a century, Canada has prided itself on being a multicultural society, one that celebrates diversity in the form of a metaphorical "cultural mosaic."[1] Since 1971, when Prime Minister Pierre Trudeau put forward a federal policy of multiculturalism, this country has moved from tolerating diversity to holding it up as one of the core features of what it means to be Canadian.

But despite this national self-identity ingrained in our common psyche (through everything from multicultural festivals to beer commercials), multiculturalism in Canada has been criticized, critiqued, and challenged by many individuals and organizations. For some, multiculturalism opens our borders too widely and threatens a historical image of Canada that many hold dear; for others, multiculturalism actually preserves power for those cultural groups that have historically held it, thus marginalizing the very people it claims to accept and celebrate. Whatever one might say about multiculturalism, it is clear that its implications are far-reaching. Conversations surrounding cultural diversity have made their way into seemingly every node of Canadian life. Yet, in some arenas, it took time for multiculturalism to be seriously discussed.

It was not until 2006 – a full thirty-five years after the advent of Pierre Trudeau's policy – that the United Church of Canada put forward its own position on cultural diversity. At its thirty-ninth General Council, following decades of various initiatives surrounding "Ethnic Ministries," it approved a vision for becoming an intercultural church.[2] In so doing, this denomination challenged views of multiculturalism held up by both federal policies and mainstream congregational practice, urging clergy and laypeople to move toward a new, more just vision of cultural diversity. In the years following the adoption of this policy, the United Church promoted its "Transformative Vision" through publications, national and regional conferences, and courses at its theological colleges.

At about the same time that the United Church was moving toward its Transformative Vision, my particular area of research interest – children's spirituality and theology – was growing into a distinct yet fluid academic field, establishing new scholarly conferences and setting up working groups within existing guilds like the American Academy of Religion. Studies surrounding children's spirituality and child theology were being published in several periodicals and by some of the most reputable publishers of academic theology in North America, continental Europe, Britain, and, to a lesser extent, other parts of the world.

While the conversations surrounding cultural diversity and the field of children's spirituality and theology were evolving and coming into their own, these distinct discourses had very little to do with one another. There are few studies of children's spirituality and theology that give particular attention to issues of culture. And even those that set their sights on culture do so from perspectives that offer either *theoretical breadth* (that is, describing the importance of cultural difference without grounding it in qualitative research that reflects such contexts), or *contextual depth* (that is, conducting research with children in particular cultural contexts without paying attention to broader issues of diversity and difference). Yet if, as some scholars argue, culture and context matter to the spiritual formation of children, then they must have an impact on young people's quests to make sense of and engage with theological matters.

The present book addresses this gap in scholarship on the spiritual and theological lives of children first by exploring how children make theological meaning in different cultural contexts, and then by using this meaning to assess and critique the very discourses in which it belongs – the context of the United Church's Transformative Vision and the field of children's spirituality and theology. By designing and conducting an exploratory qualitative study to shed light on these topics, this research makes a distinct contribution to the bourgeoning field of children's spirituality and theology.

There are, of course, many factors that influence the theological lives of children, including their families, the places they occupy along various trajectories of human development (particularly faith development), and, of course, various contextual influences such as the congregation in which they participate. Clearly, the research that I undertook fell squarely within this final area. It is the congregation of the child that I sought to isolate as the specific variable to which to attend, exploring how the theologies generated by children align with and diverge from the cultural idiom and theological ethos of their congregation. Yet as much as I set my sights on this particular factor, I recognize that there are other influences shaping the theological lives of each child involved in this study. As such, while focusing on the congregation as the primary variable under investigation in relation to children's theologies, I will at times also speak to how developmental processes and familial contexts become apparent in this research and intersect with congregational culture.

Matters of Method

To answer my research questions, I designed a multi-method empirical study in which I visited four congregations to participate in their worship services and children's ministry programs, speak with children about their theological views, and interview adults about their congregation, its culture, and its ministry with children.

Throughout 2013 and 2014, I spent time at each congregation, attending worship services and observing, participating in, and assisting with its children's programs (such as Sunday school, vacation Bible school, intergenerational congregational worship, etc.). I then spent a number of weeks meeting with children one on one or in small groups, aided, when deemed appropriate by the congregational leader, by a research assistant who took notes and assisted with asking questions.

My use of research assistants varied widely from congregation to congregation. At each community, I sought the advice of its leaders about the appropriate use of research assistants. At Parkdale United Church, my assistant was Eva, an older adolescent from the congregation whom the minister assigned to me because the children were accustomed to her leadership. My assistants at Messiah Methodist United Church varied from interview to interview. At times Jemina, a Sunday school teacher, stayed in interviews unless she needed to leave to attend to her infant child, or another matter required her attention. In some other interviews at Messiah, an administrator of the congregation was present, but acted more as a point person for the congregation rather than an assistant. The leaders of Burke Street United Church felt it was appropriate for me to bring a research assistant of my own choosing. The only congregation where I interviewed all the children without the presence of an assistant was Colkirk United Church. The members of this Aboriginal congregation and I spent several months building a relationship together, and I had come to know the children I interviewed quite well through helping with three week-long vacation Bible school programs in 2014. Because of the trust I had built among these children and the distrust this congregation has toward research, the formality of a research assistant would have undermined the relationship we had formed with one another over the previous eighteen months.

I began each interview by building rapport with the children, talking with them about their hobbies, school, and family. Then I asked if they would mind drawing a picture of God. The practice of drawing these pictures springboarded us into conversations about God, church, heaven, and many other theological matters as directed by the ideas and issues raised by the children. Through our discussions, I learned about what mattered to the children, what experiences were foundational to their spiritual and religious lives, and the sources and methods through which they generated theological ideas.

After meeting with five children from each congregation (with the exception of Colkirk, where I met with four), I held a small focus group interview in each community, where I met with ministers, Sunday school teachers, parents, and other adults who offer leadership to and have a stake in the lives of the children in their congregation. These lively conversations opened further windows into the lives of these four faith communities, helping me hear the stories that make up these congregations and letting me see the dynamics of culture and context in action. Finally, when all these conversations and interviews had taken place, I once again visited each congregation to participate in its worship and ministry with children.

Once I had completed this fieldwork, I transcribed all my interviews with children and adult focus groups, as well as my field notes. I then analyzed these conversations and notes – along with other documents I'd collected, such as bulletins and photographs – by coding them and then grouping codes under significant topics or themes. I identified a total of 129 codes and over fifteen major themes ranging from sources of theological insight and the ability to articulate theology to the children's views of God. Following this, I began describing the congregations and their cultures – especially their theological ethos – based on my experiences of participant observation and focus groups with congregational leaders. Out of such descriptive and analytical processes, I interpreted what I had learned about children's theologies, paying close attention to how their theological meaning-making reflected, and contrasted with, their broader congregational cultures.

Common methods of verifiability, while important for qualitative research, are problematic for the study I have undertaken. At certain points I considered confirming the accuracy of my study by sending my analyses of each congregation to leaders who were part of the focus group and by speaking with the children about the respective chapters in which they make an appearance. There are two important reasons that I decided that this was inappropriate. First, when I conducted interviews and focus groups, I clearly informed all participants that I would use pseudonyms

Table 1
Research Participants

Congregation	Child Participants (and age)	Adult Participants
Parkdale United Church	Jacob (5) Enoch (10) Grace (11) Angela (12) Lizzy (13)	Rev. Lynn Daniel Eva Jeannette
Messiah Methodist United Church	Dawn (9) Chris (10) Luke (11) Marion (11) Kaitlyn (12)	Rev. Ayensu Emmanuel Jemina Sophia
Burke Street United Church	Theo (5) Jeremy (6) Nicholas (8) Rebecca (9) Stephen (12)	Rev. Monica Emma Denise
Colkirk United Church	Ally (7) Ethan (8) Melissa (11) Laura (13)	Rev. Martha Arlene

and that their comments would be kept confidential (although they were aware I would write about them and that people I study and work with would read it). Because the leaders and children were often aware of one another's participation, if I had sent my analyses to them they would have been able to make educated guesses about which comments were offered by which person, and I would have violated the agreements of anonymity that I made with participants. Second, throughout this research I have been cognizant not to take advantage of the hospitality the adults and children in these communities have extended to me. To go back to them and ask for feedback on my analyses would be inappropriate for different reasons at each congregation – it was not part of my original proposal and our initial agreements as to their involvement; I would be imposing on the already busy schedules of the leaders, children, and their families; and I am no longer able to reciprocate with further assistance. For these reasons, using these sorts of verifiability methods seemed to dishonour the agreements I made with each congregation and their children, making them less of an enhancement to my work and more of an ethical violation of the relationships we had built. Ammerman and her colleagues remind us that "our object of study is, after all, a human community filled with people whose lives must be treated with respect."[3] In the case of this research, such respect for the individuals and communities who graciously gave of themselves in the course of this project meant foregoing some verifiability procedures.

During my involvement in these four congregations – and, in fact, throughout the entire research process – I kept a research journal in order to track, reflect on, and process my thoughts, feelings, and biases. While all ethnographic research is shaped by the biases of the researcher, studying issues of culture and theology have made this journey incredibly personal, forcing me to uncover my own prejudices, proclivities, and presuppositions and allow them to be shaped by the individuals and communities who joined me along the way. In this journal, I wrote about everything from necessary shifts in my research methods to frustrations in working with particular research partners; images of hope for an intercultural future, and the challenges involved in getting there. As such, the journal ranges from scribbled notes to lengthy treatises. But whether I wrote a few lines or ranted for a few pages, journaling was a necessary reflexive practice that helped me to keep track of and write myself into this project at every step, holding me accountable to the ways that my experiences and assumptions were intertwined with the research I was conducting.

Of course, like all qualitative research, the ideas within this book remain grounded in the lives of the children, adults, and congregations out of which they arose. I make no claims to universality for what I will share within these pages; each idea I explore and each interpretation I offer speaks only of the children and congregations on which my conclusions are based. In addition to not assuming that the claims in this book are universal to all children, I do not presume that the small groups of children who participated serve as representative samples of the whole of their peer group within their particular congregation. My intention was to find a comparably sized group of young people to participate within each setting in order to maintain consistency of participant groups across congregations. As it will become evident in this book, the four congregations that breathed life into this project are distinct from one another in several ways, including the number of congregants who make up the community. While in some settings the children I interviewed are simply five of a much larger group of young people, in others those five children make up the majority of the children at their congregation. It is for this reason, then, that the determination to interview approximately five children served this project well, for it ensured that even the smallest of the four congregations was able to find enough children to participate. Thus, without presuming the universality of the claims suggested by this research or the representativeness of the participants, the chapters that follow are the result of exploratory research based on a small group of children from a limited number of congregations within a single Canadian denomination.

Setting Parameters

The research in this book, like all research, is itself a cultural product, one bounded by methodological parameters – especially the size, context, and demographics of the participants – as well as my own power and positionality. Although such matters are inherent in research that relies on ethnographic methods, they are of greater significance in this study due to the fact that it engages children as the key participants and crosses cultural boundaries.

My research was a practice of portraiture.[4] That is, rather than presenting a full congregational study, this book offers images captured in precise times and places. Given the abbreviated nature of my involvement at each congregation and the realities of the relationships with which I worked, is important to note that this study does not seek to present an in-depth, longitudinal interpretation of multiples aspects of these congregations. Furthermore, the realities of the expansive landmass that is Canada required that I contain myself to engaging congregations that are located within the same broad region of the country. And I undertook this research in 2013 and 2014, when the participants were at particular stages on their faith journeys, and congregations were undergoing specific shifts in various aspects of their ongoing lives. At another time and in another place, these congregations and the persons therein may have expressed their theologies in altogether different ways, and even the theologies they expressed would likely have been distinct from those that I had the privilege of witnessing. My goal, then, has been to offer portraits, snapshots with the lens focused on the particular aspects of the participating congregations that are relevant to my central research questions.

My decision to conduct all aspects of this research in English determined additional parameters. Since each of the participants had excellent comprehension of the English language, it seemed appropriate to conduct this study in English so as to avoid the myriad methodological challenges that arise when conducting research across multiple languages or in languages that are not one's own.[5] Nevertheless, language poses a particular challenge when researching with children; younger children, especially, possess limited vocabularies through which they can express themselves. This may be even more pronounced when it comes to theological language. In their national study of spirituality and religion among adolescents in the United States, Christian Smith and Melinda Lundquist Denton found that while teens may be astonishingly articulate about some subjects, when it comes to matters of faith, many of them struggle to put language to their views.[6] This challenge may be compounded by the idiosyncrasies of language among children.[7] Not only do their vocabularies differ, but so too do their grammar and use of words. This was evident, for example, when Jeremy, a young boy from Burke Street United Church, told me his grandfather has never visited his church. Seeing this as an opportunity to have Jeremy share about his congregation, I asked, "So if Grandpy said, 'Jeremy, can you tell me about the church?', what would you say?" Immediately the young boy responded, "Then I would say 'Okay.'" In this instance, his incredibly literal use of language was quite different than what I had expected. Thus, I relied on drawing as an alternative form of communication. Of course, drawings are not exact representations of children's ideas. But when coupled with discussion, the process of drawing was often a means of having children begin to share their inner thoughts,[8] launching us into conversations that were firmly based on their ideas rather than mine.

Another set of parameters surrounding this research is related to my power and positionality. I have attempted to be cognizant of this at every stage of the research through practices of reflexivity – that is, "the need and necessity for researchers to not only acknowledge but also examine their location and how that location permeates their inquiry at every level."[9]

One way that my position affects this research is through the power that I brought to it. Factors such as age, race, gender, and education bestowed me with positions of power in my relationships with both the children and adults who participated in this research. This power was not something that could be removed from the equation, nor could it be disguised or ignored.[10] Rather, it was negotiated in many different ways with the various participating congregations and individuals.[11] For example, in my interviews with children, I occupied particular de facto positions of power due to my age relative to theirs. Yet I was able to attend to this by conducting the interviews in their congregations, where they were familiar members and I was an invited guest, and by responding to their thoughts with phrases and questions that continually gave them control over what we would discuss together.[12] While at times I was able to divest myself of certain aspects of my power, particularly by taking on the role of the invited outsider, the far-reaching arms of power worked their way into every nook and cranny of this research.

My positionality was also evident in my inconsistent relationship with participants. While I had prior relationships with at least one leader at each congregation, as these gatekeepers graciously opened their communities to me, the paths they asked me to take were quite different from one another. For example, as a predominantly White congregation, Burke Street had no hesitation about having me participate in their community based on the plan outlined in my research and ethics proposals. Colkirk was a different story altogether. Since, as Rev. Martha told me, Aboriginal communities are the most researched in Canada yet benefit least from the results, she asked me to spend time building a relationship with the congregation and its children before they could feel good about participating in this project. In her words, "we put you through all kinds of hoops in order for you to get to this moment here, to this interview, so you would have a relationship with us." Within each context, I took my cue from the local members, at times working with the congregation's administrator to book a room one evening when a child would meet for an interview, and at other times enjoying conversation over curry soup after Sunday worship services. Such flexibility was necessary for me to build and maintain trust among the congregations,[13] even if it yielded differences among my relationships with and involvement in each setting.

By getting to know the people and congregations involved in this research, my life became bound up with theirs, if only for a time. As I built relationships with them, biases took shape that affected my participation in and interpretation of the congregations. Rather than seeking to eliminate such biases – a venture that is ultimately impossible – I acknowledged that they presented an ongoing conundrum to which I continuously sought to attend. For example, the intentional ways that Rev. Lynn includes children in nearly every aspect of life at Parkdale spoke directly to my strong personal enthusiasm for empowering young people in congregational worship. Worshipping with this community revived and restored my soul. Additionally, after spending months and months getting to know the folks at Colkirk, they came to hold a special place in my heart (and I suspect that I came to be an important part of their community as well, being written into a chapter of its life[14]). More so than at any other point in the writing of this research, I was overwhelmed with the task of writing chapter 4 in a way that represented the congregation accurately. I knew that many other studies portray Aboriginal communities inaccurately and in negative light, and I wanted to ensure that I interpreted the perspectives of my friends within this community in an honest and accurate manner, one that reflected what Shawn Wilson considers vital to Indigenous research paradigms: "rather than the goals of validity and reliability, research from an Indigenous paradigm should aim to be authentic and credible. By that I mean that the research must accurately reflect and build upon the relationships between the ideas and participants. The analysis must be true to the voices of all the participants and reflect an understanding of the topic that is shared by the researcher and participants alike."[15]

In all these ways, the methodological choices I made and the power and positionality I brought to this research engendered particular parameters that shaped the nature and outcomes of the project. Even though I constructed the research process so as to ensure that it seeks the best possible answers to my central question, and despite ongoing adaptations and tweaks based on my relationships with participants, the best that I – or any other researcher – can achieve is a partial glimpse into the religious and spiritual lives of these children. To paraphrase Robert Coles, the child's house is filled with many rooms.[16] The most any of us can do is peer through a window.

Triangulating This Research

This book is an exercise in practical theology and the methodology I utilize in this research is firmly grounded within this broad and interdisciplinary field of theology and religious studies. Furthermore, it is not simply a theological study, but one that relies on methods of qualitative research in order to explore the production of theological knowledge among children who participate in broader congregational context. Thus, it is vital that I locate my research within practical theology and, further, classify it as a work of ethnographic theology.

Practical Theology

Practical theology is an umbrella term that covers a range of theological methods, all of which seek to hold practice and theory together in some sort of tension. For practical theologians, theology is not something that is only theoretical, nor is it merely concerned with religious practice; rather, it is the mutual, dialogical relationship between these two spheres that is the hallmark of this diverse field.

There is a wide range of methods that practical theologians utilize in their efforts to conceive of and maintain a relationship between practice and theory. Don Browning, for instance, outlines a fourfold method for practical theology focused on understanding that develops as dialogues and conversations, which he calls a critical or revised correlational approach.[17] Johannes van der Ven, while seeing the value of an approach such as Browning's, offers a method that relies on original empirical research.[18] Believing that theology must "expand its traditional range of instruments, consisting of literary-historical and systematic methods and techniques, in the direction of an empirical methodology,"[19] he proposes a five-stage *intra*disciplinary method that has practical theologians performing empirical research.[20] These are just two of several methodologies of practical theology, and they demonstrate the sheer breadth of the field, with some being more open to diversity in assumptions and methodologies than others.

This book is an exercise in practical theology, yet it requires a framework that has enough breadth, adaptability, and fluidity to engage in research within multiple cultural contexts. My research necessitates a methodology that is quite flexible so that it can be adapted to suit both the particularities of research questions I pose and the diverse communities and individuals who participate in it.

In his 2008 book *Practical Theology*, Richard Osmer outlines a fourfold approach to practical theology that, while similar to Browning's methodology, better lends itself to adaptation and is intended specifically for use among leaders of faith communities.[21] The first of Osmer's four "tasks" is the descriptive-empirical task, which involves collecting information about what is going on in a given circumstance, situation, or context;[22] to do so one can use informal, formal, or semiformal means, yet qualitative and quantitative methods are especially helpful.[23] The second task is interpretative in that is draws from theories – especially relevant social science research – in order to better make sense of and analyze the situation or context one is studying.[24] The next stage, which Osmer names the normative task, involves putting data gleaned in the previous task into conversation with theology in order to assess what ought to be happening in the situation.[25] Finally, one moves to the pragmatic task to respond to the present circumstance or context in light of the knowledge generated in all preceding tasks. The goal of this final stage is "forming and enacting strategies of action that influence events in ways that are desirable."[26]

As mentioned, Osmer intends his approach for use within faith communities, and it is more flexible and open to variation than those that I outlined earlier. In this book, I pay attention to each of his four tasks of practical theology, albeit in ways that are better suited to my research questions and the congregations and persons who participated in my study. I attend to the descriptive-empirical task in the first four chapters as I describe each congregation and analyze the ways that children's theological meaning-making reflects, and does not reflect, their broader congregation. The interpretive task is evident in my exploration of discourses surrounding multiculturalism in Canada and the attention scholars of children's theology and spirituality give to culture and cultural diversity. One can see the normative task as I place the knowledge generated from my research in conversation with these two discourses, allowing it to serve as an evaluative lens for the United Church's vision for becoming intercultural as well as literature on children's spirituality and theology. Finally, the pragmatic task is evident not only in the evaluations I offer, but also in the recommendations I make for the practice of ministry with children in congregations.

Clearly, my methodology does not fully align with that which Osmer proposes; but it comes close in its attention to all four of his tasks of practical theology. In drawing on his broad approach, I am better able to engage in the sort of relationship between theory and practice of practical theology that, as Robert Mager imagines, allows practice to actually have an impact on theory and, going further, sees the interplay of this relationship itself as an active practice in the world.[27]

Ethnographic Theology

Mary Clark Moschella writes that ethnography "is a way of immersing yourself in the life of a people in order to learn something about and from them."[28] Scholars in the social sciences rely on ethnography as a primary research method. Theologians, too, have come to rely on this broad approach to qualitative research. In fact, in recent years this practice has become an embryonic field that might be called, using Wigg-Stevenson's term, ethnographic theology.[29] By making use of practices from ethnography – and qualitative research methods as a whole – theologians explore how methods within these approaches can aid the work of theologians, and examine how they can be conducted in ways that are theological.

This book is the result of exploratory research that relies on ethnographic theology. That is, it aligns with theologians who make use of ethnographic research methods, along with methods from other approaches to qualitative research, to "hear the theological wisdom of the people, wisdom that is spoken right in the midst of the nitty-gritty mundane realities of group life."[30] While relying on methods within this field, my study was not an ethnography in the strictest sense. Rather, this book is a practice of the approach engendered when *ethnographic* is used as an adjective to qualify theology, the field in which my work truly lies. As Wigg-Stevenson so bluntly admits, "theologians are not ethnographers. At best, we can borrow the tools and insights of ethnography and use them in imperfect ways but nevertheless ways helpful for our purposes."[31] Along with a growing number of theologians, this book showcases how the employment of qualitative research methods within theology – especially methods borrowed from ethnography – can spark particular approaches to research. Let me share three key ways that I consider my research to be a practice of ethnographic theology.

First, I did not simply make use of qualitative methods to explore children's theologies; rather, my use of such methods was in fact a theological act, one that placed me in pastoral roles throughout this study. As I met with children and adults and spent time listening to them, I was engaged in what Moschella calls "ethnographic listening,"[32] a form of listening that she believes to be so deeply theological that she names ethnography as a pastoral practice. In listening to and speaking with the research participants, I gave them time and space to reflect on issues, topics, and thoughts that are of profound importance to them. I wonder if, in this way, I was acting as a sort of spiritual director, helping individuals to reflect on their personal experiences and perceptions of God.[33] By inviting them to share in a space that was free from judgement or correction, I found that Moschella is correct in writing that this form of ethnographic pastoral listening "validates and honors another person's experience, insight, and soul."[34]

Additionally, by relying on qualitative methods framed theologically, I acted as a companion on a theological journey with the participants, if only for a limited time. Together, as I will demonstrate throughout this book, the children and I generated theological knowledge with one another. I asked questions that stirred their theological imaginations and I created my own theological meaning when they asked me questions, many of which prompted me to reflect on things that I had not previously considered. Engaging in these rich theological conversations gave the children permission to journey to the edges of their imaginations as they wondered about God, Jesus, church, and their own lives, unfettered by the need to toe the party line or respond with "correct" answers. In these deep conversations, it became clear to me that, as Wigg-Stevenson has argued, communal theological reflection is itself a Christian practice.[35]

Second, the ethnographic methods in which I engaged were theological in their transformative power. Moschella argues that this research method can be named as a pastoral practice in its ability to evoke change.[36] Since she explores how pastoral leaders can use qualitative research to better understand their faith communities, she focuses on the transformation that can come about in the shared life of congregations. Yet she notes that individuals who participate in the research process can be significantly impacted by it.[37] By having opportunities for their deep and honest thoughts to be heard, a person can be empowered to find her or his voice.[38]

Throughout my time with them, I was able to perceive that the children's involvement in this research had an impact on them. As I will demonstrate in coming chapters, at different points in the research process I noticed children feeling a sense of validation and empowerment as I listened to them. For example, Nicholas seemed reassured and at ease knowing that I did not judge the fact that he did not enjoy Sunday school, and that I didn't like Sunday school when I was his age either; Stephen told his mother that he appreciated being able to speak freely with me about his theological ideas; and Melissa and Laura, each of whom was hesitant at first, came to value speaking opening about theological ideas in the interview so much that they asked me if we could find a time to talk again in the next day or two. While these snapshots cannot be used to demonstrate any sort of deep, ongoing, or long-term transformation, they do show that there is transformative power within ethnographic theology.

My venture into ethnographic theology also transformed me. The stories, ideas, and activities I engaged in with these children challenged my preconceived ideas. They pushed the boundaries of my faith, calling me to question my views of God, my assumptions surrounding theological integrity and research, and the ways that I practise my faith. Through practices of reflexivity, from keeping a research journal to mulling over ideas and events on the long drives home, I studied myself and opened myself to being changed by the research process.

This brings me to the third way that this exploratory study was a practice of ethnographic theology. "Sometimes," writes Moschella, "by studying a congregation's practices – the things they do and the reasons they give for doing them – we can get a vague sense of where God is in all of this."[39] During my year of participating in four congregations, I felt the presence of God, and I was often surprised by those transcendental Spirit-to-spirit moments. God was active within the conversations I had with the children, speaking to me through their voices in ways that call to mind the words of the psalmist.[40] The Divine touched my soul as I found myself becoming immersed in the corporate worship of congregations, even as I attempted to take field notes during these moments. I felt the wind of the Spirit in the hospitality and trust that these four congregations extended to me, free and without any merit on my part. In these ways and more, this ethnographic sojourn was a deeply theological practice, one that allowed me to not just speak about God with others, but to be touched by the hand of God through these encounters.

A Defining Interlude

Before moving from the task of locating my research to that of locating myself, I must briefly define some key terms used throughout this book. Theology, spirituality, belief, and faith – each of these words is incredibly common in research like mine. But the ways scholars use these terms are not always straightforward or consistent. Thus, some conceptual clarity is important.

My understanding of *theology* stems from the etymology of this term, which fuses the Greek words *theos*, meaning "God," with *logia*, meaning "utterances" or "statements." Thus, theology is concerned with utterances about God, with the meaning human beings make about God and all things related to God. While some might be prone to see theology as only involving rational ideas and concepts, solely a matter of the head, the research I undertook makes it clear that theology is something that is also felt and experienced. The utterances about God that we human beings make are not simply the products of our thinking, but also our feeling and action in the world. This understanding of theology is consistent with discourse in practical theology, which I have already described as being not simply concerned with the theoretical and abstract, but also with the realm of practice and concrete action.

Spirituality, as I will demonstrate later in this chapter, is a central concept to childhood studies and religion. It tends to speak of something broader than theology, something that is more raw and carnal. In making sense of spirituality as it relates to children, I rely on the work of Rebecca Nye, who set out to study children's spirituality among primary school children in Britain. Out of the knowledge she generated in her study, she defined children's spirituality as *relational consciousness*, which speaks of "a distinctive property of mental activity, profound and intricate enough to be termed 'consciousness,' and remarkable for its confinement to a broadly relational, inter- and intra-personal domain."[41]

Two related terms that warrant definition are *belief* and *faith*. As I use it in this book, *belief* is a noun that refers to particular statement or assertion that one holds to be true. *Faith*, on the other hand, can involve beliefs, but speaks of something broader and more abstract. As I conceive of it, faith is a gift from God, freely given to all people.[42] It is a sense of and trust in God or a higher power, and it can grow, change, and be nurtured over time. Faith does not consist solely in statements that one holds to be true. Rather, it is at some level that unnameable, indefinable conviction in something greater than ourselves, one that people can respond to with acts that extend from one's experiences of faith.

It is evident that these four terms – theology, spirituality, belief, and faith – are interrelated concepts. While I pull them apart from one another in order to provide a degree of conceptual clarity, the definitions above demonstrate that they are deeply connected with one another.

Triangulating Me

Several years ago, I had lunch with a friend during a break from a course we were taking at Virginia Union University. As we shared our thoughts from the morning's session while picking away at the food on our plates, a colleague from the course asked my friend, who was in the midst of her PhD studies, for advice as he considered enrolling in a doctoral program. She responded by asking him some questions: "What's that one question that burns within you? What issue keeps you up at night? What's the question that you can't not answer before you die?" Academic questions, she knew, are born from personal experiences. This book and the research that birthed it are the result of that "burning question" that was fanned inside of me through the convergence of several life experiences.

I grew up in the heyday of multiculturalism in Canada, a time when interest in culture and cultural diversity was bourgeoning. When I was six years old, my older sister's Brownie leader assigned her group the task of researching their family heritage. My father, being a teacher-turned-superintendent, loved to get involved in these sorts of assignments. He made an inquiry into the Hungarian club in my hometown of Sudbury, Ontario, and arranged for our family to visit the club to do some research on our Hungarian lineage. From that first visit in 1990 until university studies called me to move away from home twelve years later, the Sudbury Hungarian Society was, perhaps more than any other community, the lifeblood of my family's social world.

Each Friday night, the few dozen members of this group would meet together at Pius XII Elementary School, where we would learn Hungarian dancing, practise playing *csokors* (a term literally translated as "bouquet" that we used to refer to medleys of folk songs) on our *citeras* (folk instruments), learn the basics of the Hungarian language, and enjoy delicious Hungarian treats. On holidays like Easter, Christmas, and Hungarian National Day (15 March), the group would hold parties where we would learn and enact traditional folk tales and customs. And a few times each year, we participated in cultural galas and festivals sponsored by the local, provincial, and federal governments, where the traditional dance, music, and food of several countries would be showcased. We were even fortunate enough to make three trips to Hungary with this group – in 1993, 1996, and 1999 – that allowed us to experience the culture of this place firsthand.

My involvement with the Sudbury Hungarian Society not only allowed me to learn how to play out elements of Hungarian folklore like music and dance; it also helped me better understand some of my natural inclinations, like mannerisms, familial phrases (or *Csinosisms*, as I call them), and patterns of thought. By getting to know other people of Hungarian lineage and taking in elements of this culture's media, I came to believe that the reason why I sometimes behave, think, and relate to others the way I do is because somehow – despite growing up in a small mining city in northern Ontario – there were elements of Hungarian culture embedded in my DNA, constructing characteristics and shaping tendencies that seemed to come naturally to me.

It was through my involvement in this group that I first came to an understanding of the term *culture*. Through learning about my Hungarian heritage at the end of every week and experiencing elements of other heritages through multicultural festivals, I associated culture with ethnic heritage, with the traditional customs and ways of life that existed in the land we now call Canada for centuries or that were brought here through millions of immigrants.

The Canada in which I grew up was riding the wake of multicultural policies that played a role in my involvement in the local Hungarian group and cultural festivals that I attended throughout the 1990s. This context and local involvement gave me tools and resources that I pieced together into a simple view of culture. But it wasn't until I moved away from my home and native land that I realized the formative (and sometimes dangerous) power of culture.

In 2008 I moved to Richmond, Virginia to pursue theological studies at Union Presbyterian Seminary. Having grown up with constant access to media from the US, I did not anticipate experiencing much culture shock once I crossed the border. Sure, Richmond was part of the southern US, but I thought I had a pretty good handle on what to expect when I left Canada.

My naïveté shone through as I discovered that in moving to Richmond, I was entering a new world, a new cultural space that, while not too far south geographically, was largely defined by its history as the capital of the Confederate States of America. What particularly shocked, frustrated, and saddened me were the many ways in which this city's history of racism continued to shape the life of its citizens. Even the predominantly White seminary that I was attending and the historically Black college down the road struggled to have a mutual relationship, as power dynamics and wounds old and new festered into bitterness and division.[43]

As I navigated these new waters, I was surprised that so many people I encountered (particularly White Americans) seemed unaware of the currents that were so obvious to me. Thankfully, I met a few international students who shared my culture shock. And then I came to know some students of colour who noticed my deer-in-headlights demeanour toward these complex issues and educated me about the realities of race within the southern United States. But when I broached the topic with students belonging to the dominant culture of the US, I realized that many of them couldn't see the day-to-day effects of racism that were so blatant to me as I sat in classes, attended social events, and shopped for groceries. I wondered: *If these students can't see the problems that I see because they grew up in this culture, then are there aspects of Canadian culture that I have been socialized not to see?*

It was as if the scales had fallen from my eyes. This moment helped me realize that culture is much more than folk dancing and buffets of food at multicultural festivals. Culture is the air we breathe as human beings. Or, to use another metaphor, it is the water surrounding us that we don't realize we are swimming in until something pulls us out of it. When I left Virginia and moved back to Ontario, I brought with me a new determination to uncover those aspects of Canadian culture that I had been socialized not to see. One of the first things I needed to do on this quest was use my newfound sight to investigate the cultural narrative that was imparted to me during the first decades of my life.

I had always known that the blood coursing through my veins consisted of more than simply Hungarian DNA. My paternal grandparents were both Hungarian. My grandfather emigrated in 1926 and my grandmother's parents had left Hungary for Canada a few decades earlier, before she was born. But, as is often the case, culture is a difficult thing to pin down. My maternal grandparents crossed deep-rooted Canadian religious and ethnic divisions when they married one another. She was a Roman Catholic French-Canadian woman born and raised in St Boniface, the francophone area of Winnipeg. My grandmother's roots in Canada dated back a dozen generations to a settler who came to Nouvelle-France in 1620. My maternal grandfather's lineage stemmed from Great Britain, and he was raised in the United Church (before the 1925 union that birthed the United Church, he actually spent his first years in one of its predecessors) until converting to Roman Catholicism in order to marry my grandmother in 1939. Even my Hungarian grandparents have a history more complicated than I first realized as a child, for my paternal grandfather was raised in a poor village that had become part of Romania after World War I, and my grandmother, though a second-generation Canadian, grew up in a family of immigrants in a land that was new to them. Of course, as I will discuss shortly, I perceive culture to be much broader than ethnicity and national heritage. But this family history is the one that dominated my life story and it led me to hold, for a time, a narrow view of culture.

My research into how children make theological meaning in different cultural contexts is the most penetrating and extensive study I have undertaken into children's spirituality, theology, and culture; but it is certainly not the first. While a student at McMaster Divinity College, I conducted qualitative research into the spiritual lives of children through which I framed a four-fold typology for children's spiritual experiences. Three years later, it was published as *Children's Ministry That Fits*.[44] My Th.M. thesis from Union Presbyterian Seminary moved away from children's spirituality, but gave me experience in exploring the cultural dynamics of religion through a comparative analysis of the spirituality of emerging adults in the United States and Québec. During my doctoral studies at Toronto School of Theology, I had the privilege of taking courses about intercultural theology and ministry and working with Dr Pamela Couture to write comprehensive examinations blending multicultural/intercultural discourse in Canada with research in the field of children's spirituality and theology. During this time, I wrote, presented, and published scholarly and professional articles that flowed out of these examinations.[45] All of these prior sojourns into this subject prepared me for the research on which this book is based, research that is intimately connected to my personal history over the past quarter-century.

My Assumptions

This book is not only connected to my personal history; it is also deeply intertwined with the assumptions I bring to it. From proposal to fieldwork, coding to writing, every point along the research journey has been marked by my understandings of culture and multiculturalism, the United Church's Transformative Vision for becoming intercultural, and the field of children's spirituality and theology.

Culture and Multiculturalism

"Culture" is an incredibly complex term that has varying understandings associated with it. My assumptions regarding culture rest between modernist and postmodern notions.[46] Drawing from modernist viewpoints, I hold that culture is a universal marker of human life; that it shapes humanity but is also shaped by human beings; that the manifestations of culture are seemingly endless; and that every distinguishing feature of a group is part of its culture – as well as some features that are shared across different cultural groups. Building on postmodern ideas, I contend that cultures may be distinct from one another, but they are fluid, contradictory, and even inconsistent wholes that bind people together as a focus for common engagement rather than agreement; their boundaries are porous, so features of cultures can be shared among several societies and groups; and there can be tremendous internal diversity among a given culture, so much so that such diversity can be a central feature of a cultural group.

Cultures can be large or small, from a shared national culture to that of a small faith community or neighbourhood group. We all exist within several cultures, which overlap and combine and run into each other as they influence and are influenced by each of us who exist within them. While at times colloquial use of the term "culture" is perceived to be synonymous with ethnicity, race, and/or nationality, culture is in fact a much broader reality, overlapping with and encompassing all sorts of aspects of human life, such as religious tradition, country of origin, social class, geographic location, age, gender, sexual orientation, political persuasion, and even personal preferences such as one's taste in music, books, and movies. With so many aspects bound up with endless manifestations of culture, in reality cultures are incredibly complex entities that operate at several diverse levels of human life as they shape and are shaped by our thoughts, actions, values, and beliefs.[47]

Embedded within this book is the assumption that every congregation is in fact a particular culture, for each is a unique group of people with common ways of seeing and acting in community within their broader social context. In the landmark handbook *Studying Congregations*, Nancy Ammerman champions such a view of congregations, writing that congregations consist of "everyday patterns of life that make each congregation itself, that give it its identity."[48] As I have already noted, congregations are not unified cultures; they are internally inconsistent and complex, made up of a great many different worldviews and ways of living that converge together. Yet Ammerman notes that each possesses a distinct idiom, a mosaic of practices, artifacts, stories, and theologies that intertwine as they form a particular way of being together.[49]

Over the past half-century, cultural diversity has become a hallmark of Canadian life and self-identity. Canada is known to be a cultural mosaic, where innumerable cultures fit together in our common society. While I carry this assumption throughout the pages of this book, I also understand that the veneer of Canadian multiculturalism is replete with cracks. For one thing, not all tiles that make up this mosaic are given equal priority, and some are much more prominently placed than others. Those groups that have historically held power in Canada continue to exercise the greatest influence and benefit from privileges not afforded to other cultural groups. For another thing, Canadian multiculturalism rests on simple and surface-level assumptions about culture, seeing it as little more than ethnicity, race, and/or nationality. This is something that sociologist Phil Ryan asserts by arguing that culture in Canada is often perceived as "a sort of 'container' of individuals"[50] that holds within it all those elements that make up a culture. While there is some validity to placing boundaries around cultures, I see these boundaries as porous, containing within them a group of people that is fluid, complex, and internally diverse.

The United Church of Canada and Its Transformative Vision

The United Church's Transformative Vision seeks to step away from hegemonic and surface-level notions of multiculturalism. It urges the denomination to open its arms and more fully embrace the reality of cultural diversity that it is facing within its congregations and the society in which it participates. But it subverts its own ideals even while attempting to point to a reality that it fails to truly promote.

On my reading of the Transformative Vision – which I will more fully explore in chapter 6 – the primary view of culture that it relies on is problematically narrow and simplified. Throughout the document, culture is perceived to be little more than a synonym for ethnicity, language, and race. By identifying four categories of congregations – ethnic majority, ethnic minority, francophone, and Aboriginal – the United Church imagines cultures as settled entities, as containers that are fully distinct, bounded, and internally consistent wholes based on a few narrow cultural elements. There is little room within this fourfold classification for cultures – and congregations – that are internally diverse, shifting, and adapting to new times and places, leaving culture to stagnate into stereotype.

My positionality is that of an outsider to the United Church, yet my education and relationships provide me with access to the inside. In organizing my research, I chose to work within the categories the United Church suggests, while adapting and complexifying them to better account for my assumptions of culture. By removing the third category the denomination proposes for congregations – francophone – I maintain consistency of language across all research settings. Yet I also included a congregation that is culturally diverse, a category the United Church overlooked in its classification. Each of the four participating congregations is a distinct culture unto itself, with distinct characteristics involving ethnicity (as culturally diverse, ethnic minority, ethnic majority, and Aboriginal, to use the United Church's terms), yet also extending to the congregations' geographic settings, their sizes, their particular beliefs, and a myriad of other features that swirl together to form a unique cultural group with a particular idiom. At the same time, however, each church exists within multiple other cultures that are held in common with one another (such as their broader religious denomination and their location within a similar geographic region of Canada), and cultures that are shared with other groups yet distinct from the other participating congregations (such as their racial or ethnic identity, their location in a rural, suburban, or urban setting, their socio-economic status, and their level of internal diversity). In choosing these congregations, I am at once operating within the United Church's classification, but doing so in a way that acknowledges the complex and fluid reality of culture.

Children's Spirituality and Theology

The final set of assumptions that I carry into this research has to do with the field of children's spirituality and theology. There is a tendency within this field for scholars to overlook issues of culture and cultural diversity; among those who do attend to culture, most do not do so with adequate depth. There are some scholars, for example, who study children's spirituality within particular cultural contexts; but culture in these cases is often perceived along lines of nationality, race, and ethnicity. Furthermore, scholars may utilize culture as a primary lens for a research methodology, but continue to ignore it as a variable and framework for interpreting research findings. Thus, there is a gap within the field into which this book speaks.

If, as I assume, culture is an all-pervasive aspect of social life, then a further assumption is that all areas of human life are grounded in cultural contexts. This includes children's theological meaning-making. The negligence of culture among scholars of childhood studies and religion, however, fails to give concerted attention to this reality. Since no theology is acultural, then one can claim, as I do, that all of children's theological ideas and practices are bound up with their cultural contexts and need to be attended to as such.

Finally, research into the religious and spiritual lives of children has far too frequently been focused on generating insight into the content of children's theological ideas. These studies open windows to the inner lives of children by exploring what young people think about particular topics, such as biblical stories, perceptions of the soul, and faith practices. Yet I believe that not only is the *content* of children's theologies important to understand, but so too are the *processes* by which they come to make such theological meaning (I will discuss this further in chapter 7).

I have organized, carried out, and interpreted this research using a multifaceted set of assumptions surrounding culture and multiculturalism, the United Church's Transformative Vision for becoming an intercultural church, and the broader field of children's spirituality and theology. Throughout the eight chapters of this book, I rely on these assumptions in explicit and implicit ways in order to generate original insights into children's theological meaning-making within different cultural contexts, and utilize these insights to assess the United Church's Transformative Vision and research into children's spirituality and theology.

The Road Ahead

My practices of reflexivity and the trust that I have built with the participants involved in my study have led me to reflect deeply on the importance of relationships. While Western scholarship has tended to aim to move one's biases and personal relationships to the sidelines, Indigenous researchers have noted that such relationships and values actually belong at centre field.[51] Throughout the research process, I have sought to honour the relationships I have developed with the children, adults, and congregations that gave of themselves to participate in it, and this has caused me to make intentional decisions about the shape of this book. In particular, you will have noticed by now that I have written this book in a way that aims to make complex ideas and nuanced arguments readable for a more general audience. To do otherwise would be to betray the relationships I hold dear by telling the stories of participants – stories that do not belong to me, but were entrusted to me – in ways that might sound rather fancy and knowledgeable, but depart from the contexts of those who told them. Thus, I have attempted to limit my use of jargon and academic "in-speak" throughout this book, making it more readable, more accessible, and clearer for readers from many walks of life.

The book begins with descriptions and interpretations of children's theological meaning-making in different cultural contexts. I devote chapters 1–4 to the four congregations that participated in my research: Parkdale United Church, Messiah Methodist United Church, Burke Street United Church, and Colkirk United Church (to maintain anonymity, I use a pseudonym for every congregation and person that participated in this research). I begin each of these chapters with an overview of the congregation, paying attention to the key elements that combine together to create its particular cultural idiom,[52] including aspects of its geographical context, history, congregational demographics, worship styles, and ministry with children. I then explore the theological perspectives that contribute to the culture of the congregation by describing the theological values that its minister(s) and key leaders bring to it, as well as aspects of the broad theological ethos that seems to drive its life as a community of faith. The heart of each of these first four chapters is the "Theological Reflections" section, in which I describe the most salient characteristics of the children's theologies that arose through analysis of interviews. After analyzing and exemplifying each characteristic with excerpts from interviews, I interpret it in light of the cultural idiom and theological ethos of the broader congregation. Although this portion of each chapter is based on analysis that preceded that of the broader congregation's culture and theological ethos, I have presented the children's theologies after describing the congregation at large in order to make the parallels between the two more evident. Finally, I end each of these chapters by speaking about some manners in which the children's theologies differ from those of their faith communities.

In chapter 5 I shift the focus from the particular contexts of individual congregations to a wider view that places the children from every congregation alongside one another. This allows for a broader and more multifaceted interpretation of their theologies. Using what Emmanuel Lartey calls a "Trinitarian" view of personhood (which relies on the work of Kluckhohn and Murray[53]) to affirm that all people are "like all others, like some others, and like no others,"[54] I discuss the content, sources, and methods of children's theologies in ways that showcase commonalities held by all children, similarities expressed within particular congregations, and differences that make each child a unique theologian in their own right. With culturally based comparative study missing from the field of children's spirituality and theology, this chapter is a strategic move toward addressing the gap in the field by providing in-depth interpretation of children's theology in light of culture and cultural diversity.

Chapters 6 and 7 build on the preceding interpretations of children's theologies by using them as a lens of assessment. In chapter 6, the knowledge generated about children's theological meaning-making sheds new light on the United Church's Transformative Vision. I begin by situating the United Church's plan for becoming intercultural within its broader context of multiculturalism in Canada, describing a brief history of cultural diversity and critiques of Canadian multiculturalism. Then, after introducing the Transformative Vision, I draw from the theologies of the children and congregations that participated in this research to make three points of assessment – positive and negative – about the vision: it takes a step forward by listening to marginalized voices; it does not take into account hybrid cultural identities; and it overlooks contexts of diversity and difference.

Chapter 7 has as its focus the bourgeoning academic field of children's spirituality and theology. After placing some loose conceptual boundaries around this field, I articulate four ways that scholars within it address – or fail to address – culture and cultural diversity: by making passing references to it yet relying on implied European-American and British norms; by researching children within a specific cultural context; by conducting studies across multiple cultural contexts; and by giving concerted attention to the importance of culture and contexts in relation to research within the field. With such a perspective in mind, I draw from the theological meaning-making of the nineteen children who gave life to this book in order to evaluate research within the field and claim the following: it needs to pay attention to the processes of children's theological meaning-making and not only the products; it must explore both the individual and communal nature of children's theology; and scholars can no longer afford to ignore culture as a variable at every step of research into children's spiritual and theological lives.

In the final chapter, I offer concluding reflections by naming some directions this book proposes for future research into children's spirituality and theology, and for pastoral practice with children in congregations. In suggesting avenues that could be perused to expand and build upon the exploratory research I undertook in this book, I raise four sets of questions. Such questions invite further research into how children's congregational involvement, parents and families, additional and overlapping cultural contexts in children's lives, and longitudinal studies can all add to the knowledge I generate in this study. Finally, I highlight implications for congregational practices of ministry with children that this research leads toward: an emphasis on cultivating children's capacities for theological meaning-making; achieving consistency among children's ministry and broader congregational culture; and giving opportunities for children to talk openly and creatively about their theological views and experiences.

1 "Thank You For Making Church"

Parkdale United Church and a Theology of Community

It was 10:22 in the morning. Only eight minutes to go until the Sunday worship service began. As I sat in a pew at Parkdale United Church, I looked around the sanctuary of this historical church building. Congregants greeted one another; ushers prepared baskets for the offering; musicians set up their instruments. Amidst all this, only moments before her official words of welcome to the gathered community, Rev. Lynn stood at the communion table with Enoch, an eight-year-old boy who could hardly see over the top of the table where the congregation celebrates the Lord's Supper. The minister bent down and spoke softly to the young boy, showing him how to hold the chalice and paten that sat atop the table. During the service I would learn that these vessels were dear to the community, handmade by residents at a nearby L'Arche home and given to Parkdale by a former member of the church. As the service drew nearer, Rev. Lynn demonstrated to Enoch how he should hold the microphone and, after rehearsing some lines of liturgy, the pair moved away from the table in anticipation of the service that was about to begin.

Knowing that I had arranged to interview some of Parkdale's children during this service, Rev. Lynn recommended that my research assistant remain in worship to observe and inform me about all the ways that young people would be involved in the service, a practice that was far from irregular at this congregation. Rev. Lynn opened the service with words of welcome: "Thank you for making church today." Immediately, she asked me to stand and reminded the congregation that I would be interviewing some of their children in the church hall during the service. I moved to the front of the church and was joined by the children who were going to be speaking with me, along with a teenager who would serve as my assistant during the interview.

As we slipped out the side door and down the steps to the hall, the service continued. Worship moved along from prayers and hymns to the passing of the peace, and a sermon in which Rev. Lynn preached about the importance of diversity and the necessity of partnership among all the people of God. Following the message, Enoch took his place next to Rev. Lynn as the pair stood behind the communion table. During a future service he would join me for another interview at Parkdale, but today, he was presiding over communion. Together, Enoch and Rev. Lynn took it in turns to pray over the bread and the juice. Together they offered the words of invitation to the community, reminding the congregation that all who name Jesus as their lamp are welcome to this table. Without an indication of power imbalance or unequal authority, Enoch and Rev. Lynn presided over one of the most sacred of Christian practices. Standing side by side at that table, they demonstrated that age is no barrier to making important contributions to God's church.

From Pristine Farmland to Sprawling City

Parkdale United Church has a history that stretches back nearly two centuries to its founding in 1830. From the busy shopping centres, modest homes, and small apartment buildings surrounding the church, it can be difficult to imagine what the area around the current building looked like when it was erected amidst farmland in 1870. It is not a large church – the stone structure can accommodate about 160 people – but its stature is dominated by a steeple that reaches to the sky. The city has grown up around this once-country church, and the Parkdale United Church of today is holding onto this history as it adapts to its present neighbourhood.

Upon stepping inside this congregation's building, one is immediately struck by the eclecticism of its current décor, which blends past traditions with present circumstances. There are many elements that show this congregation's rich history – old pews, plaques commemorating congregants who fought in the world wars, large windows that flood the sanctuary with light, and wood furnishings such as a communion table and a baptismal font. But these more typical features of a congregation as old as Parkdale are juxtaposed with ones that are more unexpected – strings of lights above the chancel doors, a piano adorned with small flags from countries around the world, dusty poppies placed among memorial plaques, and a projection screen hung prominently above the centre of the platform. During my time in this congregation there were several scarves pinned on both sides of the nave, which members of the congregation had knitted throughout the summer and fall and would soon donate to a women's shelter and a Salvation Army Christmas clothing drive.

There are four doors in the sanctuary, one of which is at the small narthex and leads to the front steps of the church. The two chancel doors open on a hallway leading to a few modest offices and lined with photos and newspaper articles from the church's 185-year history. To the left of the pulpit is a door to a small but brightly lit foyer and stairs leading to the church hall, which can accommodate about 100 people and includes a small kitchen in one corner. With one wall for cupboard storage and another featuring large windows, the other two are adorned with photographs from past congregational activities and a large bulletin board filled with announcements, drawings, and posters for events in the congregation and its neighbourhood.

Parkdale is a congregation that identifies as intercultural and it makes this known in its tagline, which sometimes appears on the front of weekly bulletins: "A community of the world's peoples sharing faith and culture in our neighbourhood since 1830." About 100 people gather for Sunday worship, coming together to form a community marked by a diversity of ages, races, and ethnicities. Approximately half of the congregants are White individuals and the other half are people of colour; the majority of White congregants are Euro-Canadians, but a few are immigrants to Canada from Great Britain. While most of the people of colour are immigrants from the Philippines, others are Black Canadians and immigrants from South and Southeastern Asia. This racial diversity seems correlated with age. For the most part, the people of colour appeared to be under fifty, while most of the White congregants were seniors who looked to be seventy and older.

These demographic features are likely related to the high number of newcomers to Canada who have settled in the neighbourhood surrounding Parkdale; but they are also related to the recent history of the congregation. Around the year 2000, it began discussions with West End United Church about the possibility of amalgamating their congregations – both of which had experienced numerical decline – but neither community was willing to give up their church building. Less than a decade later, Parkdale was named a provincial heritage building, and thus the congregation was unable to close its building for any sort of amalgamation. West End United Church was not in favour of a coming together that would not see the two congregations on equal footing in terms of their buildings, so any talk of joining forces came to an end. Only a few years later, West End had to close its congregation and, after giving their building to a growing United Church congregation made up of recent immigrants to Canada, a group of elderly congregants from West End, most of them White, began attending Parkdale, although they tend to keep to themselves.

Worship services at Parkdale, like its décor, juxtapose formality and informality. Services follow a liturgy of prayers, readings, and hymns written in the congregation's weekly bulletins, which on some Sundays can reach up to twelve pages in length. Yet the formal written liturgy springs to life during the service. It is not unusual to see adults and children alike picking up simple rhythm instruments to play while dancing along to hymns, or to witness young people moving about the sanctuary as they write prayers, prepare and perform skits, or go to the hall to set up the soup lunch the congregation shares every few weeks. The rhythm of Parkdale's liturgy encourages noise, movement, and active community participation in worship services.

Each month, the youth and children in the congregation organize and lead a worship service called SingAloud which runs for about an hour before the regular service. Launched about ten years ago as a way to get young people involved in the congregation, SingAloud is a service that features more contemporary praise songs, a time of Bible quizzing, and a short "inspirational talk" in lieu of a sermon. Attendance at this service increases as it goes along, with congregants beginning to show up for the 10:30 a.m. service. If the weekly service can be classified as "informal," SingAloud can seem like downright bedlam. During one service alone, the youth led the congregation in loud music that was not terribly polished, there was an open mic time for sharing blessings and needs, and several members led an impromptu memorial for a long-time congregant and former chair of the board who recently died from complications associated with AIDS. In multiple instances it seemed as though the youth and adults alike were unsure about who was going to be leading certain parts of the service. Yet none of this informality and confusion seemed to be a problem for the congregation. And from the fact that the great majority of the service was led by young people who appeared to be quite comfortable in their roles, it seems as though SingAloud is meeting its goal of empowering youth and children to offer leadership in the congregation.

The activities for the members of Parkdale go well beyond congregational worship. Social events and celebrations are regular happenings, and two of the most common events involve sharing food together – in addition to the biweekly soup lunches, after each SingAloud service there is a simple breakfast served to the congregation. Other activities occur less frequently, but are still of vital importance. These include a summer vacation Bible camp (the most recent of which was intergenerational), a fair featuring performances highlighting the breadth of ethnic and cultural diversity in the congregation, and a retreat in cottage country a few hours away that was shared with members of a Korean congregation that uses Parkdale's building on Sunday afternoons. Although these activities are less frequent than worship services, they help build community among the members of the congregation, who speak about them with great fondness.

Making Church Together

Parkdale is all about community. From the interactive style of worship to the eclectic décor throughout the building, it's clear that the members of this congregation aren't just individual attendees – they are communal participants. Spectator Christianity is not an option here, as all are encouraged to participate in one another's lives as they gather together again and again. The conversation I had with the minister and three leaders from Parkdale showcased how much value is placed not just on community, but on each person playing a role in building and being in a community together. Eva, a teenaged leader, noted that no one falls asleep during worship services at Parkdale because congregants aren't spectators; they are part of the service. Immediately Jeannette, an adult volunteer, affirmed what this young woman said: "You're part of the service that way, but we're also called upon to be part of community together with each other." She went on to state that the communal laments and the blessings they offer over one another during worship are just some of the ways that everyone is called upon to participate in worship together. Theologically, she noted, it's a particular approach to what it means to be a congregational community.

Community has been at the heart of the theology through which Rev. Lynn has been leading Parkdale as its solo minister for the past six years. This theology is informed by "an individual theology of Sabbath" and an "impetus to live as a covenantal people." For her, a theology of Sabbath prepares individual members of the congregation for life in community. Drawing from a Hebraic notion of Sabbath, she understands the worship life of Parkdale to be one in which all people – children and elders alike – participate in worship. In fact, she encourages young people in the congregation to help lead worship; for example, by having youth like Eva (who served as my research assistant at Parkdale) and children like Enoch preside over and serve communion. In this way, the community seeks to bring "that kind of Sabbath Friday night role of the youngest child in the family [to] ask the reigning male elder around the table, you know, 'Why do we eat these foods? Why do we do this?'" But the practice of Sabbath extends beyond Sunday worship. The community encourages older children and teens to go on mission trips and retreats so that they come to value this theology of Sabbath, see the important roles they have as young people within the community, and rest, reconnect, and have powerful experiences of God. Thus, this theology of Sabbath is "codified," to use a term from Rev. Lynn, each week in Sunday worship, and in occasional events and retreats that build this practice into the faith lives of its members from an early age.

A theology of community helps the congregation to be one that values all people as participants in its life and empowers them to have a voice and a stake in the community. Although they are served by a solo minister, all members of the congregation are called upon to minister to one another. At times, such ministry involves leadership in worship services, and during my visits to Parkdale[1] I witnessed such empowerment as congregants young and old led music, wrote and shared prayers, prepared and served communion, presided over a baptism, and offered sermons. Such empowerment was given voice when Rev. Lynn began one service I attended by saying "Thank you for making church today."

Of course, empowerment of the whole community does not automatically lead to the equitable sharing of power among all members. There were times during my visits when some individuals who have traditionally held power due to their age, gender, sexual orientation, and race seemed to struggle with hearing the voices of people from whom power traditionally has been kept. Under Rev. Lynn's guidance, this community has been intentional in attempting to empower all people as active contributors to the community, as people join her in saying that it is every member's responsibility to mentor and form one another. Such a vision was highlighted in one congregant's reflections on her recent trip to Halifax for the United Church's intercultural conference. One of her biggest learnings at the event was the importance of "mutually reciprocal" relationships.

Alongside an understanding of Sabbath, Rev. Lynn's theology of community is informed by a call to go out from the community and do good in the world. In her words, out of a theology of Sabbath comes an "impetus to live as a covenantal people, caring for the widow and orphan, looking to the margins." One way she builds such a theology into Parkdale is by sharing stories that paint an image of "a loving God who accepts us and welcomes us and asks us to continue to sort of expand the stakes of our tents and welcome people in and learn how to care for one another." Worship services at this congregation are filled with moments that challenge the community to think and live and act out its mandate to care for others. For example, during the first service I participated in, a picture of Typhoon Haiyan's aftermath in the Philippines appeared on the projection screen, and the congregation, which includes a large Filipino community, was provided information about where congregants could donate funds to support the victims, to be matched by the Canadian government.

A theology of community seems to be built into nearly every aspect of the congregation. For example, it guides its understanding of food: this is a community that gathers to break bread together, both during the liturgical act of communion and the informal yet regular meals. As food brings the community together, it also shows care for those present, for Parkdale is not a high-income neighbourhood, and having food available at many ministries and activities ensures that no one leaves hungry. In fact, community is so central to Parkdale that when I began speaking with Rev. Lynn about having this congregation participate in my research and what I hoped such participation would entail, she stated that I should interview the children in pairs or small groups rather than individually. She went on to explain that everything that happens at Parkdale ought to happen among a community that does life together. This meant, therefore, that it was inappropriate for children here to participate in individual interviews.

Parkdale is a congregation that may foster community, but it does so while valuing the tremendous diversity that exists among its individual members. This congregation self-identifies as intercultural in the very broadest sense of the term, as a space in which people of incredible diversity come together to co-create community. Having studied, through her graduate research, her congregation's quest to be and become intercultural, Rev. Lynn affirms an understanding of culture much like that which I outlined in the introduction, a view that expands culture beyond race and ethnicity and to the whole life of a human community. In her words, there is "a constant collision and collaboration of 'culture' ... we need to stand apart in our difference and work together to cross barriers that can separate peoples based on (several of) race, class, age, employment status, migration history, accented language and so on."

As I observed and participated in the life of this community for a short time, it was clear to me that it is a congregation that expresses layers of diversity, including ethnicity and race, socio-economic status, nationality, age, liturgical style, and theological view. As stated previously, this congregation is made up of people of multiple ages, races, ethnic backgrounds, and countries of origin. Furthermore, there was significant theological diversity expressed during my visits to Parkdale. For example, while some congregants seemed to cringe at the use of male pronouns for God, several others regularly referred to God as "he." The involvement of people with multiple differences and diversities is openly addressed in a way that reminds people that, at times, being one community means that everyone will be pulled outside of one's comfort zone. As Rev. Lynn stated before sharing the words of lament during one service, "not all of you will like all the words every week, but it is our lament as a community of faith." Rather than seeking uniformity among congregants, this minister encourages folks to pay attention to the diversity present and build a community in which differences are respected, appreciated, and contested.

Theological Reflections

The interviews I conducted with the children at Parkdale offered glimpses into the depth of their theological lives. Yet my analysis of these conversations indicates that, overall, the ways these young people generate theology are consistent with and reflect the broader culture of their congregation. This was evident through the communal nature of their theological explorations, the importance of shared experiences, and their openness to diversity and difference.

Communal Theology

If community is at the core of life and faith at Parkdale, then it will come as no surprise that it is a significant characteristic in the theological lives of the children who are part of this congregation. Rather than offering individual thoughts and expressions of theological insight, these children generated theology with one another in communal ways. This is exemplified in the following short conversation with Grace (11) and Angela (12), both of whom were baptized and grew up at Parkdale. After I asked the girls to draw a picture of God, each of them created an image of Jesus (figures 1.1 and 1.2) and then thought together about the features that define Jesus in images:

DAVE: (*to Grace*) Is there yellow coming from Jesus's hands? What's that?
GRACE: Power.
DAVE: Okay. Because he's healing the child. (*Earlier in the interview Grace told me that she drew Jesus healing a child*) And what's wrong with the child?
GRACE: Things like … I don't know, just like …
DAVE: Nothing in particular?
GRACE: Yeah. (*Angela points to part of Grace's drawing*) That's his foot! … I know I'm a bad drawer.
DAVE: So you guys both gave Jesus black hair?
GRACE: Yeah.
ANGELA: Yeah.
DAVE: And why did you give Jesus black hair? (*Angela and Grace both shrug their shoulders*) You don't know?
GRACE: In the pictures sometimes, sometimes it's black, gray, brown.
DAVE: So the pictures in the Bible or the ones that Rev. Lynn uses or –
GRACE: Both. Yeah.
DAVE: There are different types of hair?
GRACE: Yeah. And it's like the same style. Sometimes it changes, like, the colour.

DAVE: Maybe Jesus needed a change? Dyed his hair sometimes? You never know. (*We all laugh*) So the pictures Rev. Lynn uses, they're all different? ... If you were to see a picture and – let's say it was not in a Bible and not here, you just saw a picture of Jesus ... What are the kinds of things that make you think of, that make you know that that's Jesus?

GRACE: Um, he looks kind of old.

DAVE: Kind of old?

ANGELA: He wears robes.

DAVE: Yeah?

ANGELA: In many pictures he wears robes.

GRACE: A beard.

DAVE: ... So why do you think that Jesus wears robes?

ANGELA: (*pause*) Um ... I don't know.

DAVE: Do you think if Jesus came back, like, if he was here today, would he wear robes?

GRACE: Maybe.

ANGELA: Yeah. Or if he wants to wear like a suit.

GRACE: Yeah.

DAVE: So maybe, maybe not. What makes you think he would or wouldn't?

GRACE: Because it's, like, more modern times.

ANGELA: So he'd wear more modern clothes.

DAVE: So the robes are because that's what he wore back in the day? (*Angela and Grace nod in agreement*)

(*At this point in the interview, Lizzie entered and joined us and the conversation shifted to another topic.*)

This exchange was typical of my conversations with the children from Parkdale. They would often respond to my questions and explore ideas together. In this instance, Grace's discussion with Angela led her to engage more deeply with what it is that makes pictures of Jesus distinguishable and how even superficial aspects of his life, like his clothes and appearance, were contextualized to his culture and may be reimagined in our current time and place. Yet this was only one instance among many in which these children did theology together. At another point during our interview, for example, we began talking about the relationship between God and Jesus and I asked them to say more about how they are related to one another. Grace looked to Angela as if to say, *How do you think we should answer this?*, and then responded with "They're, like, the same" – to which Angela quickly chimed in, "I think it's the same."

Theology, for these children, is not a solo enterprise. Echoing the overall theology of community that permeates the culture of their congregation, these children formulated their theological views with one another. As they drew pictures of God and talked about their congregations, they were engaged in a process of theological reflection through which they shared ideas and challenged one another as they did theology in community. And our conversation was certainly not their first opportunity to do theological reflection with one another. One way that they participate in congregational worship is by writing prayers, skits, and other pieces of the liturgy together that they then share during a future worship service. With such practices as common means through which these children do theology in community, the conversational nature of their theological thinking during my interview with them seems consistent with the way their congregation nurtures their theological imaginations in the first place.

Experienced Theology

Part of the emphasis on community that permeates Parkdale involves a focus on doing life together. This is a church offering many events and activities through which the bonds among congregants can be strengthened. From my conversations with the children here, it is clear that activities and experiences in community are of vital importance to their theologies. Worship services are certainly one form of such shared experiences. But as Angela said, it's "not just the services, but, like, things that we have done like dinners and games nights, where people come together." Angela, Grace, and Lizzy (13) – the latter of whom joined in about twenty minutes into our conversation – spoke at length about such activities, including volunteer outreach work, SingAloud, Christmas pageants, overnight retreats, and skits they had written and performed during worship. They also reminisced about a multicultural fair and told me about the types of dances – Filipino, African break dancing, and hip hop – that members of Parkdale performed.

One experience that these children shared together – and one that was highly valued by all of the children (and adults) I interviewed from this congregation – was a summer vacation Bible camp. Having in the past been led by a paid student from outside the congregation, Parkdale decided to reformat this program and asked the youth in the congregation to head it up. The result was unexpected, but has received rave reviews from the children and adults alike. As Rev. Lynn said in the adult focus group,

> I just looked at it as intergenerational camp. That's what it turned into. The youth had done all the programming for a whole week of camp. So we were a good little community. It was quite interesting ... There was about twenty of us altogether, I guess, seventeen, twenty, something like that ... I think we should just set it up that way next year ... This is what the Spirit blew, so maybe we should just go with that.

After listening to Grace, Angela, and Lizzy laugh and reminisce about experiences such as these for several minutes, I asked them why these moments mattered so much:

DAVE: Why has all that stuff been so important to you? (*They are eager to respond and a few of them try to answer at the same time*)
ANGELA: Because it's basically like how we knew each other and how we became closer to each other, and ... yeah.
LIZZY: Because it kind of, um ... it's who we are. This church is who we are. Like, if it wasn't for all the prayers we've said, we wouldn't – we wouldn't have become so faithful and like, in front of an audience, and ...
DAVE: What do you mean?
GRACE: Like, 'cause like, when we grew up we started doing things in front of the grown up – the group of people that helped us, like ...
LIZZY: We started performing at sort of a young age, sort of. And it kind of helped us come out of our little shell. Yeah.
DAVE: So you said it's kind of who you are, it's made you faithful. What do you think it means for you to be faithful?
LIZZY: That we can always, like, rely on each other and no matter what, God is always with us, and um ... yeah.
DAVE: (*to Grace and Angela*) What about you guys? What does it mean for you to be faithful?
GRACE: What she said.
ANGELA: What she said (*they all laugh*) ... To be faithful, I think, like, to be like blessed with this family that we have, and the memories

that we had with each other and all the fun things that we had, and yeah …

DAVE: Do you think you can be faithful alone?

GRACE: It's good to be alone sometimes. And then when you're with other people it's good too –

LIZZY: (*interjecting*) It's okay to be independent, but it's always good to know you have somebody to rely on.

Shared experiences are key sources for the creation of theological meaning in these children. They hold strong theologies of community, theologies forged through being a part of a congregation that invites them to participate in – and give leadership to – the ways in which they practise their faith together. By engaging in a congregation that invites them into community and sees them as participants in its life, these girls have developed an understanding of faith and faithfulness that places an importance on interconnectedness generated through sharing experiences as they do life together.

Furthermore, as the focus on community within Parkdale connects to an impetus for caring for others, the shared experiences of these children provide them with a theology of faithfulness that includes being cared for by one another. Such experiences have given them a strong sense of belonging not just to any community, but to a community that cares for them, a community on which they can rely for help. Out of the storehouses of their memories, they remember that they are cared for by their congregation. It is no wonder that Angela and Grace both drew pictures of a God (figures 1.1 and 1.2) who actively cares for others, specifically by healing and helping children with their problems. Out of their experiences of being cared for as part of a "really tight family," to use Lizzy's words, their congregation has given them glimpses of a God who works for good.

It is important to note that both the communal nature of these girls' theologies (discussed previously) and the importance of shared experiences are likely intertwined with human development. During the "tween" years and early adolescence, one's family tends to have less influence on young people like Grace, Angela, and Lizzy, who begin to place greater and greater value on relationships with one another.[2] Their friendships with peers start taking on a tremendous role in their lives as they learn to listen to others and develop the ability to engage in interpersonal perspective taking.[3] Perhaps, for these girls at least, the adolescent desire to be known and accepted by one another is kicking in and driving them to do theology in communal and experiential keys. Yet these three girls were still rather early into this new phase of life. So, while surely bound up with the increased importance of relationships at their stage of development, the communal and experimental nature of their theologies can also be attributed to the broader culture and ethos of their congregation, a community that seeks to build strong relationships through the sharing of ideas and experiences.

It is clear, then, that shared experiences are vibrant sources of theological meaning among the children at Parkdale. But they are more than simply *sources* for theology. Angela, Grace, and Lizzy spoke of the experiences they shared together at Parkdale in such a way as to interpret these things as theological *in and of themselves*. They demonstrate a position held among practical theologians: theology is not something that only exists within the realm of abstract ideas; it is also embodied in concrete practice (in their case, in the making of community). In Lizzy's words, "from this church we all became very close and, like ... from all being here together, we all became like a really tight family." Perhaps this idea was best exemplified when these three children told me about all the memories and relationships that are woven into the eclectic church building in which they meet. Only a few weeks before our conversation, a cherished older gentleman in the congregation passed away, and these girls talked about how special it was that his memory will forever live on the wall of the church – the same wall that the man and his friend had carved their initials into in 1949. As they told me about discovering this inscription and several other shared experiences, they were recounting acts through which they have done theology with their congregation. These moments and experiences that they were recounting and reflecting on as they sat with me that morning were nothing short of experiences of lived theology. Through having those experiences and recalling them in the interview, they were embodying the very theology of community that Rev. Lynn seeks to build into the core of this congregation. These children were remembering moments in which they were the living theology of Parkdale.

Open Theology

As I listened to the children discuss and generate theology together, it was evident that they were doing so while leaving room for difference and diversity. Throughout our conversations, the children shared ideas that sometimes did not align with others', yet they were not quick to discount them, but rather carefully considered different ideas. Take, for, example, this excerpt from my interview with Jacob (5) and Enoch (10), two boys who played games together on the day that I interviewed them at Parkdale:

DAVE: So Enoch, when you were drawing, you said that God can be anything. What do you mean?
ENOCH: Well, God can be anything, really. He could be one of these pencil crayons.
DAVE: What do you mean by that? That's really cool.
JACOB: Because maybe if he has powers he can transform into things that nobody else can.
DAVE: Oh wow!
ENOCH: Okay.
DAVE: (*to Enoch*) Is that what you meant, or were you thinking something else?
ENOCH: Well, yeah, kind of. Well, God just comes. There's no other way to really put it.
JACOB: ... God can transform himself into anything.
ENOCH: I'm thinking that God can just come down and just look like an animal.
DAVE: And just look like anything?
ENOCH: Yeah. Look like an animal so that he's hidden. Or like a pencil crayon or anything. So then he's hidden and nobody knows that he's there.
DAVE: Oh wow!
ENOCH: So if they do something bad, God knows and sees it.
DAVE: Oh, okay. So it's like we can see it but we don't know that that's God? (*Enoch nods*) So we can see God but he's hidden at the same time? (*Enoch nods*) Wow! And why do you think God would do that?
ENOCH: So then he'd have to know, like, not a bunch of people will come towards him and, like, ask him a question and when they

see him be good around, pretending to be really good, like "Oh here, let me help you," seeing God over there.

DAVE: So it's a way God makes sure, like, sees if people are doing good or bad?

ENOCH: Yeah. So it's a secret. Like he's a spy.

JACOB: (*at same time as Enoch*) Yeah, he could see it because sometimes when he – he can actually do stuff like Santa because Santas actually have other powers like –

ENOCH: (*interjecting*) Toy-making and elves!

JACOB: – like God.

Enoch: (*playing*) Elves, attack!

DAVE: ... Do you think that God cares about whether people are doing good or bad things?

ENOCH: Uh-huh.

DAVE: Why is that?

JACOB: Uh, because he cares if he's doing, if people are doing bad things but, I mean good things, but if people are doing *bad* things he really, really does care.

DAVE: Oh yeah?

JACOB: Yeah.

ENOCH: I think there was an old saying called, like, "Whenever you lie, [baby Jesus] cries." Or whenever you lie a lightning bolt hits you that God throws at you which you can't really see.

DAVE: Okay. So God wants people to tell the truth?

ENOCH: Yeah. To be good ... and ... because they just ... God would give a warning ... God would give a warning to those guys who are being bad so ...

JACOB: I lie sometimes, but I ... I lie sometimes, but I don't get hit by lightning bolt. I don't even know why that's true. It's really true.

DAVE: Hmm ... So you both think that God wants people to do good, to be good, like, God cares –

ENOCH: (*interrupting*) Yes, because he gives them a warning and if they don't listen –

JACOB: (*talking over Enoch*) Maybe, maybe when I lied I knew.

This snippet of dialogue is one of several in which the children at this congregation considered one another's ideas as they were speaking about issues that matter to them and "trying them on" to see if these ideas fit within their current theological imaginings. Sometimes the new ideas they encountered seemed to work well with their own emerging thoughts. For example, when Lizzy shared her understanding of faithfulness (see above), Angela and Grace both responded with "What she said." In some instances, when new ideas were not fitting very well within their current thoughts, the children tweaked their theologies in order to make room for the ideas their peers were sharing with them, which is what occurred in the conversation between Jacob and Enoch above. The idea that Enoch shared with us, that when someone lies God throws a lightning bolt to them, did not match Jacob's view, and Jacob was aware of this. But instead of discounting it altogether, Jacob demonstrated a willingness to expand his interpretation of this experience, thinking that perhaps the reason he does not get hit by lightning when he lies is because he is already aware that he lied. Thus, God need not bring it to his attention with a high-voltage warning. While this episode highlights well the fact that children of Jacob's age tend to regard what others think and do in order to better make sense of things,[4] his interaction with Enoch's idea – not discounting it yet not wholeheartedly embracing it – demonstrates a willingness to seriously consider and play with the theologies of others.

These children demonstrate that doing theology in community does not mean that all people must think and act in the same way. This sentiment is one that flows among the congregation, as exemplified by Rev. Lynn's reminders that although one's theology might "brush up against" others' at times, this is what is involved in being a community marked by diversity. Diversity is the order of the day at Parkdale, as it is continually moving toward becoming an intercultural faith community in a broad sense of what constitutes culture. This congregation demonstrates that being a community that is a "really tight family" need not necessitate that all people think in the same way. Clearly, this ethos is echoed in the conversations of the young people from this congregation, as they demonstrated a significant willingness to genuinely engage with ideas that were new or foreign to them.

Angela and Grace responded to my request to draw a picture of God by drawing images of Jesus helping others. Angela's Jesus was helping a child deal with struggles like bullies and family (figure 1.1); Grace's Jesus was healing a child from an illness (figure 1.2). As they were explaining their drawings to me, I noticed that both drawings included yellow lines around parts of Jesus's body. Grace said that the yellow streaks of light coming from his hands symbolized Jesus's power to heal others. This is not, however, the way Jesus actually heals people; for Grace, this image of Jesus's healing powers represents that "Jesus helps you and he makes things kind of better." The yellow lines behind Jesus in Angela's drawings represented rays of light, which she drew because "for some reason I think that, you know, like the sun ... I think it follows you everywhere you go. I think Jesus follows you everywhere you go."

Both of these girls were manifesting Parkdale's openness to diversity in their awareness that their images were representations of God, symbolic images of how they imagine God to be and act in the world. Such an awareness of the representational nature of their drawings calls attention to the fact that the way each person imagines God is simply that – their image – and such images are merely representations of a God who is described and imagined in different ways.

Symbols and metaphors were one way that these children demonstrated their comfort with a God beyond their imaginations. Another was through their use of language expressing their comfort with uncertainty surrounding God, which was exemplified best by Jacob. His description of God was peppered with words speaking of the mystery and uncertainty surrounding God, words like *maybe*, *it seems*, *sometimes*, and *I think*. For example, in responding to the white clothes that Enoch drew on his picture of God (figure 1.3), Jacob said, "well maybe because God's White ... or not." Just moments later, after colouring his picture of God with all sorts of colours (figure 1.4), he said, "It seems to be a rainbow-coloured body." A little while later, again in response to a question Enoch asked about whether or not God has a beard, Jacob said, "Uh, God doesn't have a beard, I think." These are just a few of the many instances in which the language these children used exhibited their comfort with uncertainty surrounding God and their interpretations of God.

At the very moment that Grace, Angela, and I were sitting in the church hall discussing their drawings, the rest of the congregants were in the sanctuary hearing a sermon about the importance of knowing that different people have different ways of naming their "lamp" and "light" and that the members of Parkdale – who call this lamp Jesus – need to work with people who name it differently. The message from the pulpit was being embodied as Grace and Angela shared their drawings with me. The children's openness to different perspectives, the representational nature of the girls' drawings, and Jacob's use of words expressing uncertainty seem to match the culture of openness at Parkdale. As the congregation seeks to be a community that celebrates diversity in many forms, such openness seems to be a characteristic of the theology of its children.

Theology All Their Own

The children from Parkdale generated and expressed their theologies in ways that were quite consistent with the wider congregation. Yet this was not always the case. Here I will investigate how some of the children at Parkdale differed from the broader theological ethos and culture of their congregation.

Jacob and Enoch both expressed theological views that seemed to be inconsistent with those of their broader faith community. The understandings of God that these boys shared with me were in some ways quite different from the loving and welcoming God that is echoed throughout worship services at Parkdale. As Jacob drew and explained his picture of God (figure 1.4), he demonstrated the "fluid and magical"[5] thinking common among young children as he told us about a God who possessed superhero-like qualities. His God lives in a castle created so that "he can protect himself by, like, if somebody was throwing something at him, the castle will block it because it's made out of brick." And a castle is not God's only means of protection; God is a mix of colours so that he[6] can blend into his rainbow-coloured castle, camouflaging himself from those who want to hurt him. What is more, God also has special powers like the ability to walk through the walls of the castle.

Jacob's understanding of God seems influenced by his interest in superheroes. His is a God who possesses special qualities and characteristics necessary for protecting himself from unspecified evil forces. Perhaps he created this image of God with Enoch and me because he had just been playing with Enoch in a superhero activity and game book. Yet the idea of God he shared is also reminiscent of Minecraft, a video game in which the player can create, explore, and engage in combat in digital worlds. As Jacob imagined a castle for God to protect himself from those wanting to harm him, so can Minecraft players build digital structures such as walls and forts to protect themselves from hostile forces. While I was not able to confirm whether or not Jacob plays Minecraft, his theology of God certainly contains parallels to the game.

This boy seems to combine this Minecraft/superhero version of God with his experience at Parkdale's vacation Bible camp, which occurred about six months before our interview. This week-long camp was an important source of theological meaning-making for the children at this congregation, a point I will explore in chapter 5. During the camp, a volunteer in a dragon costume walked around the church building from time to time. Eventually the children at the camp welcomed and accepted the dragon into the community and the volunteer took off the costume head. This practice was intended to help those present address issues of welcome and difference, showing that all people should be welcome and are deserving of kindness and friendship. During my first visit to the congregation – a few months after the camp – I saw a banner in the hall that read "Dragons Welcome" and was filled with messages from the campers to the dragon. Jacob – who was only four or five years old at the time of the camp – seemed to interpret the experience of the dragon in a manner unintended by Parkdale's leaders. The theology he generated depicts a God who is threatened by difference and must protect himself rather than welcome others into his castle. When he and Enoch told stories about the camp, Jacob's words demonstrated that he may have been afraid of the dragon; while Enoch was keen to "follow the dragon wherever it goes," Jacob distanced himself from the mythical creature, saying that "the dragon couldn't go anywhere" and making sure to say that when the dragon took off his "hat" it was somebody that he knew. Perhaps this experience was frightful for this young boy – which was clearly not the leaders' intention – and he has drawn from this experience in creating a view of a God who needs protection, much like he wanted to be protected from the dragon.

Enoch also expressed a view of God that was inconsistent with the theology of his congregation. Although he stated that "God can be anything," his drawing pictured a God who is a larger-than-life male wearing the whitest of robes (figure 1.3). This God was sporting a beard in the picture, and standing on clouds as he conversed with angels flying next to him. For Enoch, God is the creator of all that is good, while "the devil" is responsible for evil and wants to take over the world. "But," in his words, "there's only one person standing in his [the devil's] way – and it's God." Enoch also sees God as a sort of divine "spy" and judge who can come down from heaven and observe people's behaviour and offer warnings to those who are doing evil, for God wants people to do good in the world. God's judgement comes when people fail to heed these warnings: "they're doing some bad things and eventually if they keep on doing it over and over and over and over, like continuously throughout their whole life, each day, then basically they're just going to go plop (*he lifts his hand up and opens it as if to drop something*) down to hell." Conversely, people who do good in the world go to heaven to be with God.

Enoch's understanding of God is not one that I heard preached or spoken about by Rev. Lynn and the wider congregation. It actually seems to contradict the welcoming, accepting, and loving God that this minister presents to the people of Parkdale. It is, however, a relatively mainstream understanding within more conservative Christian traditions, with concepts such as God as creator and divine judge, the devil as the source of evil, and the dichotomized eternal destinations of heaven and hell. In many ways, his theology of God is based on dualisms – heaven and hell, God and the devil, good and evil – that leave no room for the ambiguity, diversity, and broad acceptance that is commonplace within the theology through which Rev. Lynn leads the congregation. Perhaps the variance of this view from that of Parkdale can be attributed to the fact that this is not the only congregation that Enoch attends. While he comes to Parkdale with his grandmother, he also accompanies her to a Baptist congregation and sometimes attends a third congregation with his mother. The theologies espoused by these churches may have helped form a view of God that in many ways does not align with the culture of Parkdale.

The understandings of God that Enoch and Jacob expressed to me both deviate from the overall theology of Parkdale in some significant ways. Yet one can also interpret such excursions as fitting within this congregation. Yes, Rev. Lynn seeks to show a God that is in many ways dissimilar from these children's views; but Parkdale seeks to be a community that is open and accepting of difference – and this includes theological difference. It can be surmised, then, that the inconsistency between Enoch and Jacob's views of God and those of the wider congregation may in fact be a manifestation of the community's broad affirmation of an interculturalism that welcomes diversity in all forms.

* * *

The five young research participants from Parkdale generate theology in ways that are consistent with the broader theology of their congregation. Their theologies parallel the congregation's theology of community in the way that they they generate and hold their views communally, the reliance on shared experiences in their theological imaginings, and their openness to difference and diversity. This is not to say that every aspect of the theologies of these children resonates with their broader faith community. In particular, some of the children developed views of God that draw from sources outside of Parkdale that result in them holding theologies that differ from the broader congregation, such as how Jacob seems to have interpreted his experience at the vacation Bible camp. In fact, this camp was a key source of theological meaning for all five of the children from Parkdale. While I will flesh out this common trend in chapter 5, we must first explore the other congregations that participated in my research and the young theologians who are part of them.

Figure 1.1 Angela's drawing

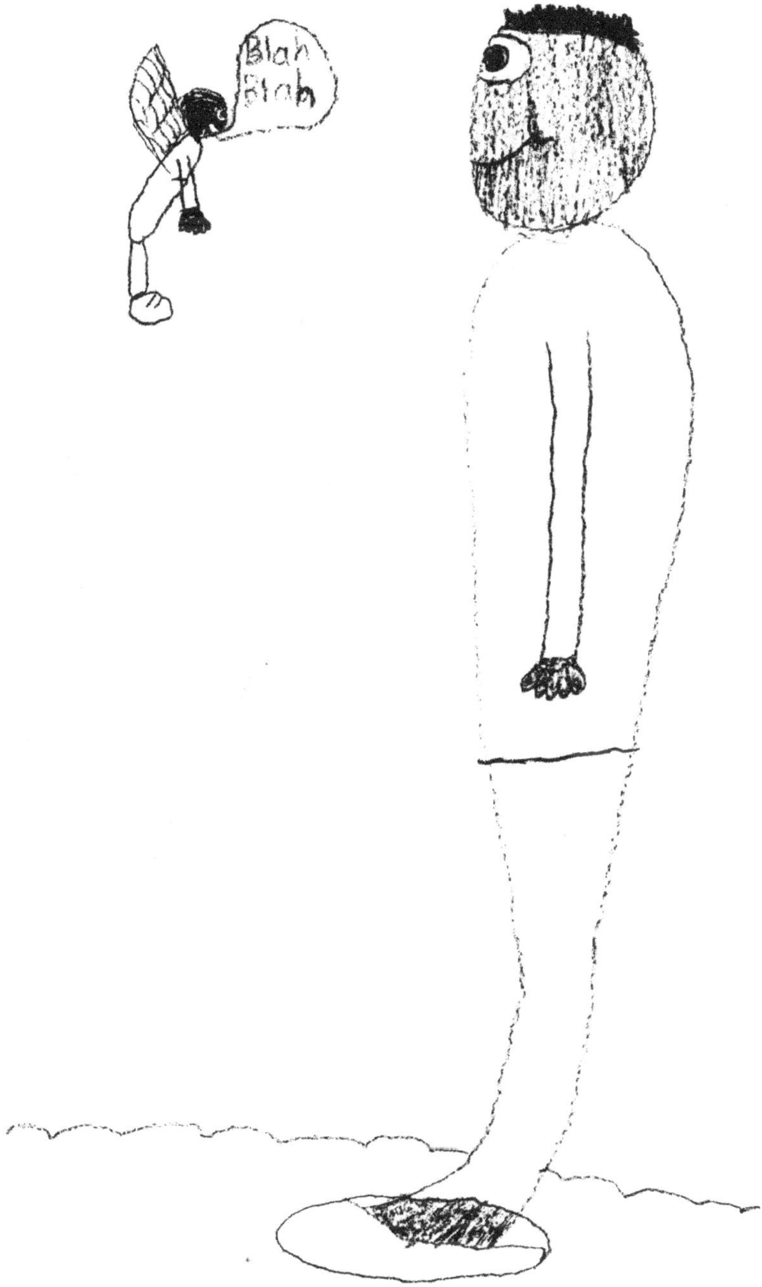

Figure 1.3 Enoch's drawing

Figure 1.4 Jacob's drawing

2 "We Put Our Tradition in It"

Messiah Methodist United Church and a Theology of Interconnectedness

Things seemed a bit chaotic in Sunday school on the first day that I joined the children at Messiah Methodist United Church. There were approximately twenty-five children ranging from three-year-olds to others well into their teens. The children twelve and younger were sitting around four large tables pushed together in the centre of the room, and the teenagers were parked on chairs at the back of the room. After standing up one after the next to recite a Bible verse that they had chosen to memorize, the children separated into two groups as the adolescents stacked their chairs and went with Emmanuel, a Sunday school superintendent, to the classroom next door. As they were making their way out, Jemina, the Sunday school teacher for the younger group, pulled me aside to say, "Dave, one of our teachers is on maternity leave, so we don't have a lot of teachers. But we manage."

I remained with Jemina's group and observed as she handed out sheets of blank paper and crayons to the younger children in the room (about three to five years old) and asked them to draw quietly as she led class for the older children. With her infant child in her arms, she asked the school-age children questions about the previous week's lesson, which focused on the story of Gideon. Try as they might, the younger children were restless as they talked to one another and wiggled in their adult-sized chairs. It was clear that the absence of one teacher meant that Jemina had combined two classes together and was doing all she could to keep one class occupied while she worked with the other. As the noise and movement among the younger children became elevated, I asked Jemina if I could help in some way. Immediately she went next door to see if Emmanuel knew whether or not there was another space in the Sunday school wing – which was currently under renovation – that was available. Before I knew what was happening, Jemina informed the children (and me) that "Uncle David" would be taking the three- to-five-year-olds to another classroom to do some activities. This wasn't quite what I had in mind when I asked if I could be of help, but I decided to roll with the punches.

I had already heard Jemina mention the Fruit of the Spirit during the class, so I asked for some paper and crayons and figured that I could talk to the young ones about the Fruit of the Spirit as they drew different fruits on their papers. It wasn't a terrible idea, as far as spur-of-the-moment lesson plans go. But it would have been better if I had been able to remember all the Fruit of the Spirit. As the seven or eight young children entrusted to my care sat in child-size chairs around a small table, I began asking them if anyone knew any of the nine Fruit of the Spirit. With not a Bible to be seen in the space, I started singing a song in my head that I used to teach to children at churches over the years: "The Fruit of the Spirit are love, joy, peace, patience, kindness, goodness, discipline, and self-control." That's only eight – I had forgotten one. No matter. I had no choice but to carry on and hope that the ninth Fruit would come to me as I matched each spiritual Fruit to the fruits that the children were drawing on their papers. Love and lemons. Peace and pineapples. Goodness and grapes.

I never did remember that elusive final Fruit before someone poked their head around the corner and told me that we had five minutes of class time left. Relieved that I didn't have much else to improvise with the group of rambunctious youngsters, I said that we needed to clean up our supplies and then asked if there was one last thing we should do before we leave to join the older children in their classroom. To offer them a hint, I put my hands together and bowed my head. "Pray! Pray!" they shouted. A young girl offered to lead our closing prayer and quickly enlisted her friend to join her. I asked the children to sit quietly and the two girls looked at each other and began to pray: "Hail Mary, full of grace, the Lord is with thee." As she continued, some of the other children joined in praying this well-known Roman Catholic prayer of intercession to the Virgin Mary. After finishing the prayer, the young leaders blessed themselves with the sign of the cross as others followed suit, saying "In the name of the Father, the Son, and the Holy Spirit." Here I was with a group of children at a Methodist congregation that recently joined the largest Protestant denomination in Canada, listening to them pray in a markedly Catholic manner – and it seemed as though I was the only one who thought this to be out of the ordinary.

A Congregation Born and Adopted

The history of Messiah Methodist United Church dates back to the late 1980s. After emigrating from Ghana and marrying a Canadian man, Jane Joiner wanted to start a Methodist congregation in her city. She began inviting other Ghanaian Methodists to meet as a prayer group in the basement of her home, and as attendance increased, the need for a space of their own became evident. But the community was divided on what it was seeking in a property, and a group of congregants broke away and found a different space. This break-off congregation experienced another schism and, in 1996, a group of members left and began meeting at a Presbyterian church in a northwest neighbourhood of their city, naming their new congregation Messiah Methodist Church.

Shortly after beginning their own congregation in the mid 1990s, the leaders of Messiah Methodist Church received a message from the lay president of Methodist Church Ghana (MCG) that the congregation should seek affiliation with the United Church, the Canadian member of the World Methodist Council. The United Church welcomed Messiah into its family, classifying this congregation under its umbrella of "ethnic ministries." To provide further clarity to its hybrid identity as part of both MCG and the United Church, both denominations signed a "Memorandum of Understanding for Cooperation" in 2013. By this time the congregation had changed its name to reflect its affiliation with the United Church and was now known as Messiah Methodist United Church.

The 2013 memorandum was a landmark event in the history of Messiah. Its leaders hold this agreement in high esteem and see it as a solidification of the congregation within the landscape of Christianity in Canada, yet in a way that keeps it connected first and foremost as a congregation of MCG. While allowing the congregation to benefit from leadership connections and resources of the United Church, this agreement gives Messiah the freedom to organize and run itself in accordance with the constitution and polity of MCG. For example, the memorandum allows MCG to appoint senior ministers to Messiah for five-year terms, with the United Church supporting such ministers with immigration assistance and denominational support staff throughout the term. Emmanuel, one of the Sunday school superintendents at Messiah, likened this relationship to finding a caretaker for your child: "It's like you have your baby, and you cannot let another person take care of it. So that's Methodist Church Ghana, in the Memorandum of Understanding. That's like, this is my child, but he is away. But I send you with a nice person. He won't hurt you, so you can take good care of him. But that doesn't mean that you own the child. It's just that you are taking care of him or her for me."

Another milestone in the history of this congregation came when West End United Church, a sixty-year-old congregation in the area, closed and many of its members began attending another United Church congregation in a nearby neighbourhood. Upon deciding to close West End, the United Church sought to keep the building within the denomination and gifted it to Messiah, which was continually growing and would benefit from a space to call its own. Since moving into this space, Messiah has gradually adapted it to reflect the unique culture of its congregation.

The building is dominated by a large, box-like sanctuary with tall windows on both sides and a platform at the front, which includes a gradually raised section for the choir. On the walls are plaques commemorating the building's sixty-year history, banners saying "I will serve the church" in English and in Twi (a native language of Ghana), the provincial flag and the flag of Ghana, and a large image of Jesus depicted as a White man holding a lamb on his shoulders. There are rows of chairs with seating for about 250 people and a communion table at the front draped with white linen. The front wall features a large wooden cross with a projection screen to the left and a banner commemorating West End United Church and Messiah Methodist United Church to the right.

The basement of the church, which is used for Sunday school, was under renovation throughout the six months that I visited this congregation.[1] At the end of a hallway was a pair of rooms that were currently used for two Sunday school classes – one for children up to age twelve and the other for teens. The other half of the basement was the site of the renovation, which was being undertaken in order to care for the building entrusted to the congregation and provide a variety of rooms for age-based Sunday school classes. The space in which the children met for Sunday school while I was a visitor was a relatively stark room with light-coloured walls, a whiteboard at the front, and four long tables pushed together with chairs around them.

Although Sunday services "officially" begin at 10:00, it is not unusual for only a handful of people to be in the large sanctuary when the choir walks up the aisle wearing black gowns and mortarboards. Congregants trickle in during the first twenty or thirty minutes, and then flood in between prayers. Emmanuel told me that the members of Messiah "are people that love noise," and its Sunday services demonstrate this: by the time the worship band begins playing loud praise songs, the room is filled with people moving about the space to hug and shake hands with one another. As the music continues, the congregants dance around the room and sing in a spirit of celebration as the lyrics are projected on the screen. Eventually the boisterous music ends and the liturgy continues with prayers, which lead to scripture readings and a sermon preached in both English and Akan. On the first Sunday of the month, members of Methodist guilds and clubs – like Women's Fellowship and The Christ's Little Band – wear their uniforms during the service, a practice shared among MCG congregations around the world.

The vast majority of congregants are people who have immigrated to Canada from Ghana, and they range in age from infants to seniors, with no age group unrepresented. While the congregation has at times included a few members who were not Ghanaian, these individuals were people of African or Afro-Caribbean descent, and during my visits to Messiah, I was the only person who was not Black. While most adults within the congregations were born and raised in Ghana, almost all of the children who are part of the congregation are second-generation Canadians. With Ghanaian culture embedded within its life, Messiah tends to function in a manner distinct from other United Church congregations. For one thing, its leaders and members rely on word-of-mouth communication, tending to keep phone calls and emails to a minimum in the organizational life of the congregation. For another thing, organization tends to happen more organically and in real time rather than through a great deal of preparation and planning. For example, even though the leaders were aware that I would be visiting and conducting interviews on particular Sundays, the interviews I held with children in this congregation were organized the morning during which they took place, with leaders speaking to me when I arrived and recruiting children and parents from the pool of individuals who were present that day.

Children's ministry in this congregation occurs through Sunday school classes separated by age groups (youth, older children, and younger children), although due to a shortage of teachers and available classroom space during my time with the congregation, there was only one class for all children under thirteen – that is, until I spontaneously held a class with the younger children. During the first part of worship services, the children sit in the back rows with their teachers, who struggle to get them engaged and have them participate in the service. Eventually they gather at the front of the sanctuary for a "Time with Children," which includes a short lesson and prayer that precedes Sunday school.

Sunday school at Messiah is in transition, as it is experiencing a shortage of teachers and undergoing renovations. Thus, during my time there, it was operating with half the leadership and half the space normally at its disposal. During this transitional period, Sunday school begins with a time when all children gather in one classroom to sing hymns and pray together. Following this, each child is called upon to stand and say a Bible verse from memory, and then the group divides into their age-based classes. The classes tend to operate out of a schooling-instructional model[2] that emphasizes memorization and knowledge acquisition. For example, in addition to sharing memorized Bible verses, Sunday school includes a lesson and discussion about a particular passage of scripture. Jemina, one of the children's Sunday school teachers who met with me for a one-on-one interview, tends to follow-up the day's Bible lesson with a "social talk" in which she discusses social issues ranging from bullying to careers. During this time, the younger children work on colouring pages or other quiet activities related to the lesson of the day.

Sunday school is not the only aspect of children's ministry at Messiah. This congregation joins others in MCG in having various guilds and fellowships for their children, like Girls' Fellowship and Boys' and Girls' Brigade. Girls' Fellowship is a time of additional lessons and conversation in which girls in the congregation participate on Saturday mornings. At times, they meet with Girls' Fellowships from other diaspora MCG congregations at large North American conventions. Brigade is a program that draws from the military in order to teach discipline to the children through marching and singing hymns together. On some Sundays, members of Brigade will march up the aisles at the beginning of the service wearing uniforms and carrying the flags of Ghana and Canada.

Putting Tradition in It

Speaking about the worship life of Messiah, Sophia – the congregation's administrator – told me of the importance of Ghanaian culture in the congregation's worship: "We put our tradition in it and it makes it work."

This is a congregation that identifies strongly as Ghanaian, and it draws from indigenous religious practices in its boisterous and free spirit of worship as well as in the theological visions that undergird this community. Perhaps the most pervasive way that a Ghanaian worldview drives Messiah is through an understanding that all aspects of life are connected. During my interview with Emmanuel, he expressed to me that Ghanaians – and Africans in general – see everything as interconnected, and this worldview allowed White people to spread Christianity throughout the continent, for Africans were able to perceive it as connected to their indigenous religions and belief systems.

Ministry at Messiah considers the whole of the person – the spiritual, physical, and intellectual, to use Emmanuel's terms. The congregation seeks to nurture faith in its members in ways that do not disconnect spirituality from other areas of their lives. For example, it helps its members not only with issues directly related to faith, but also when they face illnesses or poverty or other challenges, for the whole of one's life matters to the leaders of this community. As Jemina said to me, "under the setting of the church, everything that we do is spiritual." I experienced this understanding during my visit to the congregation one Tuesday morning to interview Rev. Ayensu. Upon arriving at the church, he led me to the sanctuary and offered prayers for my research and the well-being of me and my family. Following our discussion, we once again made our way to the sanctuary to bookend this particular aspect of my research with prayer. To this minister, my research was a deeply spiritual matter, one that he wanted to bathe in prayer in order to ask God to bless my work, my family, and their community.

The leaders of Messiah organize and implement ministry with children through a lens of the interconnectedness of all parts of life. Because they see their children as both present and future leaders of the congregation, Rev. Ayensu stated that they "take much or greater interest in the life and growth of the children – more than the adults." And as they nurture the growth and flourishing of their children, they consider all aspects of their lives. They not only want their children to grow as leaders of Messiah, but also to grow in a way that allows their faith to shine in everything they do – both inside and outside of the congregation. Thus, they teach scripture and spirituality in manners that connect them to other aspects of the children's lives. Going further, the leaders of this church also see Sunday school as a way of teaching the children – most of whom were born in Canada – about the history and culture of their parents' homeland.[3] In these ways, Messiah connects the "spiritual" with the whole lives of its children.

The interconnectedness of life not only affects Messiah's ministry with children, but also its broader worship life and theological outlook. Western society includes a tendency to classify and separate into categories various objects in the world,[4] a cultural norm that seemed removed from worship at Messiah and replaced with a focus on interconnectedness. While participating in worship services among this congregation, I struggled to understand its worship style and theological perspective, largely because I have been socialized to separate and categorize in order to understand. At different times throughout the service, elements seemed to be charismatic and liturgical, theologically conservative and theologically liberal, reminiscent of Catholic Mass and of evangelical praise services. Such an intermingling of what are ostensibly distinct theological traditions is made possible by the congregation's understanding of connectedness, which was demonstrated in Sophia's remarks (albeit not completely accurate) about the origins of the United Church: "if you look at the United Church history, it's a mash-up of all Protestant people … It is Anglican, the Methodists, the Presbyterians; they came together to come to the United Church. So in actual fact the worship is all the same." This comment showcases the congregation's propensity to focus on similarity and interconnectedness instead of difference and distinction; yet in actuality, the church union of 1925 did not erase differences among the founding denominations, and worship in United Church congregations remains tremendously varied.[5] While its Methodist roots and United Church affiliation are held in high esteem, what matters most to this community is not the theological category or denominational tradition with which its worship aligns; instead, as Rev. Ayensu said, "worship should be done in an atmosphere of freedom." As Emmanuel explained, many charismatic and Pentecostal churches in Ghana are strict in their practices of inclusion in worship, and may exclude or put stipulations on the participation of members who have breached their values or made mistakes. Yet Messiah – like other MCG congregations – emphasizes individuals' freedom to express themselves and worship God as they see fit.

Messiah may self-identify as Ghanaian, but it does so with an awareness that it is also a community that resides in Canada. This context has meant that even while the leaders of this congregation guide it in ways that align with the norms of MCG and Ghanaian culture, they have made changes to address the particularities of their current context. One such change has been the addition of a time of fellowship with tea and light refreshments after the worship service each Sunday. Unlike congregations in Ghana, the members of Messiah are spread throughout the city and its suburbs, with some families driving significant distances to attend worship each week. The physical distance between congregants necessitates greater intentionality in fostering relationships with each other, which the leaders of this church believe tends to occur more naturally in Ghana. The fellowship time after each service is a direct response to the reality of life in Canada, where members of the congregation do not always interact with one another outside of Messiah. Rev. Ayensu believes this time of fellowship is vital: "I take a cup of tea, you also take a cup of tea. We can stand and chat. For even if it's for ten minutes, it improves our relationships."

The influence of Ghanaian culture in a Canadian context shapes this congregation's ministry with children. For one thing, it makes the use of Sunday school curricula problematic. According to Emmanuel, resources from Canada do not fit well because Messiah is a Ghanaian church, and material from Ghana is also tricky because the congregation is in Canada. In light of this, Messiah imports Sunday school materials from Ghana and teachers contextualize them for ministry in its present Canadian context. Another change to Ghanaian tradition that Messiah has made has been to include children in worship. While congregations in Ghana tend to have children in Sunday school for the entirety of the service – almost a service unto itself, as Jemina told me – Messiah includes children in the beginning of its service. After an opening hymn, prayers, and some praise music, the children are called to the front for a "Time with Children" – a practice common in many United Church congregations – and then they are led to Sunday school classes. Once a month the children remain in the service for its entirety, although they sit at the back with their Sunday school teachers and do not tend to engage in worship, prayer, and other elements of the service. Although the results are mixed, the congregation's initiatives to include children in worship are a way of adapting customs from Ghanaian tradition for use within the context of Canada.

Theological Reflections

A central hallmark of African worldviews is the web of all relationships, a web that stretches far and wide from the living to the dead, those not yet born, and the whole of the world around oneself.[6] All of life is connected. Such a view of interconnectedness, which is vital to the culture of Messiah, has profound implications for how one views, understands, and interprets the world. Key characteristics of the theological lives of the children in this congregation reflect and express Messiah's vision of the interconnectedness of all things in at least three ways: first, through their tendency to draw widely from sources for generating theology; second, through viewing all understandings as accurate in some ways and inaccurate in others; and third, through sensing God's presence and involvement in their lives.

Wide Theology

I have already described Messiah as a congregation whose worship evades denominational and theological classification. Although this church grounds itself within Methodism, it does so without excluding the influence of other theological traditions, perceiving the boundaries between different denominations and theological inflections as quite porous.

Such a vision of openness to multiple theologies and traditions was evident in the lives of the five children I interviewed from this congregation in their tendency to draw widely in gathering sources for creating theology. Each of them was influenced by at least one theological tradition beyond the traditions of MCG and the United Church. Not only do all of these children attend Roman Catholic primary schools, Chris (10) and Marion (11) made their First Communion with their classes, sisters Marion and Dawn (9) attended a Roman Catholic parish before recently making the switch to Messiah, and Luke (11) attended a Pentecostal congregation until his family joined Messiah a few years ago. In my conversations with them, it was evident that these different theological traditions were influencing their current understandings. The rare instances when one of them indicated that their idea might not be accepted by their congregation only occurred when drawing from sources that were outside mainstream Christian traditions and denominations. For example, when Luke discussed what it means to be a "spirit," he admitted that he watches a television show called *Long Island Medium*, which follows the experiences of a woman who communicates with the deceased: "Church says it's not good to believe in stuff like that. But I still think it's good to believe in stuff like that because then you get closure and learn about your loved ones and how they're doing."

This tendency to draw widely from other traditions was evident during my discussion with Kaitlyn, a twelve-year-old second-generation Canadian who has been attending Messiah for as long as she can remember. It is exemplified in the following three snippets:

DAVE: Can you tell me a little bit about the drawing [figure 2.1]?
KAITLYN: Okay, well, the only part that I really like that I drew are the yellow lines, and it represents like the brightness of God. Because in the Bible when the angels tried to look at God they had to cover themselves with their wings because God is so bright.
DAVE: Oh yeah.
KAITLYN: He's just, like, God represents the light ...
D: Right. And is there a reason you picked blue [for God's clothes]?
KAITLYN: Well, I picked, I don't – I think of blue as kind of like a pure colour, kind of next to white. I think blue's just like – I don't know why. Because I think that's just like what Mary used to wear. In lots of pictures she wears blue, so probably God picked her because she was so holy.
DAVE: Okay. And what about like God's hair and moustache? (*Kaitlyn laughs*) ... I'm interested in why you drew God the way you did.
KAITLYN: The hair and the moustache, I think that God just ... I don't know, I'm not sure, but ...
DAVE: What about the way God has his hands – like that (*I open my hands like God in her drawing*)?
KAITLYN: He's kind of just doing this (*she holds her hands like the drawing*).
D: Right.
N: Like, "I'm God." So it just kind of represents himself.

* * *

DAVE: (*referring to Kaitlyn's drawing*) So the heart symbolizes that God is love?
KAITLYN: Uh-huh.
DAVE: What do you mean by that?
KAITLYN: Well, like, everything like kindness and all the virtues, I think they all lead to love. And God, he just – the reason why we're all on earth and if we all survive another day it's because God loves us and he didn't make anything bad happen to us. Because he loves us so much and he created us to love each other.
DAVE: What do you mean, "God didn't make anything bad happen?"

KAITLYN: Most of the time you need – like, God wants you to ask him [for help] first. And so he can help you because God only helps others who help themselves ... If you woke up, you know, and had a good day, went to sleep and you didn't get in a car accident or you found out one of your loved ones passed away or something, then I think that God had, he loved you so much so he kept your day going well. But most people, when something bad happens to them they always question God. Sometimes I do that too, but then I remember everything happens for a reason.

DAVE: What do you mean by that?

KAITLYN: (*immediately*) Like someone passes away maybe. God just thought those, the time on earth is done and he just wants them to be safe in heaven with him. And not like he's taking them away from you. He's just keeping them in heaven. But you can still pray to God and tell them, and tell God to tell that person or something, that you still love them. And I think God can still do that for you.

DAVE: So it's not like the relationship is over completely, right?

KAITLYN: Uh-huh.

D: What do you think it means when bad things do happen? ... Where do the bad things come from?

KAITLYN: Maybe if you get tempted to do something bad, then you turned away from God and that wasn't God's fault because you were the one who made the choice to do something bad. So if something bad happens you can't blame God for that. It's your own fault. You were just tempted to do whatever you did. You can't blame God for it ... We can choose to be with God and do the right things or we can choose to go our own way and do whatever we want. And we can't blame God for that because that was our own fault and our own choices.

* * *

DAVE: What's that like, going to a Catholic school ... ?

KAITLYN: Well, going to a Catholic school, I like it because every day that I go I get to spend, like, something learning about Jesus. At my school, after we sing "O Canada" we have prayers and in my class we usually read a religion textbook, which is good, in the morning.

DAVE: So you have religion class there?

KAITLYN: Yeah.

DAVE: Okay. And are most of the kids who go there Catholic or is it –
KAITLYN: Yeah. Most of them are Catholic. Yeah.
DAVE: Okay. And do they know that you're not Catholic?
KAITLYN: Yes, I think some of them know because, we don't really say the Hail Mary that much. Like, for Christians in the Methodist Church we don't really say it that much. So most people when they say the Hail Mary at school, I don't really say it ... I still do communion and all that stuff – just not, like, the Hail Mary.
DAVE: Right, right. There are some things that –
KAITLYN: Are different.

These three excerpts demonstrate Kaitlyn's tendency to draw from her experiences at a Roman Catholic school and a Methodist/United Church congregation in generating theological insight. In the first excerpt, she seems to be appropriating Marion iconography as she attributes meaning to the colours with which she draws God. While there are no pictures of Mary on the walls of Messiah (yet there are plenty of images of Jesus), she surely encountered images of Mary – who is traditionally depicted wearing blue and understood as pure within Roman Catholic theology – in the religion classes and Masses at her school.

The theology that Kaitlyn expresses in the second snippet is much more consistent with that which Messiah weaves into its services. She describes a God who is involved in one's life (I will say more about this in a subsection below), who protects people from harm, and who wants to help people. This vision of God was upheld at several points during worship services I participated in at Messiah, including prayers for God to "protect us from the evil one" and "expand our territory," as well as comments about having our spiritual and physical needs met through prayer. Kaitlyn's theology seems to draw from such a theological perspective, which sees God as the great provider and protector.

The final excerpt is a rare moment when Kaitlyn intentionally distinguishes between different theological traditions that influence her theology, although she does so without placing an impenetrable wall between them. She underscores praying the Hail Mary as a distinguishable difference between Methodists and Roman Catholics. Yet even while identifying as Methodist, she states that she participates in Catholic Eucharist[7] at her school, and even alludes to sometimes praying the Hail Mary with her class (i.e., she doesn't pray it "that much").[8] For her, the boundary between these two Christian traditions is one that can be crossed.

The breadth of sources for generating theology is not limited to traditions and ideas within the realms of Christianity. These children also showcased a willingness to draw from all sorts of other sources, including movies, television shows, personal experiences, their engagement with scripture, and their own imaginations. For example, nine-year-old Dawn, who recently started attending Messiah with her older sister, explained to me that although she has watched movies about Jesus, she prefers to use her imagination to think about who and what God is: "I imagine it in my imagination. Like, for example, when David and Goliath, when David slingshot a rock at Goliath's head I imagine that David was doing that to Goliath … Your imagination is very – like, sometimes it could be real … Because God formed your brain to imagine different stuff." While Dawn drew from her imagination, Luke used the 2001 BBC series *Son of God* as a way of interpreting Jesus's crucifixion:

> [In the film] you notice that he wasn't yelling at anyone; he wasn't really mad. He was only screaming out of his own pain because who wants to get a nail shoved through your hands? But he wasn't yelling at the people who threw the rocks at him. He just took it and he seemed to be in pain, but he didn't seem to be mad at anyone. And, like, calmness and stuff like that is really good traits to have because … when you're not mad, then you get to experience better things. But if you spend your whole life being all grumpy and mad then you're going to miss out on a lot of stuff.

Whether drawing from Roman Catholic iconography, television shows, or the depths of their imaginations, the children at Messiah blended multiple theological traditions and non-theological sources together as they generated theological insight. And as they did so, they gave little indication that the practice of drawing widely was outside the norm of their congregational context.

This tendency is understandable when compared to the broader theological vision of their congregation. As a Ghanaian congregation, the leaders and members of Messiah value the interconnectedness of all things, which allows their theological views to be interrelated with many other aspects of life, including those that the children draw upon to create theological meaning. Such a view is reflected in the worship life of this congregation as it makes use of hymns, prayers, and other practices that originate in a wide variety of denominational contexts. Furthermore, this worldview is reinforced in Sunday school each week as Jemina leads her class in a "social talk." Thus, the children's tendency to utilize a wide variety of sources seems to comport with the theological vision and practices of the broader congregation.

Blurred Theology

Related to the proclivity of the children from Messiah to draw widely in their sources for theological insight is their tendency to focus on similarities and avoid making distinctions between correct and incorrect theology. Rather than drawing lines between and highlighting differences among the various theological traditions and understandings that these young people have encountered, many of them seemed to speak of how all traditions, doctrines, and theological ideas are right and wrong in some ways. Luke, a twelve-year-old who has attended Messiah for the past two years, was the child who expressed this most eloquently, as seen in these excerpts from my conversation with him. The first begins as he was telling me about the congregation he attended before his family made the change to Messiah:

DAVE: Shine Church [Luke's former congregation]. Was it the same kind of thing, that you would –

LUKE: They would encourage us to think the same way [as Messiah]. Because when you go to any church they're always encouraging the same message, and that's to be holy and to be good and not to be mean to people. No matter what church you go to, whether you're Catholic, Pentecost[al], anybody who goes to any other type of church, they're all teaching you the same things. It's just where you want to go to learn about it.

DAVE: Okay.

LUKE: So, that's just what I think about.

DAVE: Okay.

LUKE: It's just different ways of teaching. So it doesn't really matter what church you're going to. You're always learning the same thing.

DAVE: Right. Okay.

LUKE: It never gets old, because it's always something you have to keep with you as you grow and ... yeah.

DAVE: So you don't think that there are some churches that are right and some that are wrong?

LUKE: Each church is right in their own way. They may not be right at everything. But they're going to be right [where] some other churches [are wrong] and they're going to be wrong where some other churches are right. So ...

DAVE: Cool. And so do you think that there are ways that, um, this church and Shine Church were, like, where Shine was wrong, this church is right? And where this church is wrong, Shine was right?

LUKE: Because Shine Church was what you would [call] an encouraging church. Like, they'll give you the message that they want you to believe in. But their message was a good message. But here, they don't necessarily give you, like, they'll still give you their message, but they'll also encourage you to think your own way.

DAVE: Here?

LUKE: Yeah.

DAVE: Whereas the other church, they wanted you to think their way, is that what it was?

LUKE: Not completely think their way. But they always had *their* message on what *they* believed in, so it was more of *their* opinion. Here, it's *their* opinion but then there's also *your* opinion. So, that's kind of what I see was different there.

DAVE: And which one would be good, then?

LUKE: Um ... either of them is fine. It's just how you want to learn, so.

* * *

LUKE: Everybody's been in that group where there's that one person who leads everyone and you never really get the chance to expose your ideas, so ...

DAVE: Yeah.

LUKE: But you do have to think about it. Because even if you're feeling bitter that they didn't let you say your idea, you notice that in a way their idea might be right too. Yours is just a different way of explaining it.

DAVE: Okay.

LUKE: Because there are people who think there's only a right way and there's a wrong way and there's a million ways to get it wrong and only one way to get it right. But that's not true. There's a million ways to make a question that's wrong, you can make it right.

DAVE: Hmm ...

LUKE: So …

DAVE: … What makes you think that's not true and there are many ways?

LUKE: Because there's not one way to solve a problem. Because you see how God said one plus one plus one didn't equal three? It equals one because they're all one person and that's his way of thinking about it. And even if it's not mathematically correct, it's still correct in its own way. But somebody who's a mathematician, if you walk up and said "What's one plus one plus one?" they would say it was three. But then you could come to someone in the church they would know what you said when you said one plus one plus one, they would think about God –

DAVE: Right.

LUKE: – and then they'd say that it's all one because they are all one person.

DAVE: Right.

LUKE: And that story where he had, like, I think five pieces of bread and two fish and he was able to divide it to feed 500 people. People who say that that's impossible, but he has the power to make anything possible.

DAVE: Right. So, from one perspective, one plus one plus one equals three and it doesn't equal anything but three.

LUKE: Uh-huh.

DAVE: But for other people, one plus one plus one equals – it could equal three or it could equal –

LUKE: (*interjecting*) One.

DAVE: One.

LUKE: That's just how I like to think. Because I don't like to think that there's only one way to do things because then you become kind of one-sided. And then you only think about, there's only a one way to make something look good and one way to make sure that it's right. But that's not how I'm trying to think. I'm trying to think that even if I don't understand this way, I can always find another way to understand the question. It's like long division and short division. People feel that long division's right and that you get a better answer. But I do short division. It's not a problem. You're getting the same answer. You're just getting it in a different way.

DAVE: Uh-huh. You know, that's what I always thought too. I could do short division and when teachers would say "Show your work,"

I'd say, "What does it matter if I show my work? I did it. I got it. It's the answer." You know?

LUKE: As long as they can use a calculator so I can think about the answer. Just, long division, when you have to put all the numbers down sometimes you get confused and you end up doing the wrong answer. But with short division, it's just the way you understand it. Because not everyone's brain works the same way. So, yeah.

DAVE: So why do you think that is? Like, do you think God made everyone to work differently?

LUKE: Yes. God purposefully made everyone work differently because then you'll learn more to adapt to what other people have to say instead of just thinking in your own way. Because you, even you think that life would be boring if everyone thought the same way because every day would just be the same thing. You would have no one who disagreed with what you said and everything would just go along. But sometimes it's okay to have people disagree with you because then you can see that they're thinking a different way. So, that's just what I try to think.

Luke's words call attention to a thread woven among the children at Messiah: a theological lens that gives all views room to be correct and incorrect in some ways, even amidst moments of disagreement. Luke may offer the clearest example of such thinking – and he certainly demonstrates the emergence of more complex and abstract thought, which is associated with children on his age[9] – but this tendency crossed developmental thresholds among the children at Messiah, demonstrating that it is certainly related to the cultural context and theological ethos of their shared congregation. For example, while Kaitlyn told me that all pictures of Jesus can be correct because "no one knows exactly what he looks like so there's no right or wrong [and] everyone that draws Jesus is a little bit right," Marion discussed names given to God and how each name expresses the same thing but is relative to the language of a people. Such understandings echo Luke's sentiments about all views being correct in some way, although these girls didn't explicitly mention that all views may indeed be incorrect in ways as well.

By seeing all views as correct in some way, these children highlighted commonalities among different groups rather than drawing lines and pointing to distinctions and differences. Take, for example, Luke's opinion about all congregations and denominations teaching "the same things." Even though he and all the other children I interviewed at Messiah had first-hand experiences with denominational traditions beyond the Methodist and United Church influences of their congregation, many of them stated that the worship styles, teachings, and doctrines of these churches were "the same" or very similar to one another. Furthermore, when discussing difference rather than similarity, Luke spoke of varieties of ways of thinking, leaving room for deeper commonalities which people might interpret and make sense of in a myriad of ways.

This tendency echoes the understanding held by some of the leaders of Messiah. For example, Sophia's explanation of the 1925 union of the United Church may not have been completely accurate, but it painted a picture focused on similarities among various Protestant denominations, for she believes that "in actual fact the worship is all the same." When such a perspective is coupled with a strong vision of interconnectedness, as it is at Messiah, it is perhaps no surprise that the children at this congregation discuss theology in a way that leaves room for all views to be correct and that they avoid placing boundaries between various views. The desire to separate phenomena into categories and classifications is a Western tendency and the African worldview at work within this congregation leads its children to challenge such separation by underscoring similarities.

The unique cultural context of Messiah was another factor that played a role in the formation of this trend within the theology of its children. As a Ghanaian congregation in a Canadian city, its leaders are continually contextualizing the resources for children's ministry that they import from Ghana and adapt for the cultural landscape of Canada. Such adaptations certainly require the leadership to examine differences and similarities between these two contexts. One difference that Rev. Ayensu named is the tendency for older teenagers and young adults in Canada to move away from home, a rite of passage that in Ghana is usually reserved for when one marries. However, as much as the practice of contextualizing Sunday school materials – and the whole of how Sunday school at Messiah functions – requires distinctions to be made between Ghanaian and Canadian contexts, it is done in a way that underscores similarities as well as differences. After all, if significant parallels did not exist between the two contexts, then it would be incredibly difficult to adapt materials from Ghana in the first place. As much as the leaders spoke about the need to contextualize resources based on the ways in which these materials do not fit within Canadian society, they must also identify how resources do fit and what similarities exist between the two contexts. This process is woven into the fabric of children's ministry at Messiah and, in fact, into everything that this congregation does. And the drawing of parallels that is so common within the life of the broader congregation is manifested in the theological insights of its children.

This tendency to focus on similarities and see all theological traditions as correct and incorrect in some ways may help explain the previous characteristic I interpreted. If, as these children believe, all traditions are similar to one another and correct in their own ways, then it stands to reason that there is nothing inherently wrong with drawing from traditions beyond the Methodist and United Churches in generating and practising one's theologies. By holding that, as Luke said, there is not "only one way to do things," these children become unfettered by denominational walls and theological traditions, and are free to explore the vast expanse of the world as they make theological meaning for themselves.

Involved Theology

The final salient feature of the theologies of the children at Messiah was their tendency to perceive God as actively involved in everyday life. For them, God is connected to and interested in them. Take, for instance, these words from Marion (11), who was born in Ghana and immigrated to Canada with her family, about the importance of prayer in her life:

MARION: Yeah. And every night we pray. Me and my family, we pray.
DAVE: Together?
MARION: Yeah. Like, we hold hands and pray.
DAVE: Oh, wow. And do you like that?
MARION: I love it a lot. If we don't pray, like, I have to even force my mom to pray for us every day.
DAVE: Wow.
MARION: Because sometimes she go to work, she come home at like 10:00. And we have to stay up. We can't sleep without praying ... Even if it's 1:00 we'll still pray.
DAVE: Why is praying so important to you?
MARION: Because, like, pray [sic] is important because if I don't know my test, I pray to God and God helped me. That's what I do.
DAVE: Wow! And do you feel that God helps you with the things you ask for?
MARION: Yeah, a lot. And sometimes God is talking to me.

DAVE: Can you tell me about that?
MARION: Sure. Like when I'm doing tests, and I'm praying and he says "Marion, you will do your best." And then I do my best actually.

Marion's younger sister Dawn (9) also described how she thinks God helps her with tests, but then goes on to say that God protects her as well:

DAVE: (*referring to when Dawn saw God in a dream*) What was [God] doing?
DAWN: He was helping me with, like, on a test, to get an A.
DAVE: Have you ever thought when you were taking a test – have you ever felt that God helps you with that?
DAWN: Yeah, because this week I got three As.
DAVE: Wow. That's great. Way to go. And so you feel that God helps you with that?
DAWN: Yeah.
DAVE: Are there other ways you feel like God helps you with things that are happening in your life?
DAWN: Yeah. When I was sleeping God protects me. He doesn't let anyone evil come.

These excerpts offer clear examples of a broader trend among the children I interviewed from Messiah: God is involved in their lives. Several times during my interviews with the children, our conversations moved toward a discussion about how God has helped them. In addition to the example of Marion above, who brought up how God helps her during a discussion about prayer, Kaitlyn's remarks about God keeping one's day "going well" show how she understands God to be connected to day-to-day life. Both girls shifted our conversations in order to speak of God's involvement in their lives, demonstrating the importance they ascribe to this theological understanding.

The children at Messiah tended to make sense of God's involvement in their lives by attributing two related roles to God: helper and protector. First, each of the four children who expressed a view of an involved God (Marion, Dawn, Luke, and Kaitlyn) explained that God has helped them to succeed on tests and school assignments, as the excerpts from Dawn and Marion above demonstrate. But God's help extends beyond their educational success into several other areas of their lives. Luke, for example, felt that God was assisting him in dealing with his unsuccessful tryout for a soccer team. Second, Dawn's statement about God's protection over her as she sleeps exemplifies the children's view of God as protector. Although held by a smaller subset of children, this was a trend clearly evident in the theologies of both Dawn and Kaitlyn, the latter of whom believes that even "if something bad happens, most of the time something good happens in the end. So you can't stop and question God if you're not like really finished with anything yet. You have to finish it and see the end result." Kaitlyn's view of God's protection is wrapped within a consequentialist worldview, for God's role as protector goes beyond the immediate and perceivable results of actions in the world; although at first it may appear as though God did not protect someone, the end result of all things is a positive outcome that God ordains. This mirrors a common aspect of Ghanaian theology: the divine protection of Jesus that Christians claim as long as they do what is right.[10]

These related ways of understanding God's involvement in one's life are not unique to these children. They are shared by the broader congregation of Messiah and expressed in its worship life. During the services in which I participated, the ministers and worship leaders at this congregation made several comments about God's assistance and protection in our lives, such as when they reminded the congregation that "God wants to care for your issues ... He wants you to open up and tell him" and when they prayed that God will "continue to protect us from any harm, [from] any plans of the enemy." This is a faith community that accentuates the involvement of God in the everyday lives of its congregants – as cosmic helper, divine protector – and its children express theologies that are consistent with this view. They are, in a way, examples of this congregational theology in action as they sense the presence of God when they sit down to take a test or wake up with a new day.

It is important to note that Marion's words above highlight a connection between family faith practices and an awareness of God's involvement in her life. It is not surprising that research underscores the significant link between the religious practices of families and the spiritual and religious development of the children.[11] Activities like praying together regularly, a practice highly valued by Marion, have a hand in shaping the religious and spiritual lives of members of the family.[12] In this particular case, it is possible to infer that Marion's tendency to see God involved in daily life is in part influenced by familial activities like bedtime prayers that allow her to connect with God in the course of everyday life. Although, as I have argued, the cultural and theological ethos of Messiah is connected in the tendency for its children to see God as involved in their day-to-day lives, Marion's words serve as a helpful reminder that the family is also a vital context for influencing the religious and spiritual lives of children.

Theology All Their Own

The three theological trends that I observed in the children at Messiah – a tendency to draw widely in theological sources, a focus on similarities and the correctness of all traditions, and experiences of God as involved in their lives – were consistent with the broader theological ethos of their congregation. Yet as with the children in other participating congregations, sometimes the young people from Messiah generated theology in ways that differed from their congregation.

In several interviews with these children, our conversation moved toward a discussion about Jesus's skin colour, often instigated by the visual portrayals of Jesus in their drawings (figures 2.2, 2.3, and 2.4). Yet Marion initiated a conversation about Jesus's complexion even though she chose not to draw a picture. Toward the beginning of our conversation, I asked her to tell me what she thought about God, and she immediately began talking about Jesus's skin colour. Although we spoke about "God," it was evident afterward that she was referring to Jesus, for she sees Jesus and God as "the same":

DAVE: Can you describe, can you tell me what you think? Like, what do you think about God?

MARION: Okay. People think that he's Black. But I think it's every colour because he bring us to earth. That's what I think.

DAVE: So God is every colour people are, or every colour?

MARION: (*interjecting*) People. Every colour that people are, that he made.

DAVE: ... What do you mean, "People say he's Black"? Who says that?

MARION: Like, all my friends. And some people – all different countries say that. They say that he's Black, he's White, he's Black and stuff. [They] make it up.

DAVE: Okay. So people, depending on where people are and what colour –

MARION: (*interjecting*) They just get coloured, they point it as God, that God is White, Black.

DAVE: Oh wow. Okay. So, have you seen pictures of God at all –
MARION: Yeah. I just saw one right now in church.
DAVE: Okay. Oh, there are pictures, then ... What are the pictures of? Which ones are you talking about? I've seen a lot of them, so I'm wondering what ones you mean.
MARION: I saw it today, you see on the board ... Yeah, it's on there.
DAVE: And what was it?
MARION: It was, like, Jesus, like, holding this, um ... Once I saw Jesus holding a sheep on his ear, and the stick ...
DAVE: Okay. Like a staff, that kind of thing?
MARION: Yeah.
DAVE: Okay. And what colour was Jesus?
MARION: White. That's what I saw. I saw a White picture. Like, he was White.

The children at Messiah – Marion included – are accustomed to seeing visual representations of Jesus; there are posters and pictures of him throughout the hallways, classrooms, and sanctuary of the church building. Yet in every image I saw at Messiah, Jesus was portrayed as a White man with brown hair (one image was actually a picture of Jim Caviezel's portrayal of Jesus in the 2004 film *The Passion of the Christ*). When I asked Marion why she thinks Messiah, a community of Black congregants, has so many images of a White Jesus, she responded with "Because sometimes I think we don't like the Black picture." To my disappointment, she did not want to say anything more about this.

Marion's theology transcends any portrayal of Jesus as belonging to a particular racial or ethnic group. It challenges the representations of Jesus as a White man that are common in images at Messiah by expanding any natural physiological realities into an understanding that infuses physical representations with supernatural meaning. For Marion, it is not Jesus's humanity that determines his complexion, but his divinity. Her understanding of his role as the creator of all humankind leads her to surmise that Jesus's skin colour is a mixture of the complexions of all the people that he has created. Such an understanding is clearly a departure from the implicit curriculum taught by the images of a White Jesus hanging throughout the church building.

Marion shares her interest in Jesus's skin colour with other children from Messiah. During my interview with Jemina, I learned that a few months after my interviews with the children, Luke used the open question time during Sunday school to pose a query about Jesus's race. Jemina recounted how this led to a thoughtful and lively discussion among the children, with some asserting that Jesus was not White and others saying that he must be White because his parents were White. Jemina told them that, as a person from Nazareth, Jesus's hair was kinky and his skin was dark: "When I recall of the ancient times, they were almost like dark skin, like almost dark. Not like dark like us, but ... How shall I call it? Like, just a little close to dark. And then their hair was like a Nazarite."[13] Because this incident occurred several weeks after the interviews, it did not have any influence on the children's theological insights about Jesus's skin colour that they shared with me. But it is interesting to note the difference between Marion's reflections and Jemina's. While this Sunday school teacher used Jesus's humanity – as a Middle Eastern man – to explain his race, Marion understood Jesus's race by focusing on his divinity – as the one who created and creates all people.

Like Marion, Luke also articulated theological insights that differed from the norms I perceived at Messiah. At one point in our conversation, he spoke about how his view of spirits is somewhat drawn from *Long Island Medium*, a television show dealing with beliefs surrounding mediumship that he thinks his church would not condone. "It may not be true, but you have to get closure in some way, even if they're just telling you random stuff that doesn't make any sense." Without admitting whether or not he believes in mediumship, he acknowledges that even the fact that he sees nothing wrong with holding such beliefs goes against the views of his congregation.

His ambivalent belief in mediumship, however, is not completely unusual. Messiah's Ghanaian roots may be intimately tied to MCG, but their cultural influence surely expands beyond a relationship with this denomination. Recent scholars into religion in Ghana and the wider continent of Africa argue that ancestor worship is fundamental to African religion. Emmanuel Lartey notes that in Ghana "ancestors are as much a part of Akan and Ga communities as the living. They are, in fact, the custodians of tradition, custom and all that is worthy in the community."[14] In his estimation, ancestor worship among this culture can be compared to the Christian idea of the "communion of saints."[15] Ancestors are the medium between the world of the living and the supernatural world, and through them the latter world becomes real.[16] Many non-Africans, however, have perceived ancestor worship as "'primitive,' 'tribal,' 'savage,' 'barbaric,'"[17] and Methodist missionaries may have caused Messiah to hold an ambivalent view of the practice. Although the congregation does not engage in any sort of ancestor worship, it holds an annual service of prayer for family and friends who have died that year, recognizing a connection with those who have gone before them. Luke's estimation that Messiah would adamantly object to mediumship may actually have more to do with a historic missionary impulse to eradicate ancestor worship than with the actual views of the members and leaders of the congregation.

Shortly after telling me about *Long Island Medium*, Luke shared that he did not believe in the devil, saying instead that there is good in every person while avoiding any conversation about evil in the world. For him, bad things just happen, and he refuses to attribute them to any particular source or entity. He then explained that he does not believe the devil exists, saying, "When you think of the devil you think about burning hot and pain and it's just what people are making you think; it's not what you're actually thinking. Because have you ever seen those old cartoons with like the angel and there's like the devil? It's what people are making you think. But you have to think for yourself every now and again." Luke has done just that. And as he thought for himself, he rejected the understanding of some of the Messiah leadership who believe in an evil being from which humanity needs divine protection. When I asked him about this theology of the "evil one" that I heard from the pulpit during one visit, he shared his interpretation of this: that the leader is telling the congregation not to sin. He concluded, "So I take in what they're saying. But I also try to think of it in my own way."

In both of these instances, Luke's self-reflection has helped him generate a theology that diverges from that of his congregation, in part due to his exposure to a television show and cartoons. In the first case, his opinion that there is nothing wrong with believing in mediumship – and that it may actually be beneficial in some instances – showcases an acceptance of a view that is not openly recognized by his congregation. In the second case, Luke's denial of the reality of the devil denounces a belief held by Messiah. Both cases highlight that the importance he places on thinking for himself has led him to question and challenge the dominant theology of his congregation and develop theological notions that diverge from the culture of Messiah.

This is where the excursions of Marion and Luke become hazy and more complex. Clearly, they both expressed theological insights that are at odds with those I saw and heard at Messiah. But in having deep and thoughtful theological engagements about Jesus's skin colour, mediumship, and the devil, these children are also incarnating an important element of the theological life of this congregation – thinking for oneself. It is indeed true that the approach to Sunday school utilized by Messiah relies on memorization and knowledge acquisition; yet it does so while encouraging the young people to engage thoughtfully with the scriptures they are memorizing and the theological ideas they are learning. This is one reason why Jemina places such a high value on the children attending Sunday school: "Their minds are growing. They want to relate ... They want somewhere where they can feel like it's our place, we are part of it, we are reading the Bible, we are interacting." Throughout our conversation, she continually used the word "engage" when describing the purposes of Messiah's ministry with children. The reason this congregation relies so heavily on a schooling-instructional model of Sunday school is not simply to "make deposits" in the minds of the children, but to help them better engage with scripture and relate it to the rest of their lives. In Luke's words, "they'll still give you their message, but they'll also encourage you to think your own way." Even while holding beliefs that are not in line with those of their congregation, these children are embodying Messiah's emphasis on thoughtful engagement with theological ideas.

* * *

Messiah United Methodist Church occupies a unique space within the landscape of religion in Canada. It is in reality an MCG congregation that has affiliated with the United Church, and its theology reflects its identity as a member of the MCG diaspora residing in one of Canada's largest metropolitan areas. Yet while worshipping on Canadian soil, much of its theology relies on an African worldview, not least its broad theology of interconnectedness. This theology was made manifest in the theological insights generated and shared during my conversations with children from Messiah in three ways: in the children's tendency to use a wide variety of sources for doing theology; in their proclivity to draw parallels between different traditions and see all views as correct in particular ways; and in the ways that they sense and make meaning of God's involvement in their lives. Yet the children also generated theology in styles that differed from Messiah's, at times drawing from sources that are not condoned by their congregation and making assertions that diverge from congregational norms, as exemplified by Marion's understanding of God's colour and the sources Luke uses to piece together his theology. These children and their wider congregation actually challenge their denomination's vision for becoming intercultural, a topic that I will take up in chapter 6. In the next chapter, however, we will dive into another congregation.

Figure 2.1 Kaitlyn's drawing

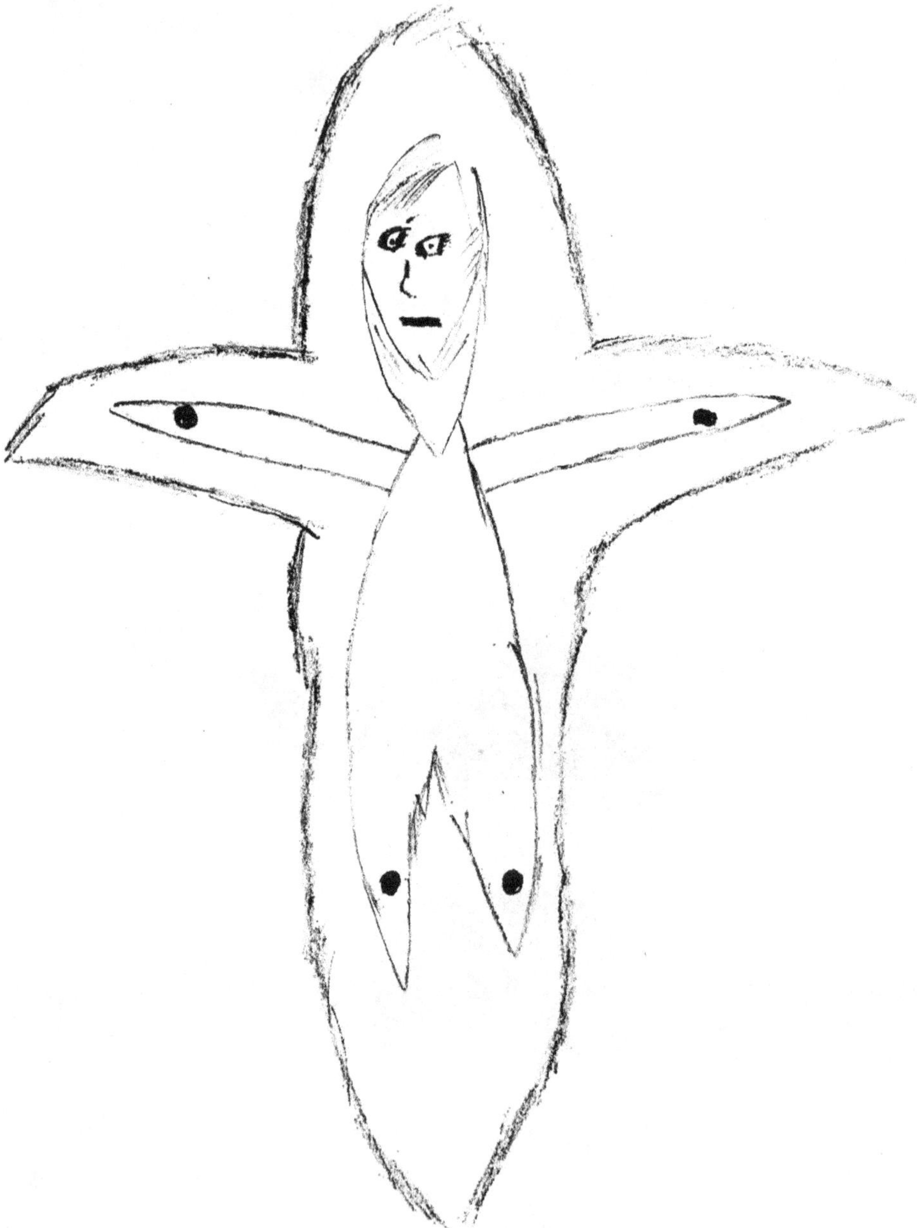

Figure 2.2 Luke's drawing
Note: Because Luke used faint lines, this version of his drawing underwent slight restoration to darken the image.

Figure 2.3 Chris's drawing

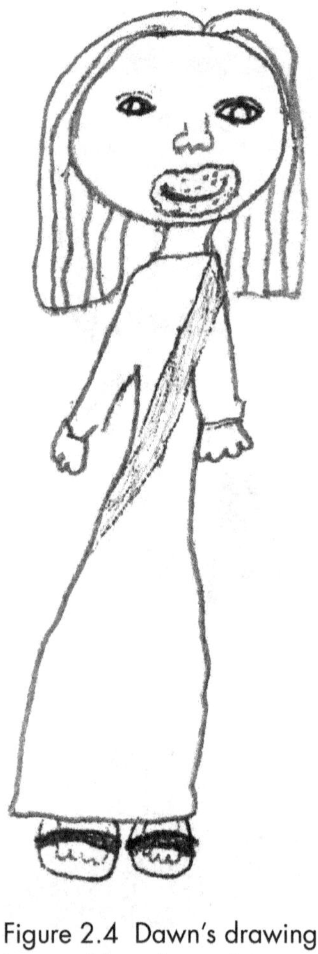

Figure 2.4 Dawn's drawing
Note: Because Dawn used faint lines, this version of her drawing underwent slight restoration to darken the image.

3 "Engaging the Stories of the Faith"
Burke Street United Church and a Theology of Speculation

The leaders of Burke Street United Church had graciously allowed me to help lead Sunday school with their school-age children. The children's programming had recently undergone a transformation – from a rotation-based model, in which small groups moved from station to station throughout the program, to a model that includes all school-age children in common activities each week. What is more, the new minister of Christian education had introduced Godly Play to the congregation's younger children (approximately six years old and younger). This imaginative, inquisitive approach to formation marked a significant change from Burke Street's previous models.

On the first day that I assisted with Sunday school, the plan was for Denise, a volunteer teacher, to offer the main teaching for the day and for me to follow up with a hands-on craft activity that reinforced the lesson, all provided by a lectionary-based Sunday school curriculum. I watched as the children sat on small mats to mark their space in a large circle. With a baptism scheduled during the worship service upstairs, the group was a mix of regularly attending children and some visitors who had joined their families to celebrate this rite. After taking attendance and leading the group in singing a well-known song as they collected the children's offering, Denise read the story of Jesus's encounter with the Samaritan woman at the well[1] using images and a toy scene of a well to capture aspects of the story. Following this, she posed questions to the children provided in the curriculum to help reinforce the story among the group, emphasizing that the Samaritan woman told others about her conversation with Jesus, and then asking the children to imagine what they might tell people if they were to meet Jesus themselves. The children were very well behaved, always raising their hands when they wished to answer a question or make a comment. Those who answered seemed quite comfortable to venture guesses when they were unsure, while others waved their hands high over their heads to indicate that they were certain they knew the right answer.

As Denise finished asking questions, she gave her place in the circle to me and I led the children in a craft activity offered in the curriculum that began by having them cut pictures of lips out of magazines. Many of the magazines that Denise had brought for this project were about animals, so there were lips of all shapes, colours, sizes, and textures. Eventually, when all the children had a few lips cut out, we gathered in a circle around a large poster board. As the children glued their lip pictures on the board, I asked them what they would tell other people about Jesus and I wrote their responses inside large speech bubbles that we drew all over the poster board. Eventually we created a collage filled with all sorts of lips saying all sorts of things about Jesus.

The next time I visited Burke Street was a few weeks after Easter. A volunteer Sunday school teacher took all the children to a kitchen adjacent to the main classroom and made "Resurrection rolls" with them. The children were eager to bake these simple pastries and roll each triangular piece of dough around a marshmallow. Eventually the children would discover that as the crescent rolls baked in the hot oven, the marshmallows melted into the dough, leaving a large sugary hole in the centre of each pastry. These tasty treats, the leader explained, symbolized Jesus's resurrection, for just as all the children there were surprised to discover that their marshmallows had disappeared, so too were Jesus's disciples shocked when they saw the empty tomb on that first Easter morning.

The scent of butter and flour and sugar wafted throughout the church basement as I gathered the children together in the main Sunday school room to lead a discussion while the rolls baked. With only minimal guidelines provided by the curriculum (e.g., "While the rolls are baking, discuss: Why do Christians say the Easter story is good news?"), I posed a number of other questions to help the children think about this topic. Some of the questions were closed questions aimed at reinforcing the lesson kneaded into the Resurrection roll activity (pun intended); others were open-ended "wondering" questions that did not have any particular correct answer. I was fascinated to see the children react to the questions. Even though only weeks before I had seen many of them raise their hands to respond to the closed-answer questions about the Samaritan woman at the well, today they were not as responsive to these sorts of questions. But when I began asking the open-ended wondering questions in the curriculum, things became much more lively. Some children shot their arms straight up in their air hoping I would choose them to respond, while others departed from this practice and simply blurted out their thoughts about the question. Maybe there was something in the air that day. Yes, perhaps it was the sweet scent of the theologically themed pastries that we would enjoy together only moments later. Or perhaps the children's active engagement with wondering questions meant something deeper.

A Church for the Baby Boom

During the years after World War II, the towns surrounding the city in which Burke Street United Church now resides were growing rapidly, and new subdivisions were being developed for families throughout the area. At the same time, membership within the United Church had been increasing steadily since the end of the war.[2] The only two United Church congregations in an ever-expanding community on the outskirts of the city were unable to meet the needs of the families moving to new housing developments nearby who considered the distance between these congregations and their homes to be too great. Thanks to the support of an existing United Church congregation and the local Presbytery, in the mid-1950s a group of over 200 charter members inaugurated Burke Street United Church in a temporary building, just in time for Christmas services.

The new congregation experienced growth at breakneck speed, and it became evident that the temporary building was insufficient for its current and foreseeable needs. There were so many children that Sunday school classes had to be held in nearby homes in order to provide space for everyone. The congregation embarked on a successive building project and worshipped at a local public school until a gymnasium and a Christian education building could be completed. Having relocated back into its own space, the growing congregation worshipped in the gymnasium for a number of years while its sanctuary was being constructed. About a decade after its founding, the people of Burke Street worshipped in their sanctuary for the first of what would be thousands of church services.

The building has not changed a great deal over the past half-century. Its sanctuary holds about 250 people in straight rows of pews with a centre aisle. The steep slopes of the ceiling are marked by wooden planks that give the entire space a warm, cabin-like ambiance. At the front is a large gold cross hanging above the platform in such a way that it seems to float above the choir, which is seated on both sides of the platform. While the sanctuary of Parkdale United Church was covered with monuments, decorations, and other items of importance to the community, Burke Street's décor is contrasted in its minimalism, with a Canadian flag and a few small banners being the only decorative elements giving colour to the rich, wood-toned hues throughout the space. At the back is a balcony – where some children like to sit for worship – that opens on the front to the sanctuary and on the sides to the small foyer through which congregants enter the space.

The basement of the church is reminiscent of a small school. The cement-block walls are painted a clean shade of white and hold bulletin boards with information about activities and events for people of all ages. There are four prominent rooms in this wing of the church,[3] the smallest of which is a library containing a desk and wall-to-wall shelves filled with books and films, most of which are for children. At the end of the hallway is the gymnasium with basketball nets at each end, where the congregation worshipped during its early years. Now people gather here for coffee, tea, and juice each week after the service, a time that is coveted by many adults and children alike. At the opposite end of the hallway are two generously sized classrooms, one of which is used for Sunday school with children in grades 2 and higher. The room is fairly stark; with no windows in the space, the lighting is provided by fluorescent tube lights. Stacks of wooden chairs are tucked away in the corner near the exit, along with a small electric keyboard. Few decorations break the monotony of the white walls, one of which is a handwritten poster containing the words to a song that the children sing as they take up the collection each week. The classroom next door contrasts this sparse Sunday school room, containing several child-size tables and chairs and interactive stations used during the Godly Play programming offered each Sunday.[4]

The vast majority of the congregation consists of older adults, with some young families peppered among the greying community. With almost no people of colour in the congregation, it's no surprise that Denise, one of the key Sunday school teachers, repeatedly described the culture of Burke Street as "White middle-class." In fact, during my interview with three congregational leaders, the participants spent time trying to name all the people of colour who attend their congregation; they were only able to think of a small handful of individuals, some of whom others in the group did not know. Burke Street is a relatively affluent community that historically consisted of "working-class management" at a local automotive production facility; and although it has in recent decades seen more diversity in terms of the careers of its members, the congregation remains fairly racially, ethnically, and economically homogenous. As a predominantly White community, members of this congregation see themselves as part of the mainstream of the United Church, a view that was particularly evident when Rev. Monica, the senior minister, remarked that one person on the board wondered why I wanted to include their congregation in research about children and interculturalism, since, in this person's estimation, Burke Street has no culture. Because some leaders identify their congregation as a typical middle-class United Church community, they struggled to name features that distinguish it from other congregations in the denomination. Yet one element that makes Burke Street more distinct is the theological and political diversity of its members – a factor that is always present but sometimes ignored, so it doesn't "rock the boat" of the strong feeling of community cherished by so many members.

Sunday services begin at 10:15, but choir rehearsals and other activities usually keep the building bustling with conversation and commotion well before the service commences. Services follow a liturgy printed in the weekly bulletin alongside a lengthy list of announcements and activities, and include an organ introit, a call to worship, a litany prayer, scripture readings, hymns, an offering, and a sermon. The liturgy is altered each week as necessary, at times including a children's message, communion, baptisms, or other rites. Services are led by Rev. Monica, who robes each Sunday, and she is assisted by Emma, the minister of Christian education, and a number of congregants. While most who offer leadership during services are adults, children join their parents at times to lead elements, such as a call to worship. The platform is framed by a choir dressed in bright green robes that sits on either side and moves to the centre to lead music.

The minister of Christian education at Burke Street has been with the congregation for less than two years, and its ministry with children has undergone some recent changes under her guidance. Until a few months before my visits with the congregation,[5] children in grades 2 and older participated in a Sunday school program that used a rotational model, which had the children focus on one biblical story for several weeks while exploring it each Sunday through a different object-lesson-based station (games, crafts, kitchen, etc.). While leaders felt this approach was successful, they struggled to find volunteer teachers who were willing to commit to teaching for several weeks in a row. Sunday school now uses a lectionary-based curriculum that guides two groups of children (grades 2–4 and grades 5–8) in learning a new Bible story each week, and leaders rotate from week to week. Children in kindergarten and grade 1 participate in Godly Play, "an imaginative approach to religious education"[6] that Emma began leading shortly after joining the staff team. Both of these programs operate during Sunday worship services; the children join the congregation for the beginning of the service and leave for Sunday school or Godly Play at a time that is dependent on the liturgy for the week (for example, if there is communion, a baptism, a musical presentation, etc.).

Engaging Faith Stories

The most prominent feature of the culture of Burke Street is its speculative approach to theology.[7] This is a cerebral congregation: it puts at the centre of its theological life "the illumination of the mind"[8] through the acquisition, development, and exchange of cognitive insight. Yet Rev. Monica does not lead the congregation in a style that requires its members to think a certain way; in fact, she said that this is "a congregation that's very open to people who have questions," and she encourages people to creatively think for themselves as they encounter scripture and engage in liturgy together. This value is shared by Denise, the lead Sunday school teacher, who remarked in our interview, "How can you believe something if you have to turn your brain off to accept it?" As mentioned previously, the individuals within the congregation hold diverse theological and political perspectives, so there are few beliefs held widely among the whole of the community. The speculative theology of Burke Street unites people not because of *what* they think, but *because they think* in the first place. Whatever they may believe, these folks emphasize God's gift of curiosity.

This aspect of Burke Street is crucial to its ministry with children. Rev. Monica's approach to children's religious education is one of "engaging the stories of the faith and getting kids to first of all just learn that there's a story, learn the fact that it is just story and then to make some application to their life ... I want the kids to realize that it's okay to understand that as a story and not that it necessarily happened." She respects the children as thinkers in their own right, and wants to see them develop their own perspectives of scripture rather than learn particular pre-packaged interpretations. This critical-application-based approach to the Bible is a manifestation of the broader congregation's speculative approach to theology. However, this minister is not directly responsible for the children's programs at Burke Street, and the two most important ways that this theology is concretely applied in children's ministry differ significantly from one another.

Emma's use of Godly Play is undergirded by this approach's goals of helping children develop a religious language through wonder, the imagination, experiencing scripture and worship, and asking existential questions.[9] Children from the age of three to first grade join Emma each week as she shares a story from scripture or about a part of liturgy using simple manoeuvrable figures and fabrics. Through "wondering" questions aimed at helping the children theologically reflect on the story (e.g., "I wonder what this could really be?" "I wonder where you are in the story?"),[10] the children develop a stance of open-mindedness and curiosity and they make their own connections between the story and their experiences. A response time following the questions provides the children with an opportunity to respond to the story in a way of their choosing, such as by working with Play-Doh or telling the story themselves using the figures. The program wraps up with a "feast," at which point the children gather in a circle and share a drink and snack. Godly Play operates from a theological standpoint that values the children's ability to make theological meaning for themselves as they wonder and encounter the story in their own ways. It reflects the speculative theology of Burke Street in its encouragement to make one's own interpretations of and connections with the story, and by leaving room for the children to engage with and ask meaningful questions.

Although it also reflects the speculative theology of Burke Street, the Sunday school program does so in a dramatically different way than the one just described. While Godly Play engages younger children in generating their own ideas, Sunday school places a greater emphasis on learning particular aspects of a biblical story, a liturgical season, or an ecclesial practice. Although she is not the only volunteer, Denise is the most frequent Sunday school teacher and offers significant guidance to the scope and shape of this program. Contrasting Emma's use of Godly Play, the theology evident in Denise's dedicated leadership of Sunday school is one that fosters Christian formation through what John Westerhoff has called a "schooling-instructional" model of religious education.[11] She organizes and teaches Sunday school from a theological perspective that regards learning stories of faith and the proper interpretations of such stories as being of prime importance to the Christian life. Thus, she struggles with the recent change from a rotational model to a lectionary-based approach. Motivated by a desire to help the children learn important and particular truths embedded in scripture, she has grown concerned that the children now move through the stories too quickly and are not able to learn what she believes they should know about them: "the kids aren't learning the story or the idea behind the story because it's a new story every week, and they don't – they're not getting it. I kind of had a small review last Sunday and it was like they just looked at me blankly." A primary school teacher by trade, Denise's desire is that by learning about Bible stories and applying this knowledge to their lives, the children in her congregation can "grow up and be gentle, loving Canadian citizens."

Its reliance on a speculative approach to theology may be the most prominent aspect of the culture of Burke Street – especially as it relates to its ministry with children – but it is certainly not the only one. Another is its emphasis on community. All three of the adults whom I interviewed emphasized that Burke Street is a welcoming congregation, one made up of people who are committed to building community with one another. Although this congregation is undergirded by an intellectual approach to theology, its emphasis on community rather than creed means that being part of the congregation, to use Rev. Monica's words, is "not so much about a theological stance as it is about community." While this leaves the door open to diversity among members of the community, its minister admits that the congregation is fairly homogenous and has not encountered a great deal of diversity in thought and practice. Thus, in some ways, its view of what it means to be welcoming is rather delicate, for some adults identified acts of being welcoming with a focus on greeting visitors ("How do you do? This is our website" … "Please come back again"), and admitted that their understanding of community has never been challenged by the presence of significant difference.

Theological Reflections

The most salient features of the theologies of the children at Burke Street all reflected the speculative theology through which their leaders guide the congregation. Each of them expressed an approach to faith focused on the illumination of the mind, yet how they did so did not entirely align with their peers. There are three features I will address in this section: the experiencing of faith through thinking and learning; the children's tendency to engage with uncertainty; and the correlation of the young people's approaches to theological meaning-making with the children's programs at their congregation.

Informed Theology

Some children expressed their ideas in manners that evidenced a view of theology bound up with increases in knowledge. Rather than creating theological insights for themselves, they placed an emphasis on theology as information learned from teachers and other leaders within the congregation. This certainly demonstrates a speculative approach to theology, one that I have just described as being embedded within the DNA of Burke Street.

This cognitive, information-based approach to theology was particularly clear during my interview with Rebecca, a nine-year-old girl who was always willing to offer answers to questions in Sunday school. As she drew a picture of God (figure 3.1), she chatted with me and my research assistant about the image that was unfolding on the paper. Her drawing depicted a city street with trees, lampposts, a playground, and a passing car. Above this scene she drew clouds and hearts and wrote, "God loves you and is all around you remember that!" After adding these elements to her drawing, we briefly spoke about why she included them before she focused on drawing other parts of her picture:

DAVE: So what are those?
REBECCA: Clouds.
DAVE: Okay.
REBECCA: Because God is all around you.
DAVE: Oh. So what do the clouds – how do the clouds show that God is all around?
REBECCA: Um, because, like, God is everywhere. Um, and … um … yeah …

* * *

RESEARCH ASSISTANT: I wonder about those hearts at the top.

REBECCA: It's for, um, God loves you.

DAVE: Okay. Why is that? So you said [on her drawing] "God loves you and is all around you. Remember that." You mentioned, like, the God being around us part. But why is it important in the picture that you show that God loves you?

REBECCA: Because if you ever do something that you don't think is right, you can always think that God loves you and he will forgive. He will forgive you if you forgive, like, do the right thing, and forgive the other person … or apologize.

DAVE: Okay. Cool. What makes you think that God loves us and is all around us?

REBECCA: Because, um … everybody says that and I want to believe in that, so, yeah.

DAVE: So when you say "everybody," who do you mean?

REBECCA: Like, people around the church, like Mrs Hill[12], Monica, Emma, a bunch of the Sunday school teachers.

DAVE: Okay. What do you mean that you "want to believe" that?

REBECCA: Because, like, I want to believe that God loves me and that he's all around me and he's protecting me.

DAVE: That seems really important to you, to know that. Why is that so important?

REBECCA: I don't know, really, but …

DAVE: But you feel it's important?

REBECCA: Yeah.

DAVE: In a way that's hard to say sometimes?

REBECCA: Uh-huh.

DAVE: Cool. Um … Is there, I wonder if there was another … like, another way that you can show that God is all around?

REBECCA: Um, you could … draw, um …

DAVE: Not that that's bad – I think what you drew is great.

REBECCA: Um, you could, like, draw a different scene or a different place where you would be. And, yeah …

DAVE: Oh. So really, you could draw anywhere because God is there?

REBECCA: Uh-huh. Yeah.

DAVE: That's cool. Have you ever felt like, have you ever felt that God loves you or that God is with you?

REBECCA: (*immediately*) Yeah.

DAVE: Yeah? Can you tell us a little about what happened?

REBECCA: Well, when I was, um … When I'm on vacation, I usually think about church and, like, sometimes we miss it, so, um, when we're on vacation. So then I think for like the day that God loves me and God is around me.

The central tenet of Rebecca's theology is reflected in the words that she wrote in the middle of her drawing: "God loves you and is all around you." Everything she put on the paper symbolized this idea. The reason she drew a town is because God is "around you when you're out and when you're in, and when you're in a different country he's always around you."

When I asked her to say more about this view, she struggled to go deeper than repeating "God loves you" and "God is all around you," yet at one point she expanded on this idea and said that because God loves people, God extends forgiveness to those who seek it, and that God's presence in her life means God is protecting her. In fact, throughout our conversation, many of her responses to my questions about her faith and her involvement at Burke Street centred on God's love and omnipresence. She said "God loves you and is all around you" five times during the interview, and talked about God loving all people six additional times; the same number of times, she mentioned that God is all around.

This understanding of God's omnipresence and divine love is one that she has learned from the leaders in her congregation. Although she has internalized it and is deeply aware of the importance of these central theological truths, it was not apparent that she had married them with first-hand experiences of God's love and presence. Each time I asked her to say more about why these ideas are so important to her beliefs, she struggled to respond without simply repeating that God loves and is all around. By writing "Remember that" and saying that this is something she "want[s] to believe," and by telling me that when she is away from her congregation she feels better when the idea of God's love and presence pops into her consciousness, she indicated that she is aware that a cognitive affirmation of such a belief is important. Yet she struggled to understand just why this is so or what this belief means in a deeper, more personal way.

This is not to say that Rebecca was unable to make theological meaning for herself during our conversation. There were a few instances in which she responded to my open-ended questions by drawing on the basic tenets of God's love and omnipresence in order to develop ideas for herself. For example, when she shared that she thinks God had no beginning and will have no end, I asked her why she didn't think God will ever end. She responded by saying, "Because he loves so many people and then there's going to be, like, new people are born, and then he will have to love them too for generations and generations." Here she was making fascinating connections between the two key aspects of the God she learned about at Burke Street – love and presence – by explaining that God's very existence is wrapped up with God's love for humanity.[13]

Other children displayed similar attributes. In addition to affirming God's presence and love for all people – albeit in less explicit ways – twelve-year-old Stephen (who happens to be Rev. Monica's son) also expressed a cognitive, information-based approach to theology. This eloquent boy responded to my request for him to draw a picture of God by sketching an image of his congregation's building (figure 3.2) because "this is where I've learned the most and experienced God the most." This was just the first of several instances in which he associated hearing, learning, and talking *about* God with experiencing God, a correlation that demonstrates the knowledge-based approach that undergirds his theological life. He was able to recount several instances when he enjoyed learning and talking about theological matters with individuals at Burke Street and at a two-week-long Mennonite music camp that he attended before I spoke with him; yet it was difficult for him to identify moments when he experienced God first-hand. For example, at one point he told me that he thinks God works through people, and when I asked him if he ever felt God working through him, he was unable to think of such a time. Much like Rebecca, Stephen's theology is one that is based on knowledge rather than experiences.[14]

Stephen also shares Rebecca's tendency to learn theology from others rather than generating it for oneself. He is extraordinarily knowledgeable in theological matters and was able to articulate his theological thinking at a greater length and depth than other children in this congregation. Yet it seemed as though Stephen was repeating understandings and ideas that he had learned from his congregation and the music camp and not ideas that he had produced for himself. For example, after sharing extensively about how the theme of the music camp was peace and how much he enjoyed talking with other campers about peace for the two-week program, he struggled to respond when asked, "What does peace mean to you?" In most instances, he responded to questions right away; but in this moment he looked embarrassed as he sat silent for a long period of time before quietly saying "I don't know."

These two children demonstrate one way that their theological meaning-making reflects the speculative theology of their wider congregation. They demonstrated a keen interest in and valuing of theological ideas that have been passed down to them, taking these insights seriously for the contributions they make to their faith lives.

Uncertain Theology

The cognitive, information-based faith expressed by Rebecca and Stephen is not the only way that the children's theological meaning-making paralleled the speculative theology of Burke Street. Some of the children at this congregation expressed a willingness to address uncertainty and doubt, a quality related to the openness to questioning that is central to Rev. Monica's leadership of Burke Street. Take, for example, this excerpt from my time with Nicholas, an eight-year-old boy who attends church irregularly with his brother Theo (5):[15]

NICHOLAS: (*talking about God*) Well ... he's actually kind of like a legend ... Because I do not know if it actually existed yet.
DAVE: If what existed?
NICHOLAS: God. If he actually did exist for sure.
DAVE: So what do you mean that it's a legend?
NICHOLAS: Well, I don't exactly know if it is a legend or if it's true or false. I don't know, like, if it actually did or not.
Research Assistant: What is a legend?
NICHOLAS: A legend is something that might be true but also might not be true.
DAVE: What do you think? Do you think it's true or not?
NICHOLAS: Not really ...
DAVE: Do you think other people think it's true?
NICHOLAS: Yeah. A lot of other people might think it, but I don't really.
DAVE: Why do you think it's not true?
NICHOLAS: Well, basically, I don't know if it is or isn't. And that's the only thing ... It's kind of hard to guess, in a way ... if you don't even know if it is true.
DAVE: Hmm. What is it that makes it hard to think that it's true?

NICHOLAS: So, I've never actually heard somebody say that somebody, like, told them that somebody has actually, or whatever, who've never known ...

DAVE: What do you think you would need to know? What would need to happen in order for you to know for sure?

NICHOLAS: Ah, well ... right now I think that he did not exist a second time. That he only actually existed once. The second time, that's kind of fiction that somebody probably made up.

DAVE: Now, when you say "he," do you mean Jesus?

NICHOLAS: Yes.

DAVE: Oh, okay.

NICHOLAS: Like how he came back a lot after he died ... That is probably fiction ... It's probably fiction that somebody just put in a story ... Just like invented it or something like that ...

DAVE: Now do you think, like, do you think stories about Jesus before Jesus died are true?

NICHOLAS: Before he died?

DAVE: Yeah.

NICHOLAS: Probably. But after he died – that's probably not. It's extremely rare that that would happen ... It might ... maybe. But it probably shouldn't ...

DAVE: So how do you know what's true and what's fiction, then?

NICHOLAS: (*immediately*) Well, what I know – do you know how I know it? It's because you – somebody with the fiction part is that, like ... The only fiction part is when he died and then came back to life.

DAVE: Okay. How do you know that's not real?

NICHOLAS: Because how do you make somebody come back to life with oil? I don't get it.

DAVE: What do you mean "with oil"? So what's the story, then?

NICHOLAS: Oil. Like, the story is his disciples were kind of friends, put this oil on him and other stuff, like, some of this stuff and then after some time he came back to life. I don't get how do you do that. And how does a person die and then come back to life. That's almost impossible I think.

DAVE: Right. Hmm. And how do you know – what makes you think that everything else that they read is true?

NICHOLAS: (*immediately*) Well, it's that it *can* happen.

This boy's speculative theology appears in his inclination to doubt the Resurrection, claiming it to be a "legend." Like Rebecca and Stephen, his theology is based on cognition, but he is less prone to simply take the information taught in Sunday school and church services at face value (he prefers to stay with his family in Sunday services, so his experience of Sunday school is infrequent). His is the faith of a skeptic,[16] and his uncertainty rests less on whether or not an event recounted in a biblical narrative actually happened or not, but on whether or not the story as told *could be possible* in the natural world. Thus, the Resurrection is impossible in his mind, because the facts of the story – as he understands them – rely on the plausibility of the miraculous.

Although this young naturalist does not believe in the viability of a bodily resurrection, his approach to generating theology is consistent with his wider congregation. After all, Burke Street is a community that encourages deep thinking about matters of theology and faith, and alignment with a particular doctrine or creed is not required for being part of this congregation. Its speculative approach to theology invites people to think for themselves about the deep questions and uncertainties embedded within Christian scripture and tradition. In fact, its understanding of belief is one that *requires* questions and doubts such as those that Nicholas shared with me. As Denise said, "How can you believe something if you have to turn your brain off to accept it?"

Jeremy (6) is another child from Burke Street who displayed characteristics of uncertainty in his theology. He attends services and Sunday school with great regularity and seems well connected to others in the congregation. Yet while Nicholas's uncertainty surrounding the bodily resurrection causes him to reject such accounts as works of fiction, Jeremy is comfortable with mystery and uncertainty in his faith. Throughout our discussion, he used his imagination and his own experiences as he drew a picture of God as a six-year-old walking in the woods with his parents on their way home from a picnic (figure 3.3). As we spoke about God and heaven, Jeremy was comfortable responding to my open-ended questions and was not shy about expressing his uncertainty about theological matters, often saying "I think" or "I don't know" before going on to respond with his ideas. While this tendency may be related to the influence of his family as well as his congregation,[17] the way that Jeremy generates theology reflects that of a mystic using the imagination to express ideas shrouded with mystery.[18]

Although Stephen's rational approach to theology is one focused on his knowledge of information regarding scripture and theological matters, his way of thinking reflects a particular level of abstraction that leaves room for uncertainty. In explaining his drawing of his church – and why it represents his image of God – he said, "I don't like to think of God as a person; more as an idea or like a thing that's always there. It's not like God is right here [pointing to a place on his drawing]. God is here [making large movements with his arms] ... It's more like a spirit that's just all around you and in you. Just not a person or one singular thing." If Nicholas is a skeptic and Jeremy a mystic, then Stephen is a metaphysicist, a budding ontotheologian who has acquired a metaphoric and abstract notion of God using church experiences and his own reflection as sources for this understanding. Such a view of God leaves open the door for God to be anything and everything imaginable. Stephen avoided boxing in his understanding of God with the words he used, being careful to use the pronoun "it" when speaking of God – even when he caught himself referring to the "thing" that is God as "he."

The ideas and opinions shared by Nicholas, Jeremy, and Stephen showcase three different ways that the wider affirmation of uncertainty and questions in the theology of Burke Street are reflected in their lives. Yet it raises questions about why the children at this congregation express a common speculative approach to theology in ways that also differ from one another. This very subject forms a third manner in which the broader culture of Burke Street is manifested in the lives of its children.

Varied Theology

Of all the congregations that participated in this research, Burke Street posed a particular challenge in the analysis of interviews with children and the generation of common themes within their theological processes and ideas. In many ways, the children at Burke Street seemed to engage in theological meaning-making using two broad styles, with some children like Rebecca masterfully increasing the storehouses of their theological knowledge based on what they have been taught, and others like Jeremy forming ideas nuanced with hefty doses of theological imagination.

Developmental theories allow us to attribute some of this difference to the various stages the children occupy along trajectories of growth in cognitive abilities and faith.[19] Yet a more accurate account of this diversity, and one more closely aligned with the core variable under analysis in this project, is found in the different theological and pedagogical approaches that undergird the ways that children participate in the worship and educational life of Burke Street. More so than their peers at the other three congregations, the children here engage in their congregation's life in manners that offer them wholly different experiences:[20] Stephen and Rebecca are regular participants in Burke Street's Sunday school program; Jeremy and Theo participate in Godly Play but do not attend with the same level of frequency as one another; and Nicholas varies his involvement between attending Sunday school and remaining upstairs with his parents, where he listens to the worship service while working in "workbooks" he brings from home. These different experiences at Burke Street correlate with the manners in which they do theology for themselves.

The children who participate in Sunday school on a regular basis are more likely to express theologies that focus on the learning of particular information that they have acquired through their involvement in this program. This focus has, however, overshadowed the making of their own theological meaning. Both Stephen and Rebecca expressed theological ideas that they attributed to their congregation's teaching (and, in Stephen's case, to the Mennonite music camp), and when I asked them questions to tease out their own interpretations and ideas, they struggled to respond at a greater level of depth and seemed embarrassed when they were unable to answer my questions immediately (even though I encouraged them to take their time). For example, when Stephen brought up the importance of interpreting the Bible in one's present context and I asked him to give me an example, he gave a detailed interpretation of David and Goliath that he said he'd heard someone say, but, in his words, "I can't really remember where," and he had difficulty responding to questions that penetrated deeper into his own thoughts regarding this biblical narrative. Perhaps the cognitive, schooling-instructional approach to Sunday school has encouraged a style of theological engagement focused on acquiring information rather than generating ideas for oneself.

Conversely, the children who participate in the imaginative, story-based experience of Godly Play (Jeremy and Theo) expressed a style of theology that in several ways aligned with the attributes of this approach. First, rather than emphasizing particular theological "points," they were much more prone to have a "storied" approach to theology. This was most clearly expressed through Jeremy, who tended to respond to my questions by telling stories that he had heard at church (e.g., the birth of Jesus and the Good Samaritan). But he went further than simply telling stories he had learned; he also created his own stories. As he explained his drawn depiction of God with "God's parents" (figure 3.3) – which he named as Mary and Joseph – Jeremy talked about how "they were at a picnic at a warm place but now they're going home from the picnic" and they are walking through the woods and must arrive home before nightfall. This example also serves to demonstrate a second characteristic of the children who participated in Godly Play: they were much more likely to be imaginative in their generation of theology. For instance, Theo's understanding of God involved the idea that God has died, but still exists in some invisible form. A third quality inherent in Godly Play that these children expressed is a slow pace in the rhythm of theological thought. While Stephen and Rebecca seemed embarrassed when they needed time to think before responding to my questions, Theo and Jeremy were not in a rush to speak when I posed a query. Perhaps this was most clearly demonstrated when Theo and Nicholas were drawing their pictures (figures 3.4 and 3.5). At one point, Nicholas told me that he was done his drawing and then decided to add something to it, and I told him that they could draw as much as they'd like to. Without looking away from his drawing, Theo added, "and as slow as you want," a line that seemed so tied to Godly Play that I wondered if Emma says it as she leads it each week.

This interpretation demonstrates the correlation among these children's approaches to theological meaning-making and their experiences at their congregation. The children who are regularly involved in Sunday school do theology in ways that are consistent with the schooling-instructional model that they participate in there. Theirs is a theology that is learned, and their ability to generate theological notions for themselves is relatively limited. Conversely, those who participate in Godly Play showcase attributes of this approach in the storied, imaginative, and slow nature of their style of doing theology.

Theology All Their Own

The particularities of Burke Street pose certain challenges when it comes to interpreting how its children's theological meaning-making departs from the culture of the wider congregation. As discussed previously, an important element of the approach to theology emphasized by the leaders at Burke Street is the value they place on independent thought. As Rev. Monica stated, children's ministry at this congregation should help the children engage with biblical stories by interpreting them for oneself and coming to one's own conclusions: "What is this story teaching you? That's just something that I wouldn't say you're just teaching that to a fourteen-year-old. You need to be teaching that to a two-year-old." This opens wide the gates to multiple interpretations, and in a congregation that is theologically diverse it can seem as though any theological idea or opinion has its place within the community. Such an open approach to theology not only makes it difficult to name theological excursions among the children; it can actually serve to encourage distinctions as the children interpret scripture and theology for themselves.

Nevertheless, it is possible to find a few instances in which the theological ideas and approaches of these five children diverge from those of the broader congregation. One such instance involves Rebecca's tendency to interpret scripture in literal ways. At a few moments during my conversation with her, Rebecca abandoned the information she had picked up from Sunday school and began to respond to my questions by starting to generate her own ideas. As she did so, she made comments that demonstrated that she interprets scripture as a biblicist. For example, when we spoke about how she is aware that some of the children in her school are not Christian, I asked her how she knew this. She responded by saying "They'll say, 'All of the stories that your church tells you aren't real.' So I can tell that he's not Christian." At another time, she explained to me that she knows God has been "real" for a long period of time because Jesus "usually mentioned God [in Bible stories], and that was a long time ago. So I knew that he would be alive for a long time." These responses to my questions pushed her to move beyond the information she acquired from Burke Street and form her own interpretations. In both instances there are hints of a literal reading of the Bible that shine through her words. In the first, she identifies believing stories in the Bible to be "real" as a mark of being Christian, while in the second she draws from a literal reading of Jesus's words about God as an argument for God's existence for "thousands of years."

This literal reading of scripture departs from the metaphorical approach that Rev. Monica seeks to form in children. Her goal is to help children "realize that it's okay to understand that as a story and not that, not that it necessarily happened ... So seven days of creation. I'm not talking about seven days. This is a story to help us understand that when God created over the universe, over universal time, and continues to create, God is continuing to say 'It is good.'" Perhaps one explanation for this departure from the norms of Burke Street is the developmental stage at which Rebecca's faith is functioning. James Fowler posited that children of about her age tend to appropriate beliefs and interpret ideas in a literal and one-dimensional style.[21] Rebecca's biblicist reading of scripture may be largely indicative not of an unwillingness but of an inability to engage in the metaphorical and symbolic interpretation of scripture valued by Rev. Monica, due to the developmental phase in which she currently makes meaning and expresses her faith.

While one reading of Rebecca's literal interpretations of scripture sees them as distinct from Burke Street's broader culture, through another lens, it appears that her biblicism does not completely deviate from that of the leaders of this congregation. In fact, it can actually appear to be consistent. Perhaps her literal reading of the Bible is a product of her willingness to think for herself, a key element of her congregation's culture. Thus, while it can seem to be wholly divergent from the broader congregational culture, her approach to interpreting scripture may actually be the result of Burke Street's encouragement to draw one's own conclusions.

This brings us to a second distinction. As explained in the previous section, both Rebecca and Stephen had difficulty generating their own theological ideas. For them, doing theology rests more on learning what they are taught than it does on coming to their own conclusions and interpretations. This in and of itself is a sort of theological excursion, for it departs from the value placed on helping the children cultivate their own interpretations and thoughts regarding scripture and theology, which was described as pivotal by Rev. Monica and Denise and is consistent with Godly Play. Thus, the fact that these two children focus on rote memorization and learning facts and information over generating theological insight for themselves goes to show that in doing so, they are choosing to do theology in a way that differs from the overall culture of their congregation.

Yet even while such an approach stands in glaring contrast to the theology espoused by leaders at Burke Street, it actually remains consistent with the pedagogical and theological practices of its Sunday school program. Rev. Monica and Denise may say that they want children to use their cognitive capacities to generate their own theological suppositions, but the actual practice of Sunday school undermines this value by promoting rote memorization and learning "the point" of biblical stories. Perhaps this difference between Burke Street's Sunday school and its broader ethos can be attributed to a choice of curriculum that departs from the culture of the congregation, or to Denise's approach to Sunday school education, or even a belief that before children can create theology for themselves they must learn basic presuppositions and tenets. Whatever the reasons, what is clear is that although Rebecca and Stephen's approach to theology differs from the broader congregation's culture, their tendency to acquire theological information that is taught to them, rather than to create ideas for themselves, is in some ways consistent with the ethos that drives Burke Street's Sunday school program.

* * *

During one of my early conversations with Rev. Monica, she chuckled as she told me about that board member who did not know why I would ever want to include Burke Street in a study about culture, since it has none. Apparently culture, for this member, was something that only applied to those who did not belong to dominant groups in Canada, groups that are also predominant at Burke Street (White, English-speaking, Canadian-born, etc.). This attitude of being part of the mainstream of both the United Church and Canada, and of possessing no distinguishing features, has made it difficult to uncover the particular theological assumptions that drive this congregation.

Yet despite some members' inability to name its own distinctive cultural markers, I have perceived Burke Street to be a highly speculative congregation, one that buttresses faith among its congregants by providing them with fodder and contexts for generating their own insights. And the children at Burke Street reflect this cultural marker in more than one way. Overall, they express very cognitive approaches to doing theology, ones that are consistent with the various theological and pedagogical assumptions that drive the programs that this congregation offers for children. And even amidst the diversity of the programs, it is still possible to name how these children break free from the broader culture of Burke Street and do theology in ways that are all their own, exemplified especially in Rebecca's theological understandings. The insight generated in this chapter, like that contributed by children in the other congregations, offers much to the fields of children's spirituality and theology, even speaking back to the norms of research in this arena. While this will become clearer in chapter 7, we move now to the final congregation we will get to know in this book.

Figure 3.1 Rebecca's drawing

Figure 3.2 Stephen's drawing
Note: Because Stephen used faint lines and included the name of his congregation, this version of his drawing underwent slight restoration to darken the image and remove the name of the congregation in order to maintain anonymity.

Figure 3.3 Jeremy's drawing

Figure 3.4 Nicholas's drawing

Figure 3.5 Theo's drawing

4 "Healing That Colonial Wound"

Colkirk United Church and a Theology of Acceptance

I wasn't sure what to expect when I arrived at Colkirk United Church on that cold, snowy morning. It was the first day of the February break for schools on the First Nations reserve in which this church resided, and I had been asked to help with an afternoon vacation Bible school (VBS) program that a few leaders at this congregation wanted to host. Since they were in need of another adult to make the program feasible, we agreed that it was a good way for me to get to know the children that I'd eventually interview and to offer some assistance to the congregation to reciprocate their help with my research.

A volunteer named Arlene and I would be the only regular leaders for the week, with Rev. Martha coming by and helping when she was able. With less than a half-dozen children expected to attend, there would be ample time for us to get to know one another. Although there was very little scheduled for the week of programming, Arlene and I had discussed several activities that we could slot into the afternoons: watching movies, doing craft projects, making pizza, reading stories, and tobogganing on a nearby hill. Throughout the week we would ask the children what they were interested in doing and try to accommodate as much as possible.

When VBS kicked off on Monday afternoon, a handful of children – three girls – arrived with their lunches and we sat around a table in the small church hall to eat together. At first the children were shy, not speaking too much with me but politely responding when I asked them questions to get to know them. After plunking away at the piano together in the sanctuary, the girls decided that they'd like to watch a movie. I helped the three of them prepare the Sunday school room by covering the windows with chart paper and plastic tablecloths as Arlene made some popcorn for everyone to share. When the film was over, the youngest girl, Ally, asked me to play a game of paddle ball with her.

We continued to get to know each other throughout the week as we did all sorts of things together. We pushed each other on toboggans down a hill that had been blessed with a fresh layer of snow. Arlene and I helped the older two girls practise speeches that they had written to present at school after the break. We ate pizza that we'd made together as they told me about powwow and hoop dancing. By the end of the week we had all become quite comfortable with one another. In fact, when two young sisters joined our small group at VBS for the first time on the Friday of that week, Rev. Martha introduced me to them by saying, "Dave's a good guy," then asking the others, "We like Dave, don't we, Laura and Melissa?" The girls smiled and nodded and Laura said "I give him two thumbs up!" After the children left and we were cleaning up from the afternoon, Rev. Martha was sure to let me know that this comment from Laura was no small gesture.

Throughout the week I'd become amazed by Rev. Martha and Arlene's ability to weave spiritual and theological lessons into all sorts of activities. While many children's programs I had assisted with in other contexts had particular times for teaching and times for playing, these leaders seamlessly interwove these two elements together, allowing teachable moments to present themselves and not letting them pass by when they did rise to the surface. When practising their speeches, for example, Rev. Martha invoked the names of Moses, Elijah, and Paul, telling the girls that although none of them were good speakers, God had given them something to say and they were going to say it regardless of what others would think of them. As we were making pizza and doing dishes together on Thursday, Rev. Martha repeatedly said that that there are sermons in everything we do. From creating chains of people out of seemingly useless scraps of paper to having two wildly different pizzas share a common baking sheet, these children were learning about love, kindness, courage, gentleness (there's the Fruit of the Spirit I had forgotten at Messiah!), and all sorts of other Christian values as we spent time together that week.

Designed to Embrace

When the members of Colkirk United Church constructed their current building, they designed it to give the impression that it has outstretched arms, waiting to embrace all who approach. The church is made up of three sections, connected in the centre by a small foyer with coatracks and a few tables with photo albums and brochures. On either side are the two "arms" of the hug, one of which contains a kitchen and small church hall with just over half a dozen round tables with seasonal handmade centrepieces. The other consists of an office, washrooms, and a short hallway leading to a Sunday school room with bright windows and walls plastered with children's artwork.

The "body" of the church building is its sanctuary, a simple space with tall windows on both sides of the room and ten rows of pews flanking a centre aisle. At the front, an upright piano rests before the platform, which is accessible by steps at the front and a ramp along the side. A Christ candle sits prominently on the end of a handrail, and an electric organ – which is rarely played – hides behind the handrail. To the right are two chairs and a simple wooden pulpit for preaching sermons and delivering announcements. At the centre of the platform are three large chairs and a communion table with a small photograph of a "homeless Jesus" statue propped up against one of its legs. This image is not the only item that decorates this space; other ornaments include a wood relief picture of Jesus, a drawing of God embracing the earth that was made by one of the congregation's children, and a simple wooden cross on the wall above the communion table. These and other items are rooted in the community, with members of the congregation having created or acquired many of them over the years. Each week there may be new images and items adorning the space. In February, for instance, there may be red, pink, and white balloons leftover from Colkirk's Valentine's Day dinner. When a member of the congregation passes away, there may be a framed photograph of that person in the sanctuary for several weeks afterwards. Such items are markers of the close web of relationships among the people within this small congregation, who adorn it with decorations that are meaningful to them.

Colkirk is an Aboriginal congregation that was founded as a Methodist mission in the middle of the nineteenth century. Since that time there have been three buildings that stood on this land. The first was a log church, which was replaced in the early 1900s with a structure that was consumed by a fire at the end of the century. The current building is the meeting place of a community that has seen significant change over the past few decades.

Only a generation or two ago, the local church was the main venue for events on the reserve. A large percentage of the broader community attended Sunday services, for there was little else to do on Sunday mornings. As Rev. Martha, the current minister of Colkirk, stated, "The church was kind of the default place." Yet much has changed since she was a child in the congregation, and attendance has shrunk in light of the expanded number of options for how community members can spend their time.

All of this means that the people who continue to remain active at Colkirk do not do so out of obligation. Rev. Martha believes that those who are part of the congregation have a sense of being called to be part of it, and this is true for adults and for the small group of children who attend Sunday services or other activities that the congregation hosts. These individuals have a strong sense of the relationships and spirit that are shared among members of this community, which extends to those who have passed on as well. This is a congregation that values connection to the past, preferring to sing from old, coverless hymnals held together with tape than to replace them with new songbooks. These hymns and the piano that accompanies them remind them of their parents and grandparents who have passed away.

Another change in recent years has been the calling of an Aboriginal minister who knows the community well. This change turned the tide from a reliance on paternalistic approaches to White "missions" among the Aboriginal community. Coupled with the formation of the United Church's All Native Circle Conference in 1988, this change of pastoral leadership has helped the congregation worship and "conduct the business of the church in a way that works for us," in Rev. Martha's words. Gradually, the dire consequences of colonialism that came about by the United Church are being addressed in the congregation, despite the ongoing challenges of defunding and perpetuated institutional racism. While becoming more aware of and involved in happenings in the wider denomination, Rev. Martha makes it clear that this community continues to be marginalized: "the broader church really has nothing to do with us because culturally, politically, socially, geographically, they're isolated from us."

Sunday services – like every other aspect of life at Colkirk – are quite informal. Worship begins sometime around 10:00 a.m., but it's not uncommon to see Rev. Martha and other adults in the community chatting and setting up for fifteen or twenty minutes after the service was scheduled to begin. There are about a dozen people – all but one of whom are Aboriginal – at any given Sunday service, and most of these folks are older adults. While it is common for only a few children to be present, it's rare to have a service with no young people involved. Services follow a simple order of worship, and begin with congregants requesting songs that they'd like to sing, many of which are from the old and tattered copies of the "blue book." After lighting the Christ candle, Rev. Martha leads the community through prayers, readings, musical interludes, a children's time, and an uplifting sermon, followed by a few moments of silence. After reciting A New Creed and praying the prayers of the people, Rev. Martha extinguishes the Christ candle and the congregation gathers in the hall for a simple lunch of soup, biscuits, cheese, and other items that congregants chose to bring that day.

Sunday services are just one aspect of congregational life at Colkirk. To address issues facing their broader community – such as systemic poverty, the breakdown of community relationships, and the rise in Sunday morning extracurricular activities – the congregation hosts a breadth of other activities aimed at building community among its members and neighbours. Such events include a knitting circle and special meals such as a Valentine's Day dinner. In recent years, Rev. Martha and volunteer leaders like Arlene have emphasized ensuring that the congregation is a safe and loving place for children. To this end, they have expanded their children's ministries from Sunday school to week-long VBS programs during school breaks and a weekly "drop in" day during the summer – all at no cost to those who attend. These programs are aimed at helping to build relationships with children who do not come to Sunday worship and to meet a need in the community for affordable (in this case, free) childcare during school breaks.

Every way that Colkirk engages in ministry with children is intended to build loving relationships with them and to value them as participants, contributors, and leaders in their congregation and community. Although each program includes regular, semi-organized activities (such as a Bible story at the beginning of Sunday school and a short chapel service each day of VBS), informality is the order of the day. Whether they show up just once or walk through the door every time there's a program for children, each child has a small storage container in which they are free to keep craft projects, school assignments, and other items that they'd like to work on while at Colkirk. The children direct the activities they engage in, which sometimes results in independent activities, and sometimes a plethora of suggestions for group activities, such as baking cookies in the kitchen, watching a movie in the Sunday school room, or flying kites in the expansive church yard. The only agenda that Rev. Martha and Arlene bring to these programs is to show the children love, invest in their self-worth, build relationships with them, and help them build relationships with one another. For the most part, any teaching or lessons they wish to impart to the children is done informally, through conversations during one of many teachable moments that arise throughout their time together.

Healing Wounds

Rev. Martha has served as the minister of Colkirk for approximately five years. Since she's no stranger to this congregation and the reserve it calls home, her leadership represents a shift toward autonomy of the local community: Colkirk no longer relies on leadership from either temporary student ministers or White clergy from off the reserve.

For this minister, leading this congregation is intimately intertwined with the history of her community. Ministering to the people within her congregation – particularly children – involves above all things working to repair the damage caused by centuries of colonialism. For most of Colkirk's history, she recounted to me, ministry had been carried out in ways that undermined the culture and context of First Nations people, with White clergy driving home the sinfulness of Aboriginal spirituality and ways of life while offering a narrow vision of salvation and life in Jesus Christ. This interpretation of the gospel has resulted in wounds that fester as they are passed on from one generation to the next, and are felt even among the very young children within this congregation. Rev. Martha explained to me how this reality shapes her ministry at Colkirk, especially that which she carries out with children:

> First Nations people are inextricably linked to history. So a lot of what's happening here in this church and in this community are just part of that river of history. This is where we are at this particular moment in time. And it's had a specific course and it has a specific course in the future. And we're trying to influence that course as much as we can based on who we are and not what Indian Affairs says we can be or not what is possible under the law, but who we say we are. So we're trying to influence that river as it goes from here. So a lot of the work that we do with the kids, as I see us trying to do it anyway, is about healing that colonial wound so that the church is no longer the place that you go to hear that you're a bad

person and you're a sinner and you can only be saved through this particular way.

A primary avenue for this restorative work is relationships. It is because relationships are so vital that Rev. Martha and Arlene spend a great deal of time simply being with and listening to people within their congregation. Rather than focusing on congregational structures and well-organized Sunday services, their emphasis on relationships blends with their congregation's informality to create a space where building community is paramount. Rev. Martha once remarked, "As Aboriginal churches, we need that. We need that time and relationship to actually know what [one another] are talking about, to know what people are all about, what we're all about." Everything from the child-led approach to children's programs to the weekly post-service meals and the passing of the peace – during which time everyone present shakes hands – are aimed at forming strong relationships with one another and with the place they call Colkirk.

Healing the colonial wound also involves the redemption of Aboriginal spirituality from the marginalized and even demonized reputation it was given by settlers and missionaries. In the many months that I spent building relationships of mutual trust and respect with the people of Colkirk,[1] I rarely heard them speak about the juxtaposition of Aboriginal spirituality and Christianity; yet I witnessed several ways that Rev. Martha and her congregation blends these two traditions together. For example, each time she lights the Christ candle, Rev. Martha draws from Aboriginal spirituality with words such as: "We light our Christ candle. And we remember that Jesus is the fire at the centre of our circle, uniting us with all our relations." Going further, there are several ways that the members of this community blend Christianity and Aboriginal spirituality in informal ways, such as one elder who shares her retelling of the Nativity depicting Jesus's birth on the reserve or a conversation Rev. Martha had with a young girl about how she doesn't need to be afraid of spirits that they see in their homes and in their church building. These are just a handful of the many ways that this minister and her broader congregation implicitly and freely synthesize elements of Aboriginal spirituality and Christianity.

Above all else, healing the wounds of colonialism among the members of Colkirk and its surrounding community involves making church a place of love. As Rev. Martha said to me, "our church is a place to go to know that you are loved and experience the love of God whenever you come here. That's what I'm trying for." This sort of love is one that this minister hopes will permeate the relationships built among her congregation. For her, this is an unconditional love that invites people to bring their authentic selves into relationship with others. She wants people to know that "the church is a place where you can be yourself and you know that you are loved by God, you know that you are loved by the congregation, that you are supported, that you are forgiven even when you mess up." For this minister, God's love is not something that is only preached from the pulpit; it is tangibly experienced as the congregation seeks to show God's love to all who walk through its doors.

The leaders at Colkirk observe that Western materialism is sweeping throughout the reserve, leaving many in the community struggling with depression, addiction, and hopelessness. In Rev. Martha's eyes, as the consequences of colonialism continue to harm individuals' lives, the rise of material resources – and in some cases wealth – results in a lack of "inner resources or connection to those things that ultimately sustain us." This in turn means that more and more people "now have better houses in which to commit suicide."[2] In light of these challenges, this congregation's leaders refer to their ministry with children as "suicide prevention." Many of the children in the community have experienced a "rough start" to life, even from their earliest years. Thus, the primary goal of Colkirk's ministry with children is "not about learning the books of the Bible or the Ten Commandments"; it is about keeping the children alive into adulthood by helping them develop the "inner resources" and relationships that can support their long-term flourishing. To achieve this, they minister with two specific emphases.

First, they support the children in developing the freedom to be themselves whenever they are at Colkirk. It is for this reason that their Sunday school and VBS programs are largely unstructured, for it allows the children the freedom to have a say in the activities they engage in within this congregation. There is a great deal of free time, during which the children can play sports and games, make crafts, read, and talk with one another, and adult helpers join them in the activities they are interested in and take advantage of the teachable moments they notice as they paint together, kick around a soccer ball, and talk. As mentioned, it's not unusual for Arlene to brainstorm with the children about what they would like to do during VBS and make plans to engage in these activities together during the week.

A second emphasis leads out of the first. Colkirk's approach to children's ministry not only gives the children the freedom to be themselves, but it also focuses on supporting them as they learn to be in community with one another. They strongly emphasize the ways that the children interact with one another as they develop healthy self-images. For them, the children need to learn that their voices matter and that the voices of others matter as well. Thus, when a conflict arises among the children, they encourage all parties to listen to one another and respect one another's feelings and opinions. In this way, they seek to help the children form healthy and sustainable ways of relating to one another in community.

Theological Reflections

The most salient features of the theological meaning-making among the children at Colkirk involve their blending of Aboriginal spirituality and Christian theology, as well as their focus on relationships and community. Both of these characteristics align with the ethos of healing the wounds of colonialism through the building of strong relations and healthy self-worth, which are so central to life and ministry at this congregation.

Blended Theology

Each of the four children I interviewed at Colkirk expressed their theological ideas in ways that demonstrated an interweaving of Christian theology with Aboriginal spirituality. Usually their blending of these two traditions was implicit and unspoken, and they seemed uninterested in discussing *how* they juxtapose these traditions, acting as though they know no other way of doing theology.

Aboriginal spirituality and Christian theology intersected throughout my conversation with Melissa (11) and Laura (13), two girls who are young leaders among the children who come to services at Colkirk (although with differing levels of regularity), participate in VBS, and attend school on their reserve. This interweaving was evidenced particularly in two snippets of our conversation, each of which bookended a lengthy period when they shared stories about the creation of the world they had learned from their congregation and school. In response to my request for them to draw pictures of God, Laura created a scene of trees at various stages of growth (figure 4.1), which she was careful to note was an unfinished drawing, and Melissa drew the backs of heads of girls belonging to different races (figure 4.2), along with words describing God, which she intended to add to but was unable to do so. I asked them why they drew these images as representations of God:

MELISSA: Because he made all those people.
DAVE: And Laura, what about all the trees?
LAURA: I don't know, just kind of like, creation of life. You get born. And then you die.
DAVE: Oh, so is that why all the trees are at different stages?
LAURA: Yeah
DAVE: And, uh, so are those roots?
LAURA: Yeah.
DAVE: And then sprouting up?
LAURA: Yeah.
DAVE: So what do you mean, like, the creation of life and the cycle of life?
LAURA: Um, he made them.
MELISSA: He made them.
LAURA: Yeah.
DAVE: God made them? Is that something a lot of people talk about at Colkirk, or –
MELISSA: (*interjecting*) I just heard it from school, I guess.
LAURA: Yeah, well we get taught, like, the Creator and stuff like that.
MELISSA: Yeah.
LAURA: But, it's like, when we come here [Colkirk], it's kind of the same thing, just in a different point of view.
DAVE: What do you mean? So at school you learn about the Creator?
MELISSA: Yeah.
LAURA: Yeah, like, Creator is like God.

* * *

DAVE: So when they tell you the stories – I don't know a lot about them. So when they tell you the stories, are the stories meant to be told, like, that's how it really happened?
LAURA: I think they change over time.
MELISSA: Yeah. A long time ago they might have been really detailed and everything.

LAURA: And now they're shortened to like five minutes.
MELISSA: Yeah.
DAVE: Why do you think that is?
MELISSA: Well, because they get passed, passed on. It passes on through a whole bunch of people.
Laura: Through generations and generations.
MELISSA: Yeah, and they might not remember all of it, but they remember the really important stuff.
DAVE: What does that feel like to you, to learn these stories that you know many generations before you have learned?
MELISSA: I guess, like ...
LAURA: It's good to know, though –
MELISSA: (*interrupting*) Yeah.
LAURA: But sometimes we know it and they keep telling you. Then it gets very frustrating.
MELISSA: Yeah.
DAVE: ... What makes it good to know? Like, why is it good to know?
LAURA: So that you're keeped [sic] up with your ... I guess –
MELISSA: (*interjecting*) Your people.
LAURA: Yeah, your people.
MELISSA: And you can relate it to things, like God.

It is possible to add several pages of dialogue among these two girls that occurred between these excerpts. For a great deal of the interview, they riffed off each other as they told me four stories that, in their words, "hook together": the story of the woman who fell to the waters and made the earth on the back of a turtle; the story of the birth of the right-handed and left-handed twins and the creation of good and evil; the story of fighting between the twins; and the story of the Peacemaker, who travelled throughout warring nations spreading a message of peace and guiding the nations to bury their weapons under the tree of peace.

Like most of the other children who participated in this research, Melissa and Laura drew pictures of God near the beginning of the interview.[3] As they explained what ideas about God were embedded in their drawings, our conversation moved to names they use when they speak of God – Melissa calls God *Creator*, while Laura refers to God as *Maker* – and they told me that they learn stories about the Creator at their school on the reserve. Believing that school and church "kind of say the same thing" about the Creator, but that sometimes at church they call the Creator *God*, they began telling me stories about the Creator that they have learned from school and from Colkirk. At times they made clear connections between Aboriginal spirituality and Christian theology, like when Melissa told me – and Laura agreed – that she sees Jesus as a person who "would help people, kind of like the Peacemaker would in the story."

However, the vast majority of instances when these girls made explicit connections between these two traditions were responses to questions I posed in an attempt to have them share their thoughts about such intersections. Left to their own accord, they were content to express their Christian faith through the stories of their Aboriginal tradition, blending these traditions together with seamlessness and subtlety and allowing the connections to exist between the lines.

One of the most significant ways that these children interwove Christianity and Aboriginal spirituality in their generation of theology was in their reliance on narrative, a central hallmark of Aboriginal knowledge.[4] Theirs is a storied faith, one that makes sense of the world around them through the stories they tell about it. Several times throughout our conversations, all four children from Colkirk expressed their faith through narratives. Ethan (8), a child who attends VBS regularly but is an infrequent Sunday school participant, explained his drawing of a river to me by telling me a story he seemed to be creating through our conversation (figure 4.3). It was a story about a God who lives at the headwaters and a people who can travel up the river to God as if they were climbing a ladder. Of course, this improvised story was not perfectly crafted according to standard dramatic structure from exposition to climax to denouement. But his ideas were expressed by building an ad hoc narrative about who God is and how humanity can encounter this God. Such a reliance on story is built into the DNA of Colkirk and is a primary means through which these children have learned about Christianity and Aboriginal spirituality, within both their congregation and school.[5]

The blending of Christianity and Aboriginal spirituality was a commonality shared among all four of the children I interviewed from Colkirk. While it is perhaps most clearly demonstrated by Melissa and Laura, who responded to my questions about God with Aboriginal stories passed down from generation to generation, Ally (7) and Ethan also expressed their theologies in ways that juxtaposed these two traditions. This commonality, however, does not equate to uniformity; these children may have relied on both traditions in generating theology with me, but they did so to varying degrees. As mentioned, in their conversation with me, Melissa and Laura moved our discussion forward in ways that demonstrated their reliance on Aboriginal spirituality in understanding who God/Creator/Maker is and how this being interacts – or does not interact – with the world. As they blend these two traditions together, they both lean on Aboriginal spirituality more than Christianity, using the former as a lens for understanding the latter. Yet while they both tend to be on the same side of the spectrum, Laura's approach is less balanced than Melissa's, as Melissa names *God* and *Jesus* more frequently than Laura. This may very well be related to the fact that Melissa attends Sunday services and Sunday school with far greater frequency than Laura, whose main involvement with Colkirk is the VBS programs during school breaks, which include a lower percentage of time dedicated to explicitly faith-based practices such as Bible stories, prayer, and hymns.

While Laura and Melissa both draw from Aboriginal spirituality more heavily than Christianity in building the mosaics that are their theologies, Ally leans predominantly toward Christianity. This bubbly seven-year-old is quite involved in Colkirk, attending VBS and participating in Sunday services with her grandparents and her mother. Her understanding of God, Jesus, and heaven reflect this high level of involvement in a Christian congregation. During the course of our interview, Ally spoke about how Jesus lived in the desert, was put on a cross, and "died for us," and she expressed an understanding of God that is largely consistent with mainstream Christianity. For her, God "lives in the sky" and "we only get to see him on pictures when we're down here [on earth], but when we die and go back up to heaven where we came from, we get to see him in real life." While her theology is largely sourced from Christianity, she joins her peers at Colkirk in blending these views with Aboriginal spirituality, although in ways that prioritize Christianity. The most prevalent way that Aboriginal spirituality informs her theology is in her understanding of God; for her, God's primary role in the world is that of creator, the one who makes all good things in nature: "He didn't make that furniture. All he made was grass, trees, leafs [sic], bark, animals ... and he makes us." Like her older peers at Colkirk, Ally's understanding of God's creative powers aligns with the right-handed twin, who, as Melissa shared, made all in the world that was good.

Relational Theology

Given the fact that the leaders of Colkirk prioritize the building of relationships among members of the congregation, it should not be surprising that one of the most salient characteristics of how the children within this congregation generate theology is the relational approach they take. One instance that exemplifies this is a vignette from my conversation with Ally. As she chatted with me on the steps of her church's platform, she told me about some prayers she recently wrote and that she's been learning "lots about God and Jesus and the Christian" for a few years. I asked her to say more about this:

ALLY: Sometimes I prayer [sic]. I change this prayer and just say something. I thank him for all he's given us.
DAVE: Wow. Have you always prayed?
ALLY: Mm-hmm. Pretty much.
DAVE: And where did you, like, what made you want to pray?
ALLY: Well, as soon as I got older, like five years old, I started to learn lots about God and Jesus and the Christian. So, yeah ... that's what started up on me starting to learn all of this.
DAVE: And where did you learn? You said you started to learn that. You're – how old are you now – six or seven?
ALLY: Seven.
DAVE: Seven. Alright, I knew that. Seven. I just forgot ... Because at the last VBS you were six. Now you're seven.
ALLY: Mm-hmm.
DAVE: So, where did you learn? You said since you've been five you've been learning about God and Jesus. Where did you learn, what do you mean you're learning about that?
ALLY: Because almost every day when I wasn't sick or I wasn't busy, I would always come to church with my grandparents and sometimes my parents.
DAVE: Every day or, like, every –
ALLY: (*interjecting*) Every Sunday.
DAVE: Every Sunday? Okay. And you come sometimes with your mom, sometimes with your grandparents.
ALLY: Sometimes we just come all as a group and sometimes I just come with my grandparents.

DAVE: Okay. I've seen you here with just your grandparents. I think the first time I met you, you were here with your grandparents.

ALLY: I think you might have sat with us.

DAVE: I did! Over there. I remember that.

ALLY: I wasn't sure who you were then!

DAVE: (*joking*) But you know who I am now, right?

ALLY: Yes!

DAVE: And I remember, you were doing something up here [on the platform].

ALLY: Oh! See that thing with numbers [the hymn board]? Each week we change the numbers. And see where there's a little space at the bottom?

DAVE: Yep.

ALLY: Because only if there's communion there's only a certain number that goes at the bottom. That's what I'm doing.

DAVE: ...You change the numbers?

ALLY: And if I get here early, like maybe fifteen or twenty minutes before church starts, Arlene wants me to help her get everything set up for church.

DAVE: Wow. And do you like helping?

ALLY: Yeah. And I really like to keep things neat a lot. My room's really clean.

DAVE: ... Let's pretend we never met at church and we met somewhere else.

ALLY: Okay.

DAVE: Let's pretend I don't know anything about your church.

ALLY: Okay.

DAVE: What would you want to tell me? If I said, "Ally, can you tell me about your church?," what would you tell me about your church?

ALLY: Um ... that it's nice and I learn a lot.

DAVE: What kind of stuff do you learn?

ALLY: Well, one time we sat here and Arlene got a whole bunch of hearts. After I'll go show you when we're finished.

DAVE: Okay.

ALLY: They're in the hallway there. You know those signs, those big things. Um, we used hearts and she cut out hearts and hands and then we wrote kind words on them.

At the beginning of this vignette, Ally told me about how she has learned about God and Jesus for the past few years and as I asked her to say more about where and what she has learned, she moved the conversation to one of sharing memories of her time at church, and of how we first met several months earlier when Rev. Martha invited me to visit Colkirk on a Sunday in order to begin building relationships with members of the community. In asking Ally to tell me more about her learning, I was expecting her to recount theological information that she had gained. Instead, she spoke about memories of times shared together at Colkirk, denoting the importance of relationships in her theological life.

I had come to know Ally from helping Colkirk with three VBS programs – in February, March, and July of 2014 – and during the final VBS I assisted with, she was aware that I wanted to have a conversation with her about her ideas surrounding God and church. In preparation for our chat, she went home and started a book of prayers that she shared with me at the outset of our formal interview. I asked her about the book and she seemed to come up with a name for it in that moment, calling it her "book of ... Christian Christ." When I asked her what "Christian" means, she responded by saying, "... almost like church? You learn Christian at church," and she could not recall what "Christ" is, although she knew it had something to do with church. At first, Ally seemed focused on using the proper language in our interview, perhaps influenced by her involvement in a conservative Baptist congregation on the reserve that she periodically attends with her mother. Yet while she knew that these words had to do with church, she was unable to articulate any sort of understanding about what they meant. This fact, when placed alongside her desire to talk about the memories she has made with people at Colkirk, may evidence the prioritization of community-building at the heart of this congregation.

Melissa, Laura, and Ethan also spoke of the importance of the community of relationships that exists at Colkirk. For example, Melissa and Laura expressed that their congregational community is like a family. They identified these familial-like connections as the most important aspects of their congregation, later speaking of how they feel more connected to their church community than to their clans at longhouse:

DAVE: What is it about this family that you seem to feel more connected to than longhouse?

LAURA: (*interjecting*) You just meet them more.

MELISSA: Yeah, like, I've just known them my whole life. I don't remember when I didn't know them.

DAVE: Is that different than longhouse?

MELISSA: Yeah.

LAURA: Because there's people, like, making other people, a lot now. And ... yeah ...

DAVE: Are there lots of people at longhouse?

LAURA: If you go to, like, bigger longhouses, then yeah.

MELISSA: Yeah. And if there's like a ceremony going on, there's going to be lots of people in it.

LAURA: It's packed.

DAVE: So, like, because it's smaller here too and less people, then you know them better?

MELISSA: And at longhouse there might be different people every time you go. So, you get to know people here because they're always here and ... they always talk to you and they're friendly.

While more articulate than Ally, these two girls express a similar understanding of the importance of relationships to Colkirk. Paralleling the broader culture of the congregation, these children see Colkirk as a place steeped in relationships with people who know them, spend time with them, and care for them.

But what do these relationships mean for the theological lives of these children? Although one can argue that they have an impact on the way children generate theology, such a view of these relationships does not fully consider their depth. These children represent what would be a paradigm shift in many United Church congregations that are predominantly White or are made up largely of members from other non-Aboriginal backgrounds. The relationships at Colkirk certainly shape the children's theology. But the relationships are in fact the theology itself. The meaningful connections that these children have with one another and with others in their congregation is the very stuff of theology, a theology embodied and expressed in these lived relationships.

This becomes clear in considering my conversation with Ethan. At some point during every interview with children from each congregation, I asked the young participants to share what they would say if someone who knew nothing about their congregation asked them to tell them about it. Ethan's response revolved around the people who spend time with him at Colkirk: "There's kids there. And they play. And there's Rev.

Martha and Arlene and Dave. And they help. And then after we go to chapel in the morning. And then after chapel, we go outside and play. And some days we make lunch." I asked him to say more about chapel, and again his response involved the people there: "We would pray and sing. And then after that we would read a book – Dave would read books." Ethan does not attend Sunday services regularly, but he and his family are well known among the congregation and he is an avid participant in VBS programs. Yet the relationships he has with the people he encounters within this congregation – including me – form the very core of his idea of what Colkirk is. His theology is not so much about knowledge that God loves him or the other theological ideas embedded in the books he hears at VBS chapel services. It is the very act of knowing and being known that is his theology. As Arlene, Rev. Martha, and the other folks at this congregation take an interest in his life and his well-being, theology is happening.

Theology All Their Own

Although Colkirk places more emphasis on helping children build relationships rather than acquire particular information, it holds certain theological truths that it wants its children to learn. Its theology is embodied in its relationships of love and acceptance, and as such it is aimed at countering a theology of guilt, inadequacy, and sinfulness that has plagued Christian mission work among First Nations communities for centuries. This is not to say, however, that the children's theologies are completely aligned with that of their congregation. Rather, just like their peers in the preceding chapters, the children at Colkirk diverge from their congregation's wider culture and create theological meaning in ways that are all their own.

Such excursions were most pronounced in Ally's theology, particularly in her understanding of church. While she holds to a relational approach to theology – as demonstrated earlier – in some instances Ally's remarks during our interview showcased that she associates church with learning particular things, a view that is not at the forefront of Colkirk's identity. For example, at the outset of our interview, three times she associated going to church with learning. In the first instance of this, she remarked that there are only a few other children in her class at school who also go to church (they attend other congregations). But she also said, "I know more than them," demonstrating that she is making associations between knowledge and churchgoing and at times assuming that knowing the right things is the marker of a good Christian. This sort of understanding counters Rev. Martha's goal of building community among the children. Yet it is perhaps not surprising when we consider the nature of thinking among children of her age; the correlation she places on knowledge and fidelity speaks to her budding abilities to form new interpretations that rely on predictability and concreteness. For her, the intangibility and abstractness of human relationships may not yet ground her faith in a way that the holding of certain bits of knowledge can. As she continues to move toward a Mythic-Literal faith in which peer relationships grow in their importance,[6] she may let go of the security of knowing and wander toward a place in which the abstractness of relationships can offer her grounding in her faith. But for now at least, this characteristic of her theological thinking marks a clear divergence from the broader culture of her congregation.

The association between going to church and learning is not the only aspect of Ally's theology that is more distinct from her congregation. This young girl seems to hold implicit and explicit theologies. Her implicit theology is evidenced by the importance she places on the relationships and experiences she has at her congregation, and it seems to align with the wider culture of Colkirk.

Yet her explicit theology is one that equates faithfulness with learning particular things and engaging in specific practices. Her descriptions of her theology reflect this view, which at times seemed to focus on earning approval among the leaders of Colkirk (in which she includes me) rather than feeling the unconditional love and acceptance of the congregation. This approval-seeking approach to faith came through in Ally's insistence on showing me her book of prayers, a book that only included one or two prayers which she began when she learned a few days earlier that we would be talking about church and God together sometime during the week. It appeared as though she wrote the book to make it clear to me that she prays regularly at home and, thus, is a good Christian. Yet this sort of behaviour – of having to prove oneself worthy and earn the acceptance of leaders in her congregation – is the very attitude that Rev. Martha and Arlene are intentionally working to counteract.

The association Ally makes between church and learning led her to speak more than her peers at Colkirk about the content of her faith. She shared theological ideas about scripture, the crucifixion, and evil, and in some instances her thoughts were those one would expect to hear from more conservative evangelical congregations rather than Colkirk. For example, she focused on the importance of believing "what it says in the Bible" as a marker of belief in God and Jesus, and she said Jesus "died for us," but was unable articulate what exactly these statements mean. It appeared as though Ally was using language and phrases that she had learned somewhere, but did not understand, demonstrating that she gives value to the content of theology, which is evidenced through proper terminology. This was most clear when we discussed where bad things come from, and she said, "Uh, what's that man's name? Oh ... hm ... No, not Samuel. Um, who's the guy who leads, um ... hell?" When I asked if she meant Satan, she immediately said "Yes, Satan makes the bad things." Ally knew that she had learned about Satan, but was unable to remember his name. From my experience with Colkirk, they do not hold this sort of theology.

If the aim of children's ministry at Colkirk is to heal the colonial wound, then the most obvious example of theological differences occurred when Ally drew her picture of God (figure 4.4). Her image was of an elderly man, and as she was colouring her picture, she searched the bin of crayons for what she called "skin colour." After struggling to find the shade she was looking for, she picked up a crayon and held it against my arm, saying "Does this look like your skin?" Her concept of God was not akin to the images of an Aboriginal Jesus found throughout Colkirk's building. God, for her, is a White man, a view based on White Westernized ethnocentric assumptions.

The damaging effects of colonialism run deep, and Christianity is bound up with them. Ally's theology – both in some of its content and in her quest to earn approval – are manifestations of a colonialistic Christianity, one that her congregation actively seeks to subvert. Perhaps these aspects of her theology are also the result of her involvement in the conservative Baptist church that she attends with her mother from time to time. Regardless of how she has come to hold these theological views, she demonstrates that as much as some children may reflect their congregation's broader culture, they will generate theology in ways that vary from it as well, drawing from sources beyond the congregation and creating theology in ways that are all their own.

* * *

Colkirk United Church is a congregation steeped in history, one that is intertwined with the paternalistic and hegemonic history of politics and mission work among Aboriginal communities in Canada. This past has negatively affected many within this congregation and community, with the ripples being felt by each new generation. The leadership of Colkirk actively seeks to heal these colonial wounds by building strong and healthy relationships among their community – especially their youngest members.

The children at this congregation generate theology in ways that reflect this ethos. Their theology redeems the Aboriginal spirituality that has been condemned by Western missionaries by holding it up and blending it with Christian theology to create understandings and ideas that are unique to their particular context and history. Additionally, they place relationships at the core of their theology, valuing the people and experiences at Colkirk as vital to their theological lives. While both of these more salient aspects of their theology are consistent with that of their congregation, these children also venture out into the theological landscape on paths that are their own, which was evident as Ally drew from sources and formed ideas that differ from the ones held by the community of Colkirk. Clearly, the ideas and stories that these children shared with me were rich with theological wisdom and meaning. In the next chapter, I will discuss this importance of story along with other salient features that arise when our focus shifts from children with a specific congregation to a multiplicity of lenses for interpreting the theologies of all the children I have introduced in the preceding four chapters.

Figure 4.1 Laura's drawing

Figure 4.2 Melissa's drawing

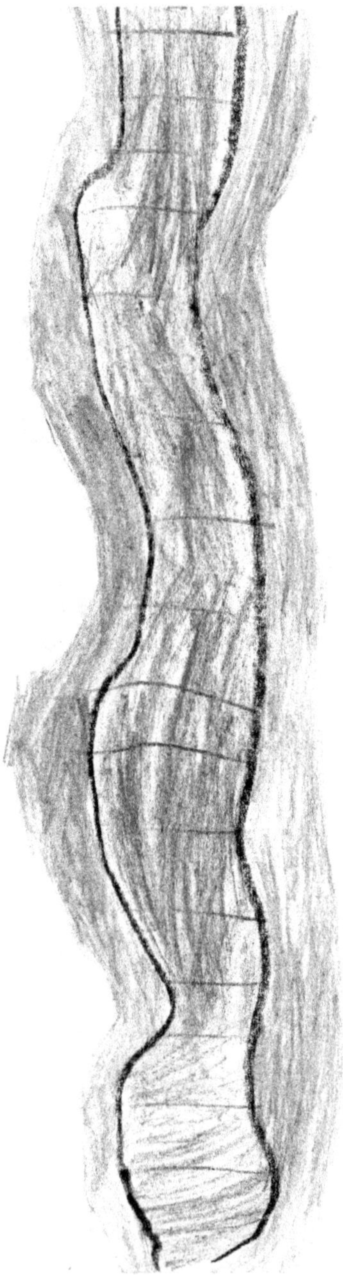

Figure 4.3 Ethan's drawing

Figure 4.4 Ally's drawing

5 Kaleidoscopic Theology
An Interpretation of Children's Theologies

In the preceding four chapters, I discuss the theologies of the nineteen children whom I had the pleasure of getting to know through my research, and I demonstrate that their theological meaning-making reflects their congregational cultures. Additionally, the theologies of these young people expand beyond those of their congregations in content, sources, and methods that work together to make their theologies their own.

This chapter widens the focus from the narrower contexts of individual congregations to a multiplicity of contexts. Rather than studying the children's theologies in light of the culture of their particular congregations, I will place the children alongside one another and analyze their theological meaning-making through a threefold framework that draws from what Emmanuel Lartey calls a "Trinitarian" understanding of personhood, one that emphasizes the universal, cultural, and individual spheres of human life.[1] Each aspect of Lartey's understanding attends to a different sphere of personhood. When taken together, these spheres move toward a truly intercultural vision of humanity. Such an interpretation of children's theologies has been lacking within the field of children's spirituality and theology. Thus, this chapter makes a strategic move toward filling the gap within the field that I identified in the introduction, shedding new light on the content, sources, and methods of children's theologies.

Finding a Framework

One of the challenges of research into multiple cultural contexts is that it too easily lends itself to analysis based on comparative evaluation, on placing different communities not *alongside* one another, but *against* one another. Rather than attempting to give equal priority to all cultural contexts and evaluating each one in light of itself, comparative evaluation can become a slippery slope toward judgements about the superiority/inferiority of various cultures, given the difficulty of achieving objectivity and impartiality among subjective human researchers. Such practices perpetuate paternalistic and hegemonic approaches to researching culture. Rather than seeing the value embedded within each cultural context, comparative evaluation allows the lens of the researcher – her or his presuppositions, values, and worldview, all of which are intertwined with the cultures that shape the researcher – to be the basis for judging and evaluating the communities and cultures under investigation. Thus, any comparative evaluation I make of the participating individuals and congregations would put me at risk of normalizing my own cultural context in such an assessment. Not only is such a framework inconsistent with the manner in which I imagined, structured, and carried out this study, but it would disrespect the people and communities who breathed life into it, and undermine my relationships with the individuals and communities who joined me on the journey.

In an essay on insider/outsider status within research, Sharan Merriam and her colleagues address the importance of representing truth embedded within research findings. In their discussion, they describe the ways in which constructivist and postmodern understandings of truth complicate the authoritative views of knowledge put forward by positivism: "Constructivists argue that knowledge/reality/truth is constructed by individuals and by human communities, while postmodernists assert that there is no single truth or reality independent from the knower."[2] Taking these words seriously, what I require in this chapter is a method of comparative interpretation that acknowledges the full personhood of the children who participated in this study, all of whom combine their unique perspectives with the aspects held in common with their peers as they search for their own understandings of truth; I require a method that allows for, in the words of Pranee Liamputtong, "the cultural knowledge of a particular group [to be] counted in its own right,"[3] rather than assessed in light of others'.

Theologian Emmanuel Lartey has written extensively about pastoral care and counselling in intercultural and diverse contexts. With a broad vision of culture in view – like the one undergirding this book – Lartey formulates an intercultural approach to pastoral care. In his words, this approach provides "many voices from different backgrounds a chance to express their views on the subject under review on their own terms. It does not then rush to analyze or systematize them into overarching theories that can explain and fit everything neatly into place. Instead, it ponders the glorious variety and chaotic mystery of human experience for clues to a more adequate response to the exigencies of human life."[4]

I have until this chapter interpreted the children's theologies by placing them alongside their congregational peers. Yet here I wish to widen my view and place all the children alongside one another. This expanded interpretation will enhance the congregation-based interpretations of previous chapters by bringing further nuance and complexity as the children's theologies are interpreted from a new vantage point.

Rather than seeking to reduce the complexity of each congregation and its members into neat categories, such an interpretation relies on a perspective of human diversity broad enough to include both shared commonalities and unique differences. Lartey uses this sort of interpretative framework in his intercultural approach to pastoral care. Drawing from a conception originally proposed by Kluckhohn and Murray in 1948,[5] Lartey uses a threefold understanding of human personhood that affirms the myriad ways that similarities and differences meld together in human beings and communities. This "Trinitarian" understanding asserts that "every human person is in certain respects 1. Like all others, 2. Like some others, 3. Like no other."[6]

Each of these assertions expresses a different aspect of human life.[7] The first draws attention to the universal characteristics of all people, such as entering the world as infants dependent on others, holding relationships with others and the world around oneself, and inevitably dying. The second acknowledges the cultural communities in which we all exist. These communities shape and influence us through their cultural attributes, and in many ways those belonging to common communities share aspects of their cultural life. The final assertion recognizes the particularities of individuality, calling attention to the uniqueness of all people. From DNA to life stories, fingerprints to feelings, each person is a unique individual who exists in personal ways that are distinct from the billions of others in our world.

Although Lartey describes these three spheres using social, psychological, and physiological ideas, I contend that each one also carries theological meaning. All human beings, for instance, are like all others in that we are made in and bear the image of God, we are beings who are marked by sin, and yet God's unconditional love permeates all our lives equally.

The second sphere allows us to acknowledge that we exist within communities that shape and are shaped by us. We are beings in relationships – with families, faith communities, and cultures – which form our identities, ethical stances, and faith. Finally, as individual persons, we are unique beings to whom God has given autonomy, consciousness, and free will, with which we have a hand in determining the trajectories of our lives and our responses to the world around us. While God has made us all in the *Imago Dei* and placed us in relationship with others, God has also given us the gift of self-determination.

When learning about people in different cultural contexts, as I have done, the most obvious of the three spheres is the second: All human beings are like *some* others. This is, after all, the level most closely aligned with culture, and it is this sphere that has been in central focus throughout this book thus far. In this chapter, however, I zoom out to include all three of Lartey's assertions – universal, cultural, and individual – as I interpret the content, sources, and methods of children's theology. By holding these three spheres in creative tension with one another, my interpretation in this chapter will affirm that all three are present in the lives of each child who participated in this study; I join Lartey in attempting to ensure that "living, growing and changing human persons is what is expected, treated as the norm, and attended to."[8] This broad formulation guards against the Western need to categorize and stereotype by making room for the multitude of ways in which people and communities hold aspects of life in common and express uniqueness unto themselves. Yet I do not overlook the irony that it does so through yet another categorization or formulation. Nevertheless, it allows the stories and relationships to truth that are embedded in this research to be attended to in their own right rather than compared against one another, letting me interpret the children's theologies in a kaleidoscopic way – that is, at multiple levels, from different angles, and with an awareness of the complexity of human personhood as it exists in all three spheres.

Like All Others

I begin my interpretation by exploring the broadest aspect of human personhood – universality. I do not assume that all children in all times and places share the characteristics I will discuss; rather, my use of the term "universal" speaks to aspects of children's theologies held in common by all the children who participated in this research. In this section I discuss ways in which the content, sources, and methods of children's theological meaning-making are held in common, particularly their concepts of God, their use of congregations as theological sources, and their conversational approach to generating theology.

God Concepts

The most salient piece of theological content shared among all the children is that each one of them held to and could describe a concept of God.[9] Of course, one reason why their God concepts may have been so prevalent in the interviews is that I used them as the starting point of our conversations by asking the children to draw a picture of God. Nonetheless, all of the children were able to express an image of God and none of them – even Marion and Lizzy, who did not draw pictures – evaded responding to my questions about their understandings of God.

Of the nineteen children, eleven expressed personified concepts of God. While children from each congregation held to this view, the majority of those who saw God as a person were from Messiah and Parkdale. Of this group of nearly a dozen children, six of them seemed to interpret God as Jesus, drawing and responding to my questions about God by talking about attributes of Jesus (such as his death on the cross, his resurrection, or pictures of Jesus within their congregation's building). Even Nicholas, who was skeptical that Jesus rose from the dead, expressed a fair amount of certainty about Jesus's existence and drew a depiction of Jesus in response to my request for him to draw God (figure 3.4). The remaining five children conceived of God as some sort of divine man, sometimes telling me about God's special powers (such as the ability to talk with angels), and – in all but one case – depicting through words and drawings that God has a moustache and/or beard although he decided to leave a beard off his picture of God, Jacob wondered aloud whether God has a beard and did not land on a definitive answer). This God concept is reminiscent of depictions of God the Father that arose during the Renaissance period and even today remain ubiquitous in contemporary television, movies, and media. With over half the children expressing a personified view of God, this was by far the most commonly held concept among these children.

The next most frequent God concept involves God's creative action in the world. Three of the children – all of whom were part of Colkirk – conveyed understandings of God's role as creator. As mentioned in chapter 4, Melissa, Laura, and Ethan all spoke about God's work as creator of the world, and the latter two drew images of nature (trees and a river; see figures 4.1 and 4.3) because they connect these natural objects with God's creative capacities.

Of the five remaining children, two of them moved this conversation from the concrete personifications expressed by eleven children to understandings firmly rooted in abstraction. Rebecca and Stephen – both attending Burke Street – depicted God in forms meant to convey God's omnipresence. While Rebecca drew a picture of her town and wrote the words "God loves you and is all around you" (figure 3.1), Stephen's drawing of his congregation's building (figure 3.2) showed where he has "learned the most and experienced God the most." He continued, "And I don't really, I don't like to think of God as a person – more as an idea or like a thing that's always there ... It's like more like a spirit that's just all around you, not – and in you. Just not a person or one singular thing."

There were two children who expressed God concepts that were more unique. While both conveyed a personified God, I do not include them in the first group of children because they do not depict Jesus or a divine "God the Father" figure. From Parkdale, Jacob's God is one that in many ways parallels superheroes and video game heroes. This God, as described in chapter 1, lives in a castle and protects himself from "bad guys" who try to harm him (see figure 1.4). Jeremy, a young boy from Burke Street, drew and told a story about a God who is a six-year-old child walking home with his parents (figure 3.3). Considering the fact that both of these boys are quite young and likely still construct meaning according to the imaginative approaches characterized by the Intuitive-Projective stage of faith, it is perhaps not surprising that their concepts of God are more fantasy-laden than those of older participants.[10] While these perceptions of God may be more unique to each of these boys, even in expressing these less conventional images, they demonstrated that they do indeed hold to particular concepts of God.

Finally, it is difficult to interpret Lizzy's conception of God. While she certainly has one – she mentioned praying to God, she explored with me and her peers what faithfulness to God looks like, and she said "God is always with us" – she arrived halfway through the interview. Angela and Grace had already discussed their God concepts with me, and after Lizzy joined us, our conversation moved toward other topics. Thus, while it is certainly possible to see elements of a caring, relational, omnipresent deity in the few words she offered about God, any additional details would be pure speculation.

Whether perceiving God as Jesus or as a superhero, all of the children who participated in this research hold to and conveyed a theology that involved a concept of God. However, these understandings are not etched in stone. Throughout my conversations with the children, their ideas about God shifted to varying degrees, calling attention to the fact that the content of their theologies – whether concepts of God or something else altogether – are in flux. None of the children expressed theological ideas or concepts that are completely fixed and impermeable. Their theological ideas, regardless of congregation, are open to transformation and change as they encounter new ideas, engage in new conversations, and have new experiences.

Congregational Influence

It is no surprise that the most evident commonality regarding the sources of the nineteen young participants' theologies is that they all draw from their congregations. The previous chapters make this clear. Yet there is not one consistent way in which they draw from their churches. In fact, their theologies are sourced from the following aspects of their congregations: theological knowledge (both explicit and implicit), experiences, and relationships.

All of the children generated theologies by using the communal theological information or knowledge of their congregations – both their explicit beliefs and their implicit theological ethos. The tendency to draw from explicit beliefs was made clear by Rebecca, who spoke often about the importance of knowing about God's love and omnipresence, two important theological assertions taught to her at Burke Street. While Rebecca's theology seemed to rely on memorizing her congregation's beliefs, Lizzy's views – such as her figurative understanding of scripture and especially her inclusive interpretation of God's commands regarding sexuality – were informed by her congregation but expressed with her own nuances. Both of these girls exemplify the tendency shared among all the children to rely on their congregation's particular beliefs or explicit theological tenets in doing theology for themselves.

This first aspect of congregational sourcing – by drawing from a congregation's theological knowledge – is not limited simply to explicit beliefs. The previous four chapters demonstrate that the broader and often implicit theology of a congregation also acts as a source for children's theologies. For example, the ethos of uncertainty and thoughtfulness that permeated the culture of Burke Street was widely held among its children, even if Sunday school programming contradicted it. Stephen and Nicholas both expressed understandings of God that included a significant degree of mystery and uncertainty, and Jeremy articulated a view of God that relied on his imagination and curiosity. Additionally, the children at Messiah relied on their congregational norms of interconnectedness in sourcing their theology. In essence, these norms gave each of them permission to draw widely, and to view sources from multiple faith traditions and those of no particular faith tradition – such as reality television – as being connected in their theological understandings. In all of these cases, the broader congregational culture served as a source through which children created ideas and knowledge about God.

A second way that children used their congregations as sources was through their experiences within these communities. Rather than drawing from certain beliefs or tenets, some children drew from the activities and events in which they have been involved. Although children from all four congregations manifested this type of sourcing, it was particularly evident among those at Colkirk and Parkdale. For example, the three girls at the latter congregation spent a large amount of time reminiscing with one another about the camps, retreats, meals, and leadership opportunities they have experienced together. These experiences were fodder for their communal generation of theology, one that is deeply rooted in a sense of community and held together by the love of the "really tight family" that has been forged through the many shared happenings among their congregation. These girls were certainly not the only children to rely on such experiences to create their theologies, but they offered a clear manifestation of this tendency.

Another method of drawing from congregations involved using relationships to generate theology. I refer here not to the communal approach to theological meaning-making like that of the children of Parkdale, but rather to the way in which the children use the relationships and community formed among the congregations as actual sources for creating theological meaning. While certainly not exclusive to their congregation, the children at Colkirk were most likely to use relationships as a source for their theological meaning-making. As chapter 4 demonstrates, these children had a relational approach to faith. The loving relationships they had developed with members of their community were sources of insight for generating theologies that sometimes appeared to be more felt than spoken. While they were less prone than some of their peers to speak particularly of God's love, their words spoke volumes about a theology of love incarnated in the relationships among their congregation. These relationships were certainly sources of insight for them as they made theological meaning.

All of the children utilized their congregations as sources in the generation of theological insight, drawing from their theological knowledge, experiences, and relationships. Yet as they did so, they also relied on several other sources, including television and movies, art, school, and other congregations they participate in to a lesser extent. Thus, not only is a reliance on congregations as a source for theology a universal characteristic among these children, but so too is their tendency to place it in conversation with extant sources. Some of the children, such as Luke from Messiah, were aware that they were drawing from beyond their congregation and interpreting multiple sources in light of one another. However, many of the children seemed less cognizant of their tendency to amalgamate sources, so they did so in tacit ways.

Theology in Conversation

When it comes to the methods that children hold in common in their generation of theology, a particularly salient feature is that they do theology in conversation. This was an important characteristic among the children at Parkdale and it was manifested in ways that were specific to them. But with a wide-angle lens in place in this chapter, it is evident that each one of the nineteen young participants shared this tendency. Whether speaking with one another or with me, it is clear that the interview was a "co-constructive process of meaning-making"[11] which provided a forum for the children to engage in a conversational method of theology. Some children – like those who participated in small group interviews – generated theology through discussion with their congregational peers. The others, however, while not having peers to do theology with during the interviews, still used a conversational method of theology, using me and my research assistants as discussion partners.

This conversational approach to theology was particularly clear at Parkdale because Rev. Lynn requested that I interview the children in small groups; their congregation attempts to avoid activities that are done individually rather than communally. Thus, the very format of these interviews may have predisposed the children to form theology through discussion with one another. Looking broadly, however, for a number of circumstantial reasons, I conducted one interview at each of two other congregations (Burke Street and Colkirk) with two children present. Therefore, out of the nineteen child participants, almost half of them (nine) participated in small group interviews. I did not organize this research with an eye toward investigating conversational theology, so no children engaged in both an individual interview and a small group interview. I am therefore unable to make informed conclusions about the effects of conversational theology. Nevertheless, it is possible for me to interpret how a conversational approach to theology played out in both individual and small group interviews.

A first approach to conversational theology involved the creation of theological insight that the children engaged in as they spoke with one another during interview sessions. I have said much about this in regard to the children from Parkdale, but I conducted small group interviews with Laura and Melissa, two friends from Colkirk, and Theo and Nicholas, brothers who attend Burke Street. In all three of these interviews, I witnessed the children engage in theological meaning-making as they spoke with, questioned, and challenged one another's views. Take, for example, the dialogical approach to interpretation that Laura and Melissa used to recount stories they had been told by their schoolteachers and congregational leaders on their reserve. They had different views of the goodness of the Creator/Maker. Laura told us that "there's sickness, right? And, I don't know, those ain't really good things. There's things like cancer. There's things like poison ivy." Melissa responded with her interpretation: "Well, I just think of that as the left-handed twin." As they shared their differing interpretations with one another, both girls appeared to open themselves to considering each other's views, for their certainty about these matters gave way to responses such as "I'm not really sure" and "I don't know." The conversational style of theology exemplified by Melissa and Laura was manifested among the other children who participated in group interviews. Regardless of congregation, as children shared their opinions and heard ideas that differed or even contradicted their own, they tended to become open to the uncertainty that such discrepancies unearthed. At times, the conversations would continue as the children engaged with one another's ideas. In other instances, such as that just described, the differences resulted in a posture of theological openness, even if the conversation about the particular topics did not continue.

A second way in which these children utilized a conversational method of theology was by engaging in dialogue with me and, when present, my research assistant. As I will consider more fully in chapter 7, some researchers into children's spirituality and theology seem to assume that interviews help reveal children's predetermined theological thoughts. Each one of the children from every congregation, however, also demonstrated that the interview process was a means by which the children actually made theological meaning. Certainly, there were moments when a young participant would respond to a question my assistant or I posed to them with what appeared to be an idea they brought with them into the interview. This was quite obvious in my interview with Stephen, a young member of Burke Street who, as explained in chapter 3, answered what in some cases were more difficult questions with responses he seemed to have learned from his congregation and at camp. Yet when my assistant asked him what peace means to him, he was unable to come to a response. Eventually, as we reassured him that this is indeed a difficult question and asked follow-up questions to help him think about when he has seen or experienced peace, Stephen started describing an understanding of peace that he may not have arrived at on his own. Stephen was generating theology as my assistant and I asked questions to help him think deeply about his theological ideas. This was a common occurrence with each child involved in this research. Their theological method relied on conversation as a way of discussing and thinking deeply about all sorts of matters, and for the duration of our interviews, I was their main companion on this journey.

Clearly, conversation was the theological method that was most clearly held in common across congregations. Each one of the nineteen children relied on dialogue with me and their peers as they generated theology for themselves. It appears, however, as though opportunities to engage in such rich and stimulating conversations are not always available in their congregations – or at least the children do not always feel that they can have these sorts of conversations with others. At least one child from each congregation admitted that some of the ideas they shared with me are ones they have not told to others. And in another instance, Laura and

Melissa approached me after our interview and asked if they could talk with me again later in the week (I conducted the interview during the summer VBS program). Unforeseen events prevented us from having a follow-up conversation, but the initiative of these often-shy girls indicated that they may not have many opportunities to engage in such theologically stimulating conversations, even though Arlene and Rev. Martha regularly make time to listen to them. Additionally, after the long drive home from Burke Street following my interview with Stephen, his mother emailed me to tell me how much Stephen appreciated the opportunity to talk with my assistant and me. In her words, the overall theme of his comments were as such:

> No offence to you Mom ... but you are my mom and Dad is dad ... I don't talk about these things with you. I know you're a minister ... but you guys are my parents. It was good to talk to them tonight ... because I said things to them that I have only thought about in my own head. It was fun to say them out loud.

Like the girls from Colkirk, Stephen indicated that our conversation was a special moment for him, one that he may not experience very much within his congregation.

Like Some Others

In this section, I redirect attention from the commonalities between all the participating children to the sphere of cultural specificity. While this aspect of human personhood has been the focus of the preceding chapters, I attend to it in a different way here. Rather than studying how the most salient ways that these children generate theological meaning are reflective – or not – of their particular congregational cultures, I will identify key commonalities of the content, sources, and methods of the theologies of children within the same congregational cultures.

Active Ecclesiology

Each group of children exhibited attributes of theological assumptions and ideas that were broadly shared among their congregational peers. The content of each child's theology – while unique – manifested parallels and similarities to those held by the other children who belong to their congregation. I will illustrate this tendency by exploring the ecclesiology that appeared among all of the children from Burke Street United Church.

At some point during each interview, I asked the children to describe their church as they would to someone who knows nothing about their congregation. Their responses to this question provide significant insights into their ecclesiologies. I was fascinated by what they tended to speak about as their "gut reaction" perceptions of church. Some children described their congregation in terms of the people who are part of it – both laypeople and clergy. But others, including each one of the children at Burke Street, closely associated church with the activities they engage in at their congregation. Theirs is a programmatic ecclesiology, one that paints a theological vision of church as activities and events in which one can participate.

Each of the five children from Burke Street responded to my request to tell me about their congregation by describing the programs it offers and the aspects of these programs. Rebecca, for example, told me about the coffee time after services each Sunday, and then went on to name parts of her congregation's Sunday school program: crafts, games in the gymnasium, stories, and cooking in the kitchen. She even gave examples of these activities, describing particular craft and baking projects that she has participated in at her congregation, such as bread-making, creating finger-puppet snakes, and a hula hoop game. Only minutes later, she named several events that Burke Street has hosted apart from Sunday morning programming, including a country dance, a talent show, pancake suppers, and movie nights.

Rebecca is certainly not alone in her tendency to associate her congregation with its programming. Her peers also described Burke Street by identifying the activities it offers. Sometimes these activities were programs, but at other times the children described the particular non-programmatic activities at their congregation as well. Nicholas, for example, does not like participating in the programming offered for children on Sunday mornings, but he described his congregation by sharing about the activities that he does to make his experience at Burke Street more enjoyable, such as workbooks that he works on while sitting with his parents during Sunday services. Here one can see an ecclesiology that not only relies on a congregation's "official" programmatic offerings, but also on the particular ways that children participate in the life of the faith community.

This focus on the "what" of congregational happenings does not mean that the ecclesiologies of these children overlook the value of relationships. Rather, the people within their congregation matter to their theologies of church in at least two ways. First, many of the children associated the programs with particular groups of people, recounting all the programs offered to children of various ages, such as the Sunday school classes and multiple children's vocal ensembles – each of which has its own name. Going further, however, the children indicated that the relationships they have with various individuals within their congregation are also an important aspect of their ecclesiologies. However, these relationships are defined by the activities and programs that have had a hand in forming and sustaining them. Jeremy, for example, held a theology of church that relied on his experience of helping to serve tea during the weekly post-service social time. This activity has allowed him to build relationships with all sorts of people at his congregation, so numerous that he didn't want to name them all. Similarly, Stephen spoke fondly of the friends he made at the local peace camp he attended, relationships that were closely tied with this program. He expressed the difficulty of knowing that this community is so intertwined with the program: "it's really hard because you meet these people and you go through these experiences with them and then you can't go there again." While relationships are certainly vital to these children's theologies of church, these young theologians often speak of them as intertwined with and even a by-product of congregational programming.

An interesting phenomenon embedded within these children's ecclesiologies is that God does not tend to feature prominently. Throughout my conversations with them, each of these children spoke about the activities at their congregations as well as their ideas surrounding God. Yet it is notable that there were very few instances when these two topics were interwoven during the course of the interviews. Their views of church tend to lack a sense of divine involvement or participation. Jeremy and Stephen, however, spoke of God in relation to their ecclesiologies. In chapter 3, I described Jeremy's drawing of God, which depicted a six-year-old God walking in a forest with his parents (figure 3.3). According to him, they were on their way home from a picnic. Jeremy's God, then, is one that, like him, participates in activities. Stephen's ecclesiology does not include a vision of a God who participates in activities the same way he does, but rather one who shows up in the very programs in which Stephen engages. This was evident when Stephen was talking about the musical he was part of during the Mennonite music camp he attended the previous summer. Without any prompting, he inserted God into the programming of the camp, saying "God was definitely there," particularly in providing patience through the many hours of rehearsal. For the most part, however, God remained absent in the ecclesiologies expressed by the children of Burke Street. And even in those rare moments when the young participants inserted God into conversations about their churches, God did not take centre stage.

The reliance on programming and activities in the ecclesiologies of the children from Burke Street is simply one example of the cultural sphere of human personhood in the content of children's theology. The children at each particular congregation expressed their theological ideas in several ways that overlapped and paralleled those of their congregational peers, demonstrating that when it comes to the content of theology, children indeed are "like some others."

Camp Theology

As was the case with aspects of the content of their theologies, some sources the children drew from in generating theological insight showcased commonalities held across congregational peers. To demonstrate one instance of this, I will interpret the use of a vacation Bible camp program at Parkdale United Church.

In chapter 1, I suggested that Jacob's theology seems to be influenced by his experiences at the small vacation Bible camp that Parkdale organized the preceding summer. Broadening this interpretation, however, it appears as though each of the children at this congregation – all of whom participated in the camp the summer before I met them – utilized this experience as a source for theological knowledge. There were at least two aspects of the children's theologies that seemed to rely on their camp experiences: their God concepts and their ethics.

For a number of years, Parkdale had been organizing summer camp programs for children under the leadership of hired directors from outside of the congregation. For the camp preceding my time among the congregation, it decided to facilitate the entire program in-house, with youth planning and overseeing the programming, and a number of adults participating in the camp as volunteer leaders. With three or four youth or adult leaders for each of the half-dozen or so children who attended the program, this year's vacation Bible camp became an intergenerational event. As outlined in chapter 1, one of the threads woven throughout the week of programming was the practice of welcoming those who are different. Over the week, a volunteer from the congregation dressed up as a dragon and wandered around the church building – inside and outside – while the children followed clues to find eggs representing values like acceptance and friendship. Eventually the group welcomed the dragon into their community. All this was meant to be an experiment in learning to accept and welcome those who may be different from oneself. This experience has become lodged deep within the collective psyche of this congregation, and as described in chapter 1, many months after the camp, a banner still hung from the ceiling of the hall, saying "Dragons Welcome."

All of the children I interviewed from Parkdale spoke with great enthusiasm about this particular vacation Bible camp, which became significant fodder for their generation of theological insight. One way that it has influenced them is in their concepts of God. This was most evident during my conversation with Jacob and Enoch, both of whom seemed to draw from the experience of the dragon, yet in different ways. In my interpretation in chapter 1, I posited that Jacob's assertion that God is in need of protection from forces seeking to harm him may have actually been the result of his experience at the camp. Perhaps the fact that a dragon was wandering around the building invoked fear and anxiety in this young boy, and he associates this feeling with the need for protection from that which is different. Of course, this was not the intended outcome of the experience, but he seems to draw from it in his concept of God nonetheless. Enoch also mined this vacation Bible camp in forming his view of God, but in a very different way. His main takeaway from the camp was the experience of having a leader dressed as an angel appear to the group: "there was an angel that came by and said to protect the egg and we had to protect the egg from the dragon." His drawing of God depicted a personified male deity talking with an angel that was flying next to his head (figure 1.3). When I asked whether the angel was small or God was large, he said that the angel was the size of a human being (which is the size the angel at the camp would have been), but that God was very large. Additionally, he went on to say that God can send angels to earth, a statement that seems lifted from his experience of having an angel appear and give instructions to the camp participants. It is important to note that there are likely developmental factors at play within the different ways that these boys utilize this camp experience. In fact, they are exemplary cases of Fowler's first and second stages of faith: "Where the Intuitive-Projective child [Jacob] fuses fantasy, fact and feeling, the Mythic-Literal girl or boy [Enoch] works hard and effectively at sorting out the real from the make-believe."[12] Although they did so in different ways due in part to the developmental capacities of their faith, both Enoch and Jacob relied on their experiences at vacation Bible camp in forming concepts of God.

While the boys at Parkdale expressed elements from vacation Bible camp in their God concepts, the girls drew from the camp in their sense of ethics. They seemed to have picked up on the intention of the dragon and egg exercise and built this into their ideas about how to treat others. Toward the end of the interview, as the girls were sharing memories of many activities and programs they had experienced together at Parkdale, Grace brought up the recent vacation Bible camp and Lizzy and Angela both remarked how much they loved the camp. Grace continued by talking about the dragon, saying, "we had to find an egg and at the end of the week we learned to accept everyone." She understood the intention behind the dragon and egg exercise and, along with the other girls, seems to have built it into the fabric of her ethics. Only minutes later our conversation shifted to discussions about what faithfulness means, and the girls expressed their frustration over people who use the Bible to support views that exclude others, particularly members of the LGBTQ community. As Lizzy was speaking about this, Grace quietly said, "Be who you want to be." Embedded within this conversation is an ethic of acceptance and welcome of those who are different from oneself. This posture was the main point intended by the dragon and egg exercise from the recent vacation Bible camp. As I sat in the hall listening to these girls that day, above us hung the "Dragons Welcome" banner, a clue about where they were drawing from as they generated this ethic of acceptance.

A Narrative Approach

In the preceding chapter, I touched on the narrative approach through which the children at Colkirk seemed to generate theology. Here I will make this phenomenon the focus of attention, as it is a prime example of how children at a common congregation make theological meaning using approaches shared among their peers. There are at least three ways that the children at Colkirk each manifested a narrative method of theology: by learning stories, by sharing their own narratives, and by narrating their theological ideas.

In chapter 4, I explained how Melissa and Laura blend Aboriginal spirituality and Christian theology through their interpretation of stories that have been passed on orally for many generations. By learning stories that are told to them, the children at Colkirk engaged in a narrative approach to theology. In some instances, particularly with Melissa and Laura, the narratives they learned were those that have been passed on from generation to generation for centuries. These include the stories of the creation of the world and the story of the Peacemaker. Other stories are ones created and shared by elders within the congregations. Laura and Melissa told me that a senior woman at Colkirk created a retelling of Jesus's birth within the context of their reserve. In Melissa's words, "When [Jesus] was born, they went to all these different houses and asked if they could stay. But there was not room for them anyplace ... There used to be a barn by the old arena, and they went there." The children also do theology through stories told during Sunday school and VBS, most of which are from Bible storybooks. For example, when imagining God, Ally pictured God wearing clothes similar to those in the illustrations of a story about Cain and Abel that I had read to the children earlier during that week of VBS.[13] Although each type of story here differs from the others, stories are at the crux of these children's theology, not only as sources but also as the methods through which they do theology – for the stories themselves are the theology.

A second way that these children use narrative as a theological method is by telling their own stories. Throughout my interviews with these children, they shared stories with me about their lives and experiences. They were neither particularly refined nor terribly lengthy, but these narratives were a primary means through which these children expressed their inner lives, their thoughts, and their emotions. This was especially true for Ally and Ethan.[14] For example, Ally had been dealing with some struggles relating to changes in her family life and difficulty with making friends at a new school. She voiced her fear and sadness over the challenges she was dealing with as she continued to settle into a new school on the reserve as she shared stories about her trials. In narrating these experiences, she expressed emerging theological ideas surrounding loneliness and hospitality as she spoke about how children at her school tend to play among themselves. Not only did these children share their stories, but at times they invited me to do likewise. At multiple times during my interview with Ally, she asked me about my school and my teacher, urging me to follow her lead and narrate my own experience of being a student.

The final way in which these children take a narrative approach to theology is through expressing their theological ideas by narrating them. I have already explored, in chapter 4, how Ethan expressed his views of God by creating a story in that moment. After drawing a river (figure 4.3), I asked him why the river reminded him of God. As we looked as his picture, he began to notice that it looked a bit like a bridge "that's crawling up, that's going to be at the top is God." This "water ladder," as he called it, became a pivotal narrative in his expression of his concept of God. Contained within it were his ideas about a God who created the world yet remains somewhat distant, as well as a distinguishing mark of faithfulness, for the ones who are able to swim against the tide are those who believe in God. In this way, he manifested the narration of theology, a theology that is not only based on stories, but relies on story as the main form of expressing one's inner thoughts and meanings.

Understanding the full meaning of narrative theology among these children involves a paradigm shift of sorts. For them, narrative is not only a means of expressing theological content or a source for meaning-making. Rather, the narrative is the theology itself. Such a premise is consistent with broader assertions about the narrativity infused into Aboriginal knowledge. Marlene Castellano, a member of the Mohawk Nation living in Ontario, names narrative as one of the primary characteristics of Aboriginal epistemology:

> Traditionally, stories were the primary medium used to convey aboriginal knowledge. Stories inform and entertain; they hold up models of behaviour; and they sound warnings. Recounted in ceremonial settings and confirmed through many repetitions, they record the history of a people. They teach without being intrusive, because the listener can ignore the oblique instruction or apply it to the degree he or she is ready to accept, without offence. Stories of personal experience can be understood either as reminiscences or as metaphors to guide moral choice and self-examination.[15]

These four children move Castellano's words from the past (as she notes, stories *were* the primary medium) to the present, showing that stories continue to be at the forefront of theological knowledge among these children. The stories that children learn, know, and tell are the very stuff of theology; theology is generated and held as stories are told and retold. These stories do not demand particular theological presuppositions or certain ethical responses; they leave themselves open for the listeners to do with them what they must. This is precisely what happened when Melissa and Laura told the narratives of creation: their interpretations of where bad things come from differed (Melissa believed it was the left-handed twin, while Laura surmised that the Creator was the source), although the story was the same. As Thomas King has said, "The truth about stories is that that's all we are."[16] When it comes to these four children, it can be surmised that the truth about stories is that that's what theology is.

Like No Other

In the final section of this chapter, our gaze narrows to the level of the individual child. Here I will explore the content, sources, and methods of children's theologies through the lens of the uniqueness of each young participant, not discussing their theologies as departures from broader congregational cultures – as I did in chapters 1–4 – but as theologies generated in their own idiosyncratic ways. Of course, it is impossible for me to consider the theology of each of the nineteen young participants featured in this research. Thus, I will speak of particular children who highlight that in very specific ways, the content, sources, and methods of children's theologies are indeed "like no other."

Contextual Theology

There is a well-known children's hymn that seeks to show the breadth of Jesus's love with the words, "Red and yellow, black and white, they are precious in his sight." This song may speak of God's love for children of all colours, but what do children make of God's colour? I did not ask them outright about God in relation to race, but some of the children raised this topic during our conversations.

Among the younger children, Ally and Enoch both made more explicit reference to race in relation to God through their drawings. Since both engage in matters of faith in ways that are largely consistent with a Mythic-Literal approach, their conceptions of God focused on concrete, anthropomorphic images, and race mattered in their depictions. When drawing God, Enoch began by using a white pencil crayon to depict God (figure 1.3) . But when Jacob asked if he was doing that because God is white, Enoch immediately said "Well, [it's] not really God [who's] white, but his clothes is white" and he sought out a brown pencil crayon and coloured over the white face he had given God. Demonstrating that conversations while drawing help children construct meaning during interviews, Enoch showed that it matters to him that God's skin matches his own. Ally, on the other hand, took a different approach (figure 4.4). Rather than depicting God with skin like hers, she wanted to be sure to give God what she called "skin colour," a colour that matched the paleness of my own complexion: "Let's look if there's a skin colour ... This looks like ... Does this look like your skin?" While neither of these children wanted to discuss the shade of God's skin in greater depth, the colour that they used to draw God mattered to them.

Luke and Marion, both from Messiah, demonstrate how children's understandings about race in relation to God become more complex as they gain the ability to think in more abstract terms. In my conversation with Jemina, she recounted a moment during an "Ask Anything" time in Sunday school when Luke said (in her words), "Aunty Jemina, why is Jesus painted White all the time?" She went on to say that she asked other children what they thought: "I remember Chris saying that he's not White. Then another thought maybe his parents were White. And I came in to give a little explanation and I said I would research more and give it to them. Because I told them that from the history of Israel, I know that the Israelis are not, like, White people. Yes, they are not White. So then they are not dark like us and they are not White people. They are in between." Luke did not speak about Jesus's race in our conversation – perhaps because that Sunday school discussion satiated his curiosity – but it is evidently a topic that interested him.

It is eleven-year-old Marion's view of God in relation to race that I want to focus on as an example of how the content of children's theologies are in some ways like no other. A relatively new member of Messiah, this girl articulated her beliefs in a way that demonstrated her emerging recognition of the contextual nature of theology. Her theology includes a belief that ideas about God and Jesus are related to one's broader culture (which, of course, is a central argument of this book).

As we sat together in a Sunday school room at Messiah, Marion opted to describe her concept of God to me with words rather than a drawing. Right away she said, "People think he's Black. But I think it's every colour because he brings us to earth ... Some people, like all different countries, say that. They say he's Black, he's White, he's Black and stuff." Here she alludes to but does not specifically name her awareness of theological contextualization. Yet she also inserts her own particular viewpoint into this discussion, arguing that God is every colour (at least every possible shade of human skin) since God created all people, regardless of the colour of one's skin, and this diversity is reflected in God's very being. Shortly afterward, as we were speaking about the relationship of God and Jesus, she said, "It's just that [God] has so much different names. Like here, they call – sometimes they call him Jehovah." When I asked her why she thinks people refer to God using so many different names, she responded, "That's what they think. Maybe their language. How other languages [say God's name]." In saying this, she further nuances her view by naming language as a particular variable at work within the contextualization of theological beliefs.

While Marion is not alone among these nineteen children in the belief that theology is relative to one's context (Melissa, Laura, and Stephen, for example, all alluded to similar ideas), the uniqueness of her theology lies in the depth and theological maturity through which she articulates such a belief. Not only is she more eloquent and nuanced in her understanding of theological contextualization by actually naming this belief, she also described its specific incarnations by giving examples of how particular contextual phenomena – such as one's country and language – might shape one's theological ideas surrounding God's colour and name. Going further, Marion showcased her sophistication by holding herself to the same standards as others. She demonstrated clearly her belief in the contextual nature of theology, going so far as to say that people who believe that God is either Black or White actually "make up" this idea, that it is not necessarily grounded in the reality of who she believes God to be. Yet this young girl also applied this view to her own theological meanings. As she spoke about her personal beliefs, she separated them from those of other people she has met, but she qualified her claims with phrases like "that's what I think," indicating a self-recognition that if the beliefs of others are related to their contexts, then hers must be as well.

Marion's views regarding the contextual nature of belief set the content of her theology apart from that of her peers, both at Messiah and at other congregations. Perhaps her distinct experiences of diversity – as a child born in Ghana and now living in Canada who used to attend a Roman Catholic parish and now worships at Messiah – had a hand in forming this particular aspect of her theological ideas. However she has come to hold to this view, this aspect of Marion's theological meaning-making is a prime representation of the uniqueness of the content of theology in each and every one of the children.

Dreaming Theology

Dawn, who happens to be Marion's younger sister, exemplified how children build their theology from unique theological sources by drawing from her dreams. During our forty-minute conversation, Dawn told me about two dreams, which she believes are ways that God communicates with her. In the first dream, she told me that God took her to heaven:

> So I was flying up past the sun and I didn't melt … And in my head I was thinking it was impossible, right? And I went past and after I went to heaven and I seen the gates and angels beside them … I went through the gates and I seen different stuff. Like, I seen different kinds of plants and different kinds of people … And pathways golden. And there's a lot of gold in heaven … I seen Jesus. But I didn't see him well … He was doing different stuff, like helping prepare meals and other stuff.

I asked Dawn if there were other instances in which God spoke with her in this way, and she went on to tell me about a dream in which God appeared to her at her school. Although she did not describe this dream in much detail, she mentioned that God "was invisible but I was the only one that could see [God]. Like, I had been at school. All my friends couldn't see God but I could." I gently asked her to describe what God looked like, and she responded by saying, "he has brown hair and he spoke my language [a Ghanaian language]."

In keeping with a characteristic of Christianity in Ghana,[17] Dawn utilized these dreams as significant sources of theological insight. The second dream in particular revealed aspects of who God is that she wove into her drawing of God (figure 2.4) and subsequent explanation. For one thing, this vision of God paralleled the image of Jesus – although unclear – that she witnessed in the first dream. This led her to believe that God and Jesus are connected somehow, and she placed this view alongside scripture by reminding me that "in the Bible, they said God came to life and he formed himself as Jesus." Going further, while she did not directly weave the fact that God spoke her native language into her theology, it surely conveys something about the intimacy she feels in her relationship with a God who speaks to her in dreams and helps her with aspects of everyday life, such as tests at school. This is a God who knows her so well that he speaks to her in her first language, the language that had a hand in forming her worldview.

The first dream that Dawn shared with me is a storehouse of insight from which she can draw to generate theology on any of a number of topics. It offers insight into angelology, providing her with ideas about what angels look like and what their roles may be in heaven; it provides information about cosmology, offering Dawn a "sneak peek" into heaven, a place of great beauty filled with gold and unique creations; it speaks of Jesus as a person who even in heaven takes on the role of a servant as he goes about his way busily preparing meals; it even provides fodder for a soteriology, for, echoing St Paul's writing in 1 Corinthians 13:12, Dawn interpreted the blurriness of Jesus to mean that "if you believe in God you can see [Jesus] one day." Using St Paul's words, the promise of heaven for Dawn is that of no longer seeing "dimly," but seeing Jesus "face to face" with full clarity.

Dawn's dreams are rich with resources for making theological meaning, and she explained them to me with great passion and conviction. Yet she admitted that I was the first person with whom she shared both of these dreams. While she told the first dream to her mother, who didn't believe her at first, I was the only person given the privilege of hearing about the second. Dawn's fear of being told that the things that happened in these dreams did not really occur – which she expressed to me with tears in her eyes – keeps her from feeling free to tell them to others.[18] Grateful for being able to hear about them, Dawn's divine dreams showed me the uniqueness through which children construct a theology that is all their own.

Mysterious Theology

Two boys – Jacob, from Parkdale, and Stephen, from Burke Street – both expressed a theological method that relies on a comfort with mystery and uncertainty, which was particularly evident during our discussions about God. However, how they utilized this approach shaped their theological ideas in ways that were unique to each of them.

I have already interpreted, in chapter 1, the comfort with uncertainty that Jacob exhibited during my interview with him and Enoch. As these two boys spoke with me after starting to draw their pictures of God, Jacob articulated his ideas in a way that left God shrouded in mystery. He used words like "maybe" and "I think" as he described what God might look like, demonstrating an awareness and comfort with uncertainty surrounding who exactly God is and how this God appears.

Although he is twice Jacob's age and attends a United Church congregation with a radically different culture, Stephen's method of doing theology also relied on mystery and uncertainty. Rather than drawing a physical being – even a representation of what God might look like – Stephen drew a picture of his congregation's building to demonstrate that this is the place where he has learned and experienced God more than any other place (figure 3.2). In our conversation, he was quick to say that, for him, God is an "idea" or a "thing that's always there" rather than a "person or one singular thing." His theological method seems to use mystery as a starting place for making meaning about God and other theological matters, and this reliance on mystery and uncertainty is a trait he shares with the young boy from Parkdale.

What sets these two boys apart from each other is how this common characteristic nuances their theological ideas, which is most clearly visible in their approaches to describing God. For Stephen, the mystery and uncertainty surrounding God dissuades him from pinning down any particularities about God's character and being. I asked him to say more about his ideas after he told me why he drew a picture of Burke Street's building, and he used metaphorical language to convey that God is like an omnipresent spirit. In saying, "It's more everything," he even avoided tying any sort of personified pronoun to his theology of God. As I continued asking questions, he skirted around any language that would place conceptual constraints on God: "Um ... it's hard to explain ... just kind of like a spirit that loves you no matter what. And is always there." This leads me to interpret his theological method as leading him to avoid describing God in any sort of detail. Perhaps for Stephen, to do so would be to lose the mysterious aspect of who and what God is.

Jacob, on the other hand, had no qualms about providing details – in words and images – about God. Over the course of our interview, he eagerly went into great detail about several of God's qualities, including where God lives, what colour God is and why God is that colour, and how God defends himself from forces that seek to do him harm. His is a God that he imagines with great creativity, and he was completely comfortable telling me about God's qualities, such as his ability to walk through walls or change himself into things that nobody else can see. And as he explained several aspects of who God is to me, his mystery-laden approach to theology left room for his assertions to be inaccurate, which he demonstrated with words like "maybe" and "I think." He found a way to speak with great detail about a God who remains cloaked in mystery.

Stephen and Jacob share a common theological method that weaves mystery and uncertainty deep within it. Yet despite this similarity, the uniquenesses and idiosyncrasies of their individual theologies appear in the dramatically different ways that they speak – or perhaps in Stephen's case, do not speak – about God. This is simply one way that, once again, children generate theology in ways that are all their own.

Tending to Tension

This chapter shows that the children who participated in this research make theological meaning in ways that are held universally with one another, that are shared in common with their congregational peers, and that are unique to each one at an individual level. As I have already stated, the tendency of research such as mine is that it can fall prey to prioritizing the cultural sphere of human life and ignoring the other two spheres. Yet holding up any one sphere at the expense of the others can lead to ethical violations that theologians would name as sin: a focus on the universal ignores difference and can allow those in power to impose their experiences as normative to others; prioritizing the cultural can lead to conflict and widespread disagreement among different groups, as well as scapegoating those who are not seen to be part of one's own cultural group; and a focus on the individual can result in nihilism, selfishness, and isolation at the expense of collaboration and community. Thus, some sort of tension among all three spheres is necessary to avoid these trappings.

This chapter has moved toward maintaining a degree of tension among all spheres, and by doing so it seeks to honour the fullness and complexity of children's lives. By analyzing the children's theologies in light of these three spheres of life, I have steered away from theologically trivializing them as active in only one aspect of human life. Their theologies demonstrate that children are full human beings, that they are active members of communities, and that they are also individual people who possess agency in the world. For example, in analyzing the sources of their theological meaning-making, had I only explored how these children are like one another, I could have made assertions about the influence of congregational culture on the theologies of all children. But in doing so I would have overlooked the fact that the children at each congregation sourced their theologies in ways that were unique to their particular contexts. I would have also focused so much on the universality of children's theological sources that I would have overlooked the fact that they are not merely passive recipients of the theologies of their broader congregations, but active theological agents who create meaning for themselves in distinct, nuanced, and personal ways. Likewise, had I focused solely on the idiosyncrasies of the children's individual theologies, I would have had to gloss over the enculturating role of communities and the ways that children, as full human beings, possess commonalities shared among all others. By using Lartey's Trinitarian view of personhood as an interpretive lens, I have attended to the fullness of children's theological lives, seeing them at one and the same time as whole human beings, members of communities, and active self-determined agents.

* * *

In this chapter, I have used a number of differently angled lenses to interpret the generation of theological insight among the children who participated in this research. Relying on Lartey's threefold understanding of human personhood, this kaleidoscopic interpretation sheds light on the ways in which children from different cultural contexts make theological meaning at the universal, cultural, and individual levels. It is evident that these children are like one another in their holding of particular God concepts, their tendency to source their theology from their congregations, and the dialogical approach through which they generate theology. Some content, sources, and methods of theology are also held in common by their congregational peers, as evidenced by the programmatic ecclesiologies of the children at Burke Street, the use of a recent vacation Bible camp as fodder for theology among those at Parkdale, and the narrative approach to theology shared by all the children at Colkirk. Finally, one can see the uniqueness of children's theological meaning-making through Marion's contextualized ideas, Dawn's reliance on her dreams as sources of insight, and an approach to theology that relies on mystery and uncertainty utilized in different ways by Jacob and Stephen.

6 Toward Transformation

An Analysis of the United Church's Vision for Becoming Intercultural

This chapter marks a shift in emphasis from practice to theory, even though both are interwoven throughout this book. But at this point, I use the information generated through this study – which I have already interpreted in previous chapters – as a launching point for critiquing two discourses: the United Church's Transformative Vision for becoming an intercultural church, and, in the next chapter, the academic study of children's spirituality and theology.

The present chapter responds to the question I asked at the outset of this book: *How does the theological meaning-making of children within these four diverse congregations confirm or challenge the way that the United Church constructs its vision for becoming intercultural?* By foregrounding children's theologies and the lives of their congregations, it is possible to bring to light new perspectives on how the United Church's Transformative Vision is – or is not – reflective of the realities of individuals and congregations who make up this denomination. To frame this discussion, I will begin by offering background information about multiculturalism in Canada as well as key critiques of it. Next, I describe how the United Church sought to respond to problematic aspects of Canadian multiculturalism with its vision for becoming intercultural. I then interpret the Transformative Vision through the lens of the theological lives of the children and congregations that I discussed in previous chapters. Such an approach prompts three significant assessments of the United Church's report for becoming intercultural: a strength of it lies in the priority it gives to voices on the margins; it simplifies culture by leaving little room for cultural hybridity; and it overlooks the ways that individuals and congregations within the denomination are already expressive of interculturalism in and of themselves.

Multiculturalism in Canada

Multiculturalism is a contested term within Canada, one that carries with it multiple meanings and understandings. Richard Day, among other scholars, argues that *multiculturalism* can be used in at least three distinct ways.[1] First, it can refer to the fact of diversity, a fact that is often perceived as problematic and in need of government solutions.[2] Second, multiculturalism can speak of an ideology or a "bottom-up narrative,"[3] which Rinaldo Walcott sees as a product of civil rights, postcolonialism, and new social movements that arose during the latter half of the twentieth century.[4] The result, in May Chazan et al.'s estimation, is that many Canadians believe there is a consensus that "some version of multiculturalism – whatever its limitations – is here to stay, lodged deeply at the heart of Canada's national identity both at home and abroad."[5] Finally, multiculturalism can reference a particular set of policies or what Grace-Edward Galabuzi names a "top-down approach" resulting from public demands to officially recognize and accommodate diversity among the Canadian population.[6] While these policies can imply that official multicultural legislation is static and settled, the reality is much more complex.[7] Although there is general consensus surrounding these three understandings of multiculturalism, some scholars add additional definitions of this term. Mark Leman, for example, adds a fourth perspective, which he does not expand upon beyond the following definition: "the process by which racial and ethnic minorities compete with central authorities for achievement of certain goals and aspirations."[8]

A (Brief) History of Contemporary Multiculturalism in Canada

Day posits that throughout the early 1900s, the English language was seen as the "great assimilator" for immigrants to Canada, ensuring that English Canada remained fairly monocultural.[9] But in the 1960s, there was a growing awareness that Canadian society was – and has been for some time – fragmented by its cultural diversity; this fragmentation was a problem to which Canada needed to respond.[10] As immigration policies became more liberal and newcomers increasingly hailed from regions outside of Europe, policies of *assimilation* into English Canada developed into those of *integration,* which allowed immigrants to retain some elements of their home cultures.[11] Day critiques the racism and imperialism implicit in the transition from assimilation to integration, which did not actually involve a significant shift in how the Canadian government addressed the reality of "others." In his words, "each method is thus based upon the transformation of a problematic Other into a non-problematic – 'eliminated' or 'participating' – Self."[12]

The 1963 Royal Commission on Bilingualism and Biculturalism was a landmark event on the journey of multiculturalism in Canada.[13] Launched to recommend action to forge equal partnership between Canada's "two Founding nations" (the British and French),[14] the commission's report (known as the "B&B Report") included an entire volume about "the Cultural Contribution of the Other Ethnic Groups," which addressed members of the population who were not of British or French heritage.[15] According to Clifford Jansen, this volume of the B&B Report carved a path for an official policy of "multiculturalism in a bilingual framework" put forward by Prime Minister Trudeau in 1971.[16] Trudeau claimed that Canada had two official languages but no official culture, which in turn made culture a key marker of differentiation among citizens.[17] According to George Elliott Clarke, this policy marked the first instance in which the government positively recognized that non-White, non-British, or non-Aboriginal persons were also Canadian.[18] Fifteen years later, in 1986, the Employment Equity Act was passed, which, in Patience Elabor-Idemudia's estimation, sought to remove barriers to meaningful employment for "visible minorities" and other marginalized Canadian groups.[19] Day remarks that this year also marked the first time that the federal census allowed Canadians to select multiple identities as their "ethnic group."[20] Since 28 per cent of Canadians chose to do so, it appeared as though hard-and-fast cultural groups could not always conceptualize, organize, and capture Canadian diversity. Two years later, Prime Minister Mulroney passed the Canadian Multiculturalism Act, enshrining multiculturalism into the Canadian Charter of Rights and Freedoms and demonstrating that it transcended political parties.[21]

While aspects of multicultural policies appeared to be well for some time – at least among members of dominant groups – it became clearer and clearer that there were cracks in the multicultural veneer. In particular, contemporary scholars believe that the events of 11 September 2001 blew a hole in multiculturalism, which suddenly became open to being revised and challenged.[22] And in recent years, the attention Aboriginal people are bringing to Canada's legacy of residential schools has also gone a long way toward challenging federal policies for managing cultural diversity. Yet according to Chazan et al., even as governments revised multicultural policies, they continued to pay little attention to objections and criticisms,[23] despite the fact that trend-tracker Michael Adams has found that many Canadians continue to regard multiculturalism as an integral part of our national identity.[24] It is to these criticisms that I now turn.

Critiquing Multiculturalism

Multiculturalism may be for many a central source of Canadian pride, but it has been a point of contention among scholars and authors who witness and experience its underside. Three such thinkers are Lawrence Hill,[25] Neil Bissoondath,[26] and Himani Bannerji,[27] who call attention to the fact that multiculturalism proliferates limitations and creates challenges. I will describe three critiques that they lob against Canadian multiculturalism: it simplifies cultural identity; it sanitizes and stagnates culture; and it allows those groups who have traditionally held power to continue to dominate cultural "others."

SIMPLIFICATION

Through stories about being "Black and White in Canada" and informal interviews with thirty-four Canadians with one Black and one White parent, Hill raises critiques that speak to the simplistic notions of culture that Canadian multiculturalism at best leaves intact and at worst encourages and reinforces. Throughout his memoir, he demonstrates that multiculturalism leaves little room for hybrid cultural identities (in Hill's case, hybrid racial identities). He and the people he interviewed state that they have been asked countless times "what" they are and where they are "really from." Hill shares that he struggled to assert his Blackness, was not perceived as White, and was continually challenged by fellow Canadians who refused to give him room to explore his identity as a child of a Black father and a White mother.[28] Although self-identifying as Black, he acknowledges that "I have many different sides. They all fit together into the configuration of who I am."[29]

Hill calls attention to the fact that in contemporary Canadian contexts, wider, fluid, and more complex perspectives on culture – like that to which I subscribe – tend to get stripped down and simplified into one contained and racially defined culture or another. Canadians, he argues, ignore such racist simplifications of culture: "In this country, racism is like a fleet-footed bedbug that runs for cover under a sweet-smelling duvet stuffed with politeness and tolerance for multiculturalism."[30] Such simplifications shut the door on possibilities for the mixing, regeneration, and creation of cultures and cultural elements in the complex realities of human life.

SANITIZATION AND STAGNATION

Born in Trinidad to parents of Indian descent, Bissoondath identifies a number of ways that Canadian multiculturalism (specifically multiculturalism as government policies) affects "our individual and collective selves."[31] Analogizing its tendency to sanitize culture to the sanitization of the jungle at Disney World, he argues that multiculturalism commodifies culture and puts it on display in ways that allow others to have a "taste" without experiencing its full flavour.[32] Multiculturalism assigns members of non-dominant groups the role of the "other" who must preserve their stereotyped and de-contextualized cultural heritage rather than evolve and adapt to new times and places.[33] In his words, "Culture becomes an object for display rather than the heart and soul of the individuals formed by it."[34]

Bissoondath's critique rests on a vision of culture as a living organism that multiculturalism makes stagnant. "Culture is life," he writes. "It is a living, breathing, multi-faceted entity in constant evolution ... Stasis is not possible. A culture that fails to grow from within inevitably becomes untrue to itself, inevitably descends into folklore."[35] In his mind, multiculturalism promotes a culture of festivals and folklore in which participants can become exposed to "theatre" rather than the people who breathe life into culture, where "easily digested stereotypes"[36] are the order of the day and culture is stripped of its power and weight as it is "manipulated in social and political usefulness."[37] In the end, what is left of culture is a stagnant, sanitized commodity that upholds what is simple and appealing at the expense of a fuller understanding of culture that includes breadth, shadows, shame, and ugliness.[38]

DOMINATION

A Bengali-born sociologist who spent her career teaching at Toronto's York University, Bannerji focuses on race and gender in her outline of how multiculturalism acts as an apparatus of the state for maintaining hegemonic control of those deemed to be "other." Canada, she argues, is constructed by citizens of European descent who categorize people of different skin colours and ascribe "otherness" in order to manage those who diverge from the (White/male) status quo.[39] This management of otherness, she contends, is an integral aspect of multiculturalism,[40] which through social policies and racist ideologies "supplies an administrative device for managing social contradictions and conflicts" within a settled and homogeneously perceived Canada.[41]

Rather than maintaining a simple binary categorization of citizen and non-citizen, Bannerji identifies a paradoxical third category of "insider-outsider" for those who simultaneously belong and do not belong.[42] For her, these "nominal citizens"[43] – among whom she includes herself – are non-White persons who, because of their racialization, are "part of [Canada's] economy, subject to its laws, and members of its civil society. Yet we are not part of its self-definition of 'Canada' because we are not 'Canadians.'"[44] Bissoondath makes a similar argument, stating that hyphenated identities imposed upon (non-British, non-White) Canadians are not meant "to define the word 'Canadian' but to mark a distance from it, the hyphen that links them a sign of acceptable marginalization."[45] Bannerji argues that multiculturalism is a means of racialization through which the Anglo-Canadian culture maintains its dominance while "tolerating" and organizing others as "multiculture."[46] It is a way of tolerating otherness, but inasmuch as otherness does not threaten to disrupt the status quo; it is not meant to dig into deeper issues like social justice and equality.[47] In the end, multiculturalism maintains power among those dominant cultural groups that have historically held power by legitimating inequalities already present and containing disapproval and wariness.[48]

Transforming the United Church's Vision

In 2006 the United Church sought to respond to the shortcomings of multiculturalism in Canada with a vision for transforming the denomination into one that honours and respects its internal cultural diversity. In this section, I will use broad brushstrokes to describe the role of culture and diversity within the United Church from its founding to the early twenty-first century, tracing its move from the assimilation of cultural others to the celebration of diversity through interculturalism.

When the United Church was established in 1925, its leaders envisioned a "national" church made up of and reflecting the ideals of White, Protestant, British Canadians.[49] Yet United Church theologian Greer Anne Wenh-In Ng notes that as Canada became increasingly diverse, the denomination likewise became marked by greater levels of diversity.[50] In response to changes in government policies regarding multiculturalism and immigration during the last few decades of the twentieth century and the first decade of the twenty-first,[51] the United Church has recently become an active participant in discourses about multiculturalism and diversity in Canada.

Over the past nine decades, the United Church has evolved from a denomination of assimilation to one that celebrates diversity. In an essay about ethnicity in the United Church, Ng states that for more than the first half-century of its life, the denomination addressed pluralism by fostering assimilation to English Canada among its congregations and ministries.[52] Yet gradual shifts occurred in the United Church that led it to re-examine its relationships with non-dominant cultural groups, a process that began with the formation of the National Ethnic Committee in 1972, a committee of the Division of Mission in Canada.[53] Over twenty years later, after the establishment of two additional committees – the Ethnic Ministries Working Unit in 1988 and the Feasibility Task Group on Ethnic Ministries in 1992[54] – the United Church inaugurated the Ethnic Ministries Council in 1996 with the purpose of adding non-dominant voices and supporting non-dominant congregations and laypeople to fully participate in the denomination.[55] This council was to bring under its umbrella all United Church congregations and missions that were non-Anglo, non-francophone, and non-Native and organize them into "associations" and "coalitions."[56] A decade later, the Ethnic Ministries Re-visioning Task Group – a committee established in anticipation of the tenth anniversary of the Ethnic Ministries Council – put forward "A Transformative Vision for the United Church of Canada" at the 2006 General Council. This report prompted the General Council to declare the United Church to be a "national church where the intercultural dimension of ministries is emphasized as a denominational priority."[57] The Transformative Vision put forward the notion of shifting away from the assimilation of non-dominant cultures and toward an acceptance of diversity, a vision marked by a change in language from *multicultural* to *intercultural*. Since that report, the United Church has produced resources and organized conferences to foster the appreciation, understanding, and celebration of diver- sity among the denomination.[58]

Becoming Intercultural

According to Adele Halliday, team leader for Transformational Ministries in the United Church, the Transformative Vision evolved out of a feeling among several non-dominant groups that "the United Church needed something *like* multiculturalism, but that would go *deeper* than superficial interactions and a desire to be more transformative."[59] In an effort to "go deeper" – to envision more than the problematic notions of multiculturalism criticized by Bissoondath, Bannerji, and Hill – the United Church took a stance of becoming *inter*cultural.

At its best, interculturalism[60] moves away from the simplification, sanitization, and domination of cultures to what United Church ethicist Roger Hutchinson refers to as "encounters among persons and groups with cultural differences."[61] As the Transformative Vision states, interculturalism moves the point of focus from issues of tolerance, assimilation, and integration to relationships of "mutually respectful diversity and full and equitable participation."[62] In choosing to become intercultural, the United Church acknowledged that the forms of multiculturalism prevalent in Canada since the 1970s are not appropriate and have failed to address the inequality of power and wealth.[63] It sought to move the denomination toward recognition that one single cultural group no longer dominates a space, speaking instead about how, as Hutchinson states, "the public realm is, and should be, both *shared* and *contested*."[64]

Central to the Transformative Vision is the realization that this is not a vision of present realities, but one of future possibilities; the authors of the document admit that "it is a vision of a United Church of Canada that we want to become but are not yet."[65] Thus, the report includes an appendix that outlines a three-year plan (2006–2009) for building a program of intercultural ministry into the United Church, a plan that involved recruitment and hiring of staff members, national consultation, and reporting recommendations for further action. It seems, based on the 2009 report from the Task Group on Intercultural Ministries, that a number of the steps for further action have been taken, which has led the

Ethnic Ministries Unit to be renamed the Intercultural and Diverse Communities in Ministry Unit.[66]

Maintaining the Centre

The Transformative Vision represents a significant shift in the self-understanding of the United Church. Rather than seeing itself as a denomination led by one culture yet open to others, the United Church has discerned the need to shift its centres of power so that those who have been part of their community – yet are underrepresented within it – can take their places alongside those who have traditionally maintained power.

While steps have certainly been taken to move toward becoming an intercultural church, there are aspects of this vision that uphold problematic power dynamics related to cultural groups. Ren Ito's analysis of the Transformative Vision has led him to argue that the White, Anglo majority of the United Church is largely undiscussed in this landmark document. In his estimation, this signifies a tacit view of culture that exempts White people from the visions of cultural equality that it imagines.[67] This interpretation seems to parallel the opinion of the board member at Burke Street who remarked that their congregation has no particular culture. Such an assumption about what is in fact a very specific congregational culture indicates a tendency among members of a dominant culture to perceive their ways of life to be the norm, from which others can only deviate. For example, the term *visible minority*, while common among discourse in Canada, assumes that there is an *invisible majority* who holds the privilege and power to do the seeing and naming of that which is visibly "other." The power dynamics behind the comment by Burke Street's board member are also present within the Transformative Vision in at least two ways.

First, there are significant moments in which this document uses terminology that implicates the United Church in the dominating tendencies of multiculturalism. Ito believes that while White Anglo cultures are largely absent from the report, the language of the Transformative Vision not only covertly keeps such cultures within the document, but actually reinforces their power. It implies, for example, that the true core of the denomination consists of "White Nations peoples" (to use the document's dubious phrase) who are making the decision to more fully embrace those non-dominant people who remain on the margins of the

United Church.[68] It also uses terms like "us" and "we" in ways that demonstrate a binary distinction between those cultural groups that have historically held power ("us") and those that have not (an implied – if unnamed – "them"). While this presumption is read between the lines, perhaps it is nowhere clearer than with these words: "White Nations peoples were also once strangers loved by God. There are now new strangers outside the United Church, loved by God but not by us. There are even those within the United Church, also loved by God, yet whom we consider strangers and do not love. If God indeed 'shows no partiality' (Acts 10:34–35), then we are challenged to humble ourselves."[69] Furthermore, in one instance the document goes so far as to ask, "Are we willing to risk letting go of our hold on our cultures to God's transformation and grieve the passing of old structures and unearned privilege?"[70] It appears as though the "us" in this statement – the persons being asked to relinquish "our hold on our cultures" – are members of dominant cultural groups like the members of Burke Street, for only those who have benefited and continue to benefit from these structures and privileges would grieve their passing. Others, like the members of Parkdale, Messiah, and Colkirk, may actually celebrate it. This implication betrays the vision of interculturalism that the report is offering by engaging in the practices of "otherizing" that Bannerji unearths within Canadian multiculturalism at large. The very individuals and groups that the Transformative Vision calls the church to more fully embrace are set up as a "multiculture" and managed in order to maintain the status quo.[71]

Power dynamics can also be perceived in the use of the term "inclusive" in various places throughout the report. For example, there are multiple instances in which the authors speak about the decision to become intercultural as "in keeping with the United Church's justice-seeking and inclusive history."[72] At first glance, the United Church's quest to become inclusive is laudable. But a closer look reveals it to parallel Canadian multiculturalism by legitimizing colonialist power dynamics and allowing those groups who have historically held control to retain it. The United Church's own resources surrounding interculturalism lend themselves to this criticism. A resource "for educating toward racial justice"[73] edited by Greer Anne Wenh-In Ng and published two years before the Transformative Vision names the concept of inclusivity as "problematic in that it assumes that one individual or group is in a position to decide whether to 'include' or 'exclude'; marginalization and tokenism often still result."[74] Even though the report is the product of conversations and consultations with voices on the margins, the overall tone of the document is one in which those who have historically held power in the United Church retain their grip on it, and even reinforce it by choosing with whom to share it. In the end, although the United Church feels as though "God is calling [its members] to transformation," the proposed changes re-inscribe the denomination's position as an assimilator into the dominant Canadian culture[75] rather than helping it move beyond this historic role.

Assessing the Transformative Vision

The maintenance of pre-existing power dynamics is not the only critique one can make of this document. In fact, when read in light of the children and congregations that participated in the research on which this book is based, three points of assessment become evident in Transformative Vision. The first applauds the path it marks away from late twentieth-century political and social understandings of Canadian multiculturalism with all its problems and toward more just and equitable relationships among various cultural groups. This becomes particularly evident in its tendency to look to voices on the margins of the denomination and hear what they have to say as gifts that can help the United Church move toward a more just vision for becoming intercultural.

But while this is certainly a helpful step in a positive direction, the document actually replicates some of the criticisms lobbed against multiculturalism and brings with it new sets of challenges and limitations. There are at least two additional points that surface by evaluating the Transformative Vision in light of the children and congregations considered in earlier chapters: it fails to account for hybrid cultural identities and it leaves little room for contexts of diversity and difference. I will discuss each of these assessments in turn, beginning with the more positive of the three.

Gifts from the Margins

The children and churches introduced throughout this book affirm the call to take seriously the voices of those on the margins of the United Church, a call that the Transformative Vision offers to the denomination. According to this document, such people offer "guidance, wisdom, and insightful leadership as gifts for the wholeness of the church."[76]

In a spirit of "collaboration, accompaniment, and partnership," the Transformative Vision seeks to bring together those in the United Church who are from non-dominant cultural groups as well as those who are part of cultures that have tended to hold sway in the denomination. In this way, it can continue to move toward being an inclusive and justice-seeking church. This laudable task was undertaken through a number of steps that led to the Transformative Vision. First, the members of the Ethnic Ministries Re-visioning Task Group, who put forward this document, are part of many different cultural groups within the United Church, both those at the centre and on its margins.[77] Second, they engaged a two-phase re-visioning process, the first phase of which included holding focus groups with a diverse cross-section of individuals from across Canada in order to evaluate the purposes of the Ethnic Ministries Unit and explore new visions for it.[78] The second phase consisted of a broad strategy of consultation with leaders from several cultural groups – for example, Aboriginal, francophone, and urban ministry leaders – as well as staff at the General Council Office, conference level, and among Presbyteries.[79] In all these ways, the task group took seriously a wide range of voices from many cultures, especially those from non-dominant cultures.

As people who do not traditionally hold power within congregations, the children who participated in this research demonstrate that voices on the margins can lead churches toward new understanding and action. Take, for example, the conversation between the three girls at Parkdale as they spoke about how to interpret the story of creation in a way that allows people to, in their words, "be who you want to be." These words challenge the congregation toward a theology of radical acceptance. Or consider the invitation toward a theology of mystery that Nicholas can offer his community as he makes meaning of the Resurrection, wondering aloud how it can be possible for someone to rise from the dead and doubting the validity of this theological tenet. His is a challenge to think deeply about the claims of faith that may be so commonplace within congregations that members overlook just how radical or miraculous they really are. It's no wonder, then, that Rev. Lynn calls the children at Parkdale prophets: "The prophets are the ones I continually tell, 'You need to be speaking and doing and you need to be active in church, because that's what prophets do.'"

By holding meaningful theologies that are pregnant with transformational potential for their broader congregations, these children affirm the

United Church's belief that the people on the margins of their denomination ought to be seen as leaders within the church and that theirs are voices worth hearing. Yet just as I intentionally sought to listen to the voices of children and Rev. Lynn makes a point of calling Parkdale's children prophets, those who have historically held power need to be intentional in receiving the leadership of persons from non-dominant cultures. This commitment has been integrated into the Transformative Vision through the diverse task group that penned it and the focus groups and consultations that they initiated in order to evaluate past proposals and envision a path toward becoming intercultural.

Overlooking Hybridity

The Transformative Vision rests on problematic and narrow understandings of culture, which simplify this broad term by boiling it down to little more than a synonym for ethnicity and, to a lesser degree, race and language. This is clearly demonstrated in the report's frequent naming of particular cultural contexts: "Aboriginal, Francophone, ethnic minority, and ethnic majority peoples."[80] By naming particular groups based on these categories, the report simplifies culture from an incredibly broad and complex concept to one that hinges on only three manifestations of human diversity: language, race, and ethnicity.

The research in this book shows that culture is much more complex than the Transformative Vision imagines it to be. The children and their congregations defy the narrow fourfold classification with which the United Church makes sense of cultural diversity. Ethnicity, race, and language alone fail to capture the multifaceted complexity and layers of diversity that are inherent in the identities of these individuals and communities. To demonstrate this, I will turn our attention to the children at Messiah Methodist United Church.

Before moving to the children, however, it is important to underscore the fact that the identity of Messiah is exponentially more complex than simply being a community with roots among one particular cultural group. It is at one and the same time both African *and* Western, Ghanaian *and* Canadian. Thanks to its 2013 "Memorandum of Understanding for Cooperation," it is a member of both Methodist Church Ghana and the United Church of Canada. Thus, in many ways, Messiah's cultural identity may be best described as hybrid, a mixture of multiple elements stemming from various sources that blend together into a continually evolving cultural identity that shapes and is shaped by its individual members. Such hybridity is evident at Messiah within its worship practices and its ministry with children.

First, the liturgy and structure of Sunday worship services at Messiah reflect a blending of both African and Western, Ghanaian and Canadian elements. The relaxed and fluid nature of a start time is reflective of Christian worship in Africa, as are the dancing and boisterous singing that are regular features of musical worship during services. Yet the procession of the choir and, on some Sundays, the procession of flags at the beginning of services, as well as a "Time with Children," are elements stemming from Western and North American norms for liturgy and congregational worship. Furthermore, the use of both Akan and English indicates a linguistic hybridity among congregants, for if all members of the congregation spoke either language, there would be no need for services to include both. Following worship, the community stays together to enjoy tea and light refreshments, a common practice in congregations in Canada but largely absent in MCG communities in their homeland. These are just some of the ways that the people of Messiah have adapted their worship services to reflect their identity not only as Ghanaians, but also as Canadians.

The hybridity of Messiah's identity is also evident in its ministry with children through its approach to Sunday school and their inclusion in corporate worship. In chapter 2, I explored how Emmanuel, Jemina, and other leaders at Messiah have struggled with their curricular choices for Sunday school. As a hybrid culture, this congregation does not neatly fit into the intended audiences for curricula produced by either Ghanaian or Canadian publishers. Thus, the leaders are continually adapting, rewriting, and creating resources to more adequately suit their unique needs. Additionally, Sunday school has moved away from its traditional role in Ghana as the sole worship and formational experience for children in congregations, as Messiah takes steps toward including young people in congregational worship not only for a portion of each service, but also for an entire service once each month. Such a move is reflective of recent conversations among Western scholars and practitioners about the importance of including children in corporate worship.[81] But, as Jemina has said, it departs from the tendency of churches in Ghana to have separate programs and services for children for the entirety of corporate worship. Formational efforts for children at Messiah – through Sunday school and partial inclusion in corporate worship – demonstrate the dual space of the congregation, a space that is both Ghanaian and Canadian.

The children at Messiah engage in theological meaning-making in ways that, reflecting their wider congregation, speak of a hybridity of Ghanaian and Canadian culture. The five participating children, most of who were born in Canada, are the living embodiment of the blending of Ghanaian and Canadian identities. The theological themes I identify in chapter 2 – a tendency to draw widely in theological sources, a sense of the interconnectedness and commonalities of theologies, and a view of a God involved in the details of their lives – all reflect the broader Ghanaian culture out of which their parents have come. Yet their location within Canada also shapes their theology.

This hybridity was exemplified in my discussion with Dawn surrounding her dreams, which I explored in greater detail in chapter 5. Within Christianity in Ghana, it is not uncommon to infuse one's dreams with theological meaning.[82] Yet Dawn has not found her friends in Canada to be receptive to such experiences. When I asked her why she hadn't told anyone about one of her dreams, her eyes filled with tears: "Because really, like, people, like ... they say, 'Oh no, you didn't have this dream.' And they don't really believe me because ... because, like, if I told my friends they won't believe me. Because last time when I told them a story ... they didn't believe me." Dawn's tears speak of a struggle she experiences because of the hybridity of her theology. Since mining dreams as sources of theological meaning and speaking of them with the seriousness and importance that Dawn has ascribed to them may be a natural impulse of Ghanaian Christianity, this girl thought nothing of sharing about them with friends not as fantastic adventures in the subconscious mind but as journeys through time and space on which God has taken her. Dawn told me that her dreams were very special to her, so when she told some of her friends about it and they did not infuse it with the same depth of meaning, she learned that it might be best not to tell others about her dreams in the future. The hybridity of Dawn's theology shines through this incident as she straddles two cultures that perceive her dreams in contrasting manners. No doubt she will continue to wrestle with how to interpret her dreams theologically as she explores how both Ghanaian and Canadian cultures have something to say about the matter.

The children at Messiah engage in theological meaning-making in ways that speak to the swirl of cultures in their broader congregational context and wider lives. While each of the characteristics that I describe in chapter 2 are evidence of the depth of such hybridity, the manner in which Dawn experienced and interpreted her dreams is a particularly clear example. She, like her peers at Messiah, engages in theology within a context that is at once both Canadian and Ghanaian, United Church and MCG. In so doing, she offers a critique of the narrow and simplified classification of cultural contexts within the United Church's Transformative Vision. This landmark document does not envision hybrid identities and the sorts of dual relationships to cultures and contexts that intermingle in the lives of congregants like Dawn. Thus, this report cannot adequately make room for the complexity that comes with hybrid cultures – leaving communities like Messiah and the individuals therein at risk of being misunderstood or oversimplified.

Ignoring Intercultures

Another critique of the Transformative Vision is that it ignores congregations that are *in and of themselves intercultural.* Ironically, contexts of interculturalism are not named in the fourfold categorization repeatedly included in the document, which only views "mutually reciprocal relationships"[83] occurring between different cultural groups, rather than recognizing them as a prominent feature of a particular culture itself.

Overall, the Transformative Vision assumes cultures to be internally consistent wholes and points of consensus among members. In the introduction to the report, the authors share that participants in the diverse focus groups that led to the document made clear that "a denominational emphasis on intercultural ministries needs to include ethno-specific or language-specific congregations as well as culturally diverse congregations."[84] Yet this recognition of congregations that are internally diverse, inconsistent, and intercultural does not appear to impact the visions and ideas shared within this document. This was most evident in a section that outlined the rationale and history of the re-visioning of the Ethnic Ministries Council. In an effort to "de-construct the benevolent assimilation of minorities into the dominant culture," the Transformative Vision redefines "multicultural" to include "any congregation or group of people with monocultural similarities."[85] While their goal may be to include groups under the umbrella of multiculturalism that have previously been overlooked, the use of the term *monocultural* conveys the idea that cultures are fundamentally based on uniformity and internal consistency.

The realities of life within the children and congregations central to this book challenge such assumptions about consistency and consensus among individuals. They demonstrate Kathryn Tanner's assessment that cultures are common points of engagement rather than agreement;[86] internal consistency, or, to use the report's term, "monocultural similarities" are not a requirement for a culture to be considered a culture.

Internal diversity and inconsistency were most apparent among Parkdale United Church, a congregation whose identity as an intercultural community is at the core of its collective heart. The children here demonstrate that the culture of a group – in this case, a congregation – can include difference, diversity, and disagreement. Their minister, Rev. Lynn, subscribes to a very broad view of culture, and her leadership of Parkdale has helped its layers of diversity – including ethnic, linguistic, national, racial, socio-economic, sexual, generational, and theological diversity – to be perceived not as a burden to overcome, but rather as a mark of distinction to be worn with pride. Of course, as stated in chapter 1, such diversity brings significant challenges that the congregation must face, such as expectations for congregational worship and disagreements about theologies and the language used to express them. Rather than shying away from such disagreements, Rev. Lynn names them before the congregation, indicating that their community can maintain strong relationships among its members even though the many aspects of this interculture will resonate differently with those who make it up.

The children within this congregation hold what I called in chapter 1 an "open theology"; they expressed their theological ideas and practices in ways that opened them to recognizing that other people – even those within their congregation – may subscribe to very different theological meanings and may even disagree with their thoughts. Not only did the language of some of the children express this openness – through words like "I think" and "maybe" – but so did the general postures that they brought to the task of drawing a picture of God and talking freely about their theological ideas. For these children, being part of a congregation that feels more like "a really tight family," to use Lizzy's words, need not require that all people think and act alike, proving that diversity and disagreement can be a central hallmark of the culture of a faith community.

Even within the other congregations, where interculturalism was not part of their self-identity, children still demonstrate that their congregational culture can leave room for internal inconsistency and disagreement.

For example, in chapter 3 I consider the diversity among the children's programming at Burke Street, with younger children participating in Godly Play and older children engaging in an approach to Sunday school that diverges from the norms and values inherent in the former program. This inconsistency correlated with the approaches through which the children generated theological insight, with some weaving imaginative ideas freely into their theologies and others focusing on ensuring that they gain knowledge of the ideas that Sunday school presents to them. Yet both of these incredibly different approaches to children's ministry and their own styles of generating theological insight are at home within their congregation, showcasing that culture need not require agreement to be valid.

The distinct manners in which children made theological meaning that I explored in chapters 1–4 are yet another indicator that culture can indeed include difference and diversity. I have demonstrated that, while children's theological meaning-making is reflective of their congregational cultures, at times their theologies diverge from those of their congregations. Children, as members of the culture of a congregation, showcase disagreement over the theological norms of their broader culture, and some of them are aware of this. For example, in chapter 2 I mentioned that Luke draws from the reality show *Long Island Medium* in creating meaning surrounding the ideas of spirit, while cognizant that this diverges from the broader culture of Messiah. Yet such difference and disagreement need not push this boy to the fringes of his congregation. Rather, it indicates that he can be a vital participant in the community even while holding inconsistent theological ideas.

These examples testify that the United Church's understanding of culture within its Transformative Vision is far too narrow and simplistic to include the reality of life within many of its congregations. Not only does it ignore the differences and diversities that exist within congregational cultures, but it actually ignores those congregations in which diversity and even disagreement are a cultural hallmark. How then can the denomination move toward becoming an intercultural church on a large scale when it overlooks the ways that individuals and congregations like Parkdale are working out this vision for themselves? In naming four particular categories of culture – Aboriginal, francophone, ethnic minority, and ethnic majority – the Transformative Vision assumes that cultures are homogenous wholes that engage in relationship with one another. This book demonstrates that cultural groups like congregations can be sites where differences intersect and converge with one another.

* * *

Interpreting this document through the lens of the children and congregations whose voices form the backbone of this book enables me to offer three assessments of the Transformative Vision: the report gives serious consideration to voices on the margins of the denomination; it does not leave room for congregations and members who ascribe to hybrid cultural identities; and it ironically overlooks congregations that are charting their own path toward interculturalism.

The Transformative Vision may be riddled with problems as discussed above, but my interpretation nonetheless shows that the vision signifies a step toward a more just future for the denomination. The children and congregations detailed in previous chapters offer some important correctives that can help the United Church continue to move further toward the intercultural church it seeks to become. Of course, what will come of this vision is not yet known. Rev. Martha, minister of Colkirk, reminds us of this: "If we truly allowed our church to change and be influenced by different people, none of us can imagine what that church would look like because it would be formed in the formation of it."

7 Renegotiating a Field of Study

An Analysis of Scholarship in Children's Spirituality and Theology

In this chapter I allow the children and congregations at the centre of this book to evaluate the bourgeoning field of children's spirituality and theology. Having been forged through significant studies and partnerships from the last decade of the twentieth century, this field continues to grow and produce significant research into all sorts of topics related to the spiritual and theological lives of children. After offering some conceptual clarity around the parameters of this field, I address four ways in which culture and cultural diversity are or are not attended to by scholars of children's spirituality and theology. Building on this, I draw from the research I conducted to make three assessments of the field: it neglects the processes of children's theological meaning-making in favour of products; scholars need to consider children's theologies not only among individual persons, but also as collective and collaborative phenomena; and studies must attend to culture at every stage of research, particularly in the analysis of knowledge generated through qualitative and ethnographic studies.

Clarifying Blurred Boundaries

Children's spirituality and theologies of childhood are distinct subfields of childhood studies and religion, yet ones marked by blurred boundaries. Contemporary scholarship often overlaps these subfields in its quest to explore the spiritual, theological, and religious lives of children. Thus, for the sake of clarity amidst growing complexity in these fields, I use *children's spirituality and theology* to denote the shifting scholarly space that these two subfields occupy. Despite the significant overlap between these subfields, it is possible to make some clear distinctions between them.

The field of children's *spirituality* has as its focus children's inner lives. Scholars of children's spirituality explore children's quests to connect with that which is beyond themselves and their awareness and consciousness of these searches for connection. This field is conceptualized broadly and includes scholars who conduct research from confessional and non-confessional perspectives as it relates to the human spirit as manifested in children. Throughout the 1990s in particular, children's spirituality gained momentum through the publication of landmark works such as Robert Coles's *The Spiritual Life of Children*[1] and David Hay and Rebecca Nye's *The Spirit of the Child*.[2] These works, alongside the *International Journal of Children's Spirituality*, which began publication in 1996, set the stage for how scholars explore the inner lives of children in relation to spirituality.

But what is children's spirituality? While the breadth of this term makes arriving at any one definition challenging, several scholars have attempted to do just this. The International Association for Children's Spirituality – which consists of a range of scholars from confessional and non-confessional perspectives – relies on its former president, Jack Priestly, in setting forth an understanding of spirituality. While believing that it cannot be defined, Priestly states that spirituality is "a concept of constant motion or at least of potential motion which can on rare occasions be stilled."[3] He goes on to note that, although spirituality may intersect with religion, it cannot be contained by religious traditions.[4] It is, thus, something that seems to be universal – if difficult to identify – among human beings. Despite Priestly's aversion to placing any fences around an understanding of spirituality, in an article in the organization's journal, Vivienne Mountain argues that children's spirituality tends to focus on relationship as a dominant theme.[5] For example, Nye's groundbreaking research in Britain led her to define children's spirituality as "relational consciousness."[6]

As a field of inquiry, children's spirituality leaves room for confessional and non-confessional perspectives. In confessional circles, more effort has been devoted to offering further precision and conceptual clarity to definitions of children's spirituality, perhaps due to scholars' desire to identify themselves and their research as grounded in particular religious and theological traditions. In North America, for example, the Society for

Children's Spirituality: Christian Perspectives defined children's spirituality as "the child's development of a conscious relationship with God, in Jesus Christ, through the Holy Spirit, within the context of a community of believers that fosters that relationship, as well as the child's understanding of – and response to – that relationship."[7] The focus on relationship and the child's consciousness of relationship is shared among both confessional and non-confessional colleagues. But as this definition shows, those who study children's spirituality from a confessional perspective may place the triune God and the faith community at the centre of these relationships, while acknowledging that children who do not identify as Christian are still spiritual beings.

The area of *theologies of childhood* explores what it means to be a child and to experience childhood in light of scripture, tradition, and religious experience (particularly Christian, although there is growing religious diversity within the field). In addition to giving thought to children and childhood from confessional perspectives, some scholars of theologies of childhood explore the theological ideas of children and the ways in which they generate and communicate these ideas. Like its sister subfield, theologies of childhood is difficult to pin down. For some, it centres on uncovering historical theological understandings of what it means to be a child and experience childhood,[8] as well as the quest to generate new understandings in contemporary contexts.[9] Others' area of concern lies with the desire to "examine and reform the themes of Christian faith and doctrine through the eyes of a child."[10] Yet whether learning from children's theological meaning-making, bringing to light historical understandings of childhood, or offering new theological visions of what it means to be a child, theologies of childhood provides a forum for giving concerted attention to the many ways in which theology and children converge.

Considering Culture

Despite exponential growth in research surrounding children's spirituality and theology, scholars have paid little attention to culture and cultural diversity, and among those who do address these issues, many do not go deep enough in their consideration and analysis. There are four broad ways that scholars of children's spirituality and theology address culture and cultural diversity: in passing references and assumptions that imply unnamed European-American and British dominance in the field; through studies of children and childhood within a particular cultural context; by conducting research into children's spirituality and theology across multiple cultural contexts; and through critical attention to the importance of cultural context when studying children's spirituality and theology. I will describe these four general uses of culture in the field of children's spirituality and theology by introducing one or two primary examples in each category.

Passing References

The first general way that scholars of children's spirituality and theology address culture is through passing references. Without placing culture and diversity at the centre of their gaze, these scholars speak of them from time to time and their arguments and ideas are situated within specific, if unnamed, cultural contexts. Two strong examples of this tendency are David Hay and Rebecca Nye's *The Spirit of the Child*[11] and John Westerhoff's *Will Our Children Have Faith?*[12]

Hay and Nye, in their 1998 landmark text, speak of culture in relation to their quest to better understand what exactly children's spirituality is. Building on scholars such as Robert Coles, who thematically investigated "the ways in which children sift and sort spiritual matters,"[13] Hay and Nye perceived a lack of details regarding what exactly children's spirituality looks like.[14] Relying on zoologist Alister Hardy's arguments about the evolutionary survival value of spirituality to human beings and Nye's own qualitative research among children in British primary schools, Hay and Nye posit that spirituality is an inherently biological phenomenon, and they go on to propose a definition of children's spirituality as "relational consciousness."[15] Drawing from research in psychology, anthropology, and neurophysiology, Hay demonstrates that spirituality is culturally mediated and always exists within particular cultural contexts[16] which shape how it is expressed,[17] understood,[18] attended to,[19] and manifested,[20] as well as how it evolves in human beings.[21] Hay does describe an important role for culture, which he regards as a variable that affects nearly every node of spiritual life.

Yet Hay and Nye sweep culture under the rug, almost to the point of ignoring it completely, when they discuss Nye's qualitative research into children's spirituality. Using Hay's assumptions about the biological nature of children's spirituality as a foundation, Nye conducted research aimed at gaining a sense of the contours of children's spiritual lives. She met with thirty-eight children (twenty children aged six to seven and eighteen children aged ten to eleven) for up to three one-on-one interviews per child. Despite Hay's assertions about the influence of culture on spirituality, Nye's research sample was quite monocultural: all the child participants attended public primary schools in predominantly lower-middle-class areas of "two large industrial cities in the English Midlands (Nottingham and Birmingham)";[22] the authors identify all the children as "Caucasian," with the exception of one child of "African-Caribbean origins";[23] and twenty-eight of the children had no religious affiliation, with four identifying with the Church of England, four with Islam, and two with the Roman Catholic Church.[24] While there are certainly some aspects of cultural diversity represented among this small group, it is predominantly monocultural in socio-economic status, geographic location, race, and religious affiliation. From this culturally limited sample, Hay and Nye draw conclusions regarding the spirituality of children, naming this phenomenon "relational consciousness." In Nye's words, "children's spirituality was recognized by a distinctive property of mental activity, profound and intricate enough to be termed "consciousness" and remarkable for its confinement to a broadly relational, inter- and intra-personal domain."[25]

Another prime example of considering culture in passing is Westerhoff's now-classic 1976 text *Will Our Children Have Faith?* At the core of this book are Westerhoff's arguments for moving from a view of Christian education based on socialization to one of enculturation, which shifts the process of education from a focus on how individuals are shaped by other members of a community to "the process of interaction between and among persons of all ages ... In enculturation one person is not understood as the actor and another the acted upon, but rather both act, both initiate action, and both react."[26] Although Westerhoff does not often explicitly speak of culture, he writes about the importance of community, which he argues requires a high degree of consensus of identity in order for diversity and pluralism to be possible.[27] Community, for him, is at the heart of the formation of children, and he speaks of communities of faith in ways that allude to the fact that they are distinct cultural contexts for formation. In his afterword to the 2000 revised edition of this text, he states that in the quarter-century since the first edition, ethnicity and culture have become more important than race as social categories.[28] While he does not define any of these terms, he states that "ethnicity and culture sometimes overlap, but the culture of the rich and the poor, the literate and the illiterate, the city and the country, the North and the South differentiate persons within any single ethnic group."[29]

Westerhoff's arguments rest on unnamed European-American norms that run throughout the history he traces and the present circumstances he outlines. This is most clearly evident in his reference to "ethnic churches" as those made up of congregants who are part of particular (non-dominant) cultures.[30] By having a specific (and brief) section dedicated to "ethnic churches," one might surmise that he holds a similar assumption to the Burke Street board member who thought that congregation was simply cultureless. Similarly, Westerhoff does not explicitly refer to the fact that all congregations are indeed "ethnic," and, going further, they possess the fullness of culture and all those elements that are woven into it – including ethnicity, language, patterns of thinking, and so on.

And yet Westerhoff's updated comments make a case for seriously considering the ways that children's spiritual and religious experiences – as well as the meaning they make of these experiences – may differ by cultural context. Even in the first edition, he states clearly that increasing pluralism among communities leads to competition among different ways of life and understandings,[31] and in the updated publication he names (but does not elaborate upon) the difficulty of maintaining "unity and common mind" while honouring diversity within a community.[32] Of course, Westernoff's purposes, as well as those of Hay and Nye, are not to place culture in a position of focus. Yet both groundbreaking texts do in fact help make the case for research into children's spirituality and theology that seriously considers culture (as I attempt to do), even as they exemplify a tendency within the field to make passing references to culture without offering critical attention to this topic.

Culture in Context

Some scholars give more concerted attention to culture by studying children's spirituality and theology within a particular cultural context (often a culture based on a shared national or geographic context), rather than across different cultures and in contexts of cultural diversity.[33]

A notable example of a study within this category is Martin Ubani and Kirsi Tirri's research into the perceptions of spirituality and religion among preadolescents in Helsinki, Finland.[34] Perceiving the majority of research into the relationship between spirituality and religion as theoretical and philosophical, these scholars wished to add empirical data to the discussion.[35] To do so, they studied 101 students in grade 6 (twelve or thirteen years old) at a school for higher-achieving children, asking what meanings these Finish students attribute to spirituality and religion and what differences exist between their understandings of these concepts.[36] Their research generated "over 700 written opinions on the concepts of religion and spirituality."[37] After asking groups of students to brainstorm ideas surrounding religion and spirituality (a task offered in an English handbook for religious education[38]), Ubani and Tirri grouped responses into three broad categories: the institutional dimension, the supernatural dimension, and the humanistic dimension. Under these three dimensions fell eleven categories of responses, most belonging to the first and third dimensions, which they analyzed in light of whether the children raised them in reference to religion or spirituality.

This study does not adequately consider cultural context in data analysis, even though Ubani and Tirri explicitly address culture by naming the particular context in which it rests. In their report, the authors note that in a "multicultural world," spirituality can be expressed and understood in many ways and by many different kinds of people,[39] and they provide important background information about the cultural context of the children in their research, particularly religious education classes in the Finnish public school system.[40] Yet while sharing the results of their research, Ubani and Tirri do not place the particularities of the culture of contemporary Finland at the fore of their analysis, instead tending to address in a more broad and a-cultural approach the words that these young people regard as important for their understandings of spirituality and religion. For example, while the authors refer to how the grade 6 religious education program and predominance of Lutheranism in Finland may have contributed to the children's perceptions of religion and spirituality,[41] much of their analysis ignores the broader cultural context in which these children participate. Additionally, the study is problematized by a lack of critical consideration of the fact that, as the authors admit, the term "spirituality is all but absent from the Finnish religious education curriculum, and the single time it makes an appearance its counterpart in the Finnish translation is "religious."[42] Thus, their use of an English-based assignment to inquire about children's perceptions of religion and spirituality seems to add a degree of confusion based on the sheer fact that the major terms (*religion* and *spirituality*) do not clearly translate into a Finnish cultural context.

By overlooking the dynamics of culture, Ubani and Tirri's findings are posed in an a-cultural way, which allows the dominant (educated, English-speaking, metropolitan, Lutheran-based) culture to dictate and direct the conversation. Although they admit that "in a pluralistic world it is important to study how different populations perceive religion and spirituality,"[43] they failed to take their own advice by neglecting to attend to a cultural analysis of their findings. All this leads one to wonder if perhaps their stated purpose – "to investigate the meanings given to the concepts of religion and spirituality by Finnish Grade 6 students" – should be rewritten as "to investigate the meanings given to the concepts of religion and spirituality by English-speaking Grade 6 students who happen to be Finnish," which better reflects that lack of attention to the cultural contexts of these students in their analysis.

This study by Ubani and Tirri is exemplary among those that explore children's spirituality and theology within a particular cultural context, but do not adequately consider culture in the analysis and interpretation of research findings. While still holding significant merit within the field, had they prioritized culture, Ubani and Tirri could have shed new light on their findings. For example, they could interpret the fact that the children used the term *religion* 65 per cent more than *spirituality* in light of the lack of usage of the latter term in everyday language in Finland.[44] Although they make some brief connections between the knowledge their study generated and the cultural context of the child participants – such as correlating their associations with the term *religion* with the current themes of public religious education classes – the overall framework and interpretation of their study has very little to do with the culture with which it is connected.

Considering Diversity and Difference

While above I spoke of the small number of studies surrounding children's spirituality and theology within a particular cultural context, here I examine the even smaller number that address this topic across multiple cultural contexts and amidst contexts of cultural diversity.[45]

Kelsey Moore, Victoria Talwar, and Sandra Bosacki's qualitative research into perceptions of spirituality among a diverse group of children residing in a large Canadian city[46] exemplifies this third category. These researchers argue that the majority of studies into spirituality focus on practice, overlook spiritual experience, and – at least among Canadian studies – rely on assumptions and measures based on Christian ideologies.[47] To respond to this, Moore conducted a study that examined perceptions of spirituality among children "across diverse religious and spiritual backgrounds within Canada – a pluralistic society."[48] Acknowledging that "differences in religious beliefs, practices and affiliations are often interwoven with other cultural features"[49] and that religion and spirituality – and perceptions thereof – are embedded within social contexts,[50] she conducted short interviews (in English) with sixty-four children belonging to a range of ethnic groups and religious traditions within a single Canadian city. The authors state that a primary goal was to "explore the spiritual experiences of children from different cultural, religious, and spiritual orientations."[51] As such, the children who participated came from a broad range of ethnic backgrounds and religious affiliations, as well as no religious affiliation. Moore's analysis of the data generated from this study highlights a number of themes that emerged from the children's narratives, and ideas shared by a wide spectrum of this diverse group of children. The six broad themes the authors identify are: positive feelings during prayer, the location of God, perceptions of God as a helper, viewing God as a listener, the human soul and spirit, and identifying God as a comforter.[52] In the end, they argue that research needs to be conducted in order to formulate measures of spirituality that consider and reflect "the diversity and breadth of children's spiritual beliefs within a multicultural context."[53]

These authors make a significant contribution to a gap they perceived in current research, yet they overlook culture and diversity in the analysis of Moore's findings. Although they name religious affiliation and, to a lesser degree, ethnicity as the most significant markers of cultural diversity among participating children, and they design and carry out the study with these distinctive aspects of culture in mind, their analysis is solely focused on the generation of themes that were held in common among this group of children. After explaining each theme, they include two or three quotes by various children that substantiate their findings, and are careful to include the religious affiliation and ethnic heritage of the quoted child. Yet there is little reason for having these identifying features, as they do not interpret the theme and, more specifically, these quotes in light of these cultural features of the children. Any differences or distinctive features of the children's perceptions that may be related to their religious or ethnic traditions are omitted from the authors' discussion, glossing over the "diverse views" that they name in the subtitle of this essay. Despite their admission that "definitions of religion and spirituality are continuously evolving and may be culturally dependent,"[54] the authors make no headway in identifying how this may be so, leaving this task to future studies such as the one I conducted.

The research of Moore, Talwar, and Bosacki is one example of the handful of studies that consider children's spirituality and theology in multiple cultural contexts and amidst contexts of diversity. While scholarship within this category considers culture with more intentionality and complexity than that of categories previously discussed, such studies remain limited by a lack of more critical attention to how children's spiritual and theological lives are bound up with culture. It is such attention that forms the basis for the fourth and final category I will outline.

Culture Matters

The final way that researchers consider culture in relation to children's spirituality and theology is through critical attention to the importance of issues surrounding culture.[55] This landscape is sparsely populated, but one scholar who exemplifies it through both theoretical and empirical research is Joyce Ann Mercer.[56]

Throughout her book *Welcoming Children*, Mercer keeps a keen watch on surrounding cultural contexts as she explores how to construct a "child-affirming church and theology."[57] Drawing from Pierre Bourdieu's position that practices form and are shaped by larger *habitus*, or social contexts,[58] she assesses how a capitalist consumer society affects practices and beliefs relating to children's religious education within Christian communities of faith.[59] For example, an assumption that undergirds her book is that mainline churches have often unintentionally adopted practices and beliefs surrounding consumerism that affect their ministry with children – and ministry in general.[60] She writes, "this method will lead me to examine the larger 'habitus' in which belief and practice take shape – that wider social and cultural space within which people experience and learn a way of life."[61] Unlike Westerhoff and Hay and Nye, who make reference to but do not adequately explore the formative power of culture, Mercer chooses a methodology that seriously considers cultural context and investigates how culture shapes different elements of Christian belief and practice, including perspectives of children and childhood.

In fact, she argues that *habitus* is not simply a one-dimensional social context in play in this formative process, but that children – and all human beings, in fact – exist "in multiple and often competing communities exercising formative, shaping influences of the child's identity."[62] Furthermore, these various cultures (or habitus) vie for formative influence and compete for control of cultural reproduction, which occurs "as dominant groups, able to disguise the power relations in such impositions of cultural arbitraries, thereby set the agenda for what other groups aspire to as they seek to alter their status and power positions. In effect, a particular way of doing things comes to be seen as commonsensical, natural, and self-evident."[63] In this careful attention to the formative power of habitus, Mercer sets the stage for considering children's spirituality and theology in light of a more robust and complex understanding of culture and context.

Through her leadership of the "Children in Congregations" study, Mercer engages in ethnographic research that grounds her theories in the lived realities of faith communities.[64] Over nine months, her research team spent between twelve and fifteen hours per week at one of three Presbyterian (USA) congregations in the San Francisco Bay area, each of which was "distinctive from the other two in terms of size, socio-economic and demographic situation, and theological orientation."[65] Their primary aim was to study congregational practices that nurture children's faith.[66] While not using this terminology, Mercer perceives each congregation to be a distinct cultural context, a site where particular practices are shared among parties as they "create 'webs of meaning' and action that form a more comprehensive matrix."[67] She and her colleagues describe each congregation in detail, paying attention to aspects of its history, demographic location, and congregational practices, which weave together to create a unique cultural tapestry. After describing a congregation, they identify and analyze a contextual practice that this congregation engages in for nurturing faith in children.

Mercer's assumptions about culture demonstrate a more broad and complex understanding than those of the scholars described above, one that in many ways aligns with the assumptions surrounding culture that I laid out in the introduction. For one thing, she holds that the relationship between a culture and its individual members is mutually influential, for not only do congregations shape children, but children also shape congregations.[68] She also assumes that cultures do not necessarily contain internal consensus, for she admits that within congregations, the experience of and meaning ascribed to practices will vary among members,[69] and she states that shared practices are sites of resistance.[70] Furthermore, Mercer reveals a complex and fluid understanding of culture in her thoughts on the multiplicity of communities that are operative in the lives of individuals and the competitive nature of cultural influence. This is also evident in her depiction of each congregation in the "Children in Congregations" study as a distinct culture with attributes shared not only among the congregations, but also among their broader social contexts. Mercer's critical attention to culture, both theoretically and practically, makes her research unique in the field of children's spirituality and theology.

Assessing Children's Spirituality and Theology

The ideas and interpretations generated through my research offer particular points of critique for the field of children's spirituality and theology to consider. By turning the tables on the field in this way, I create a new interpretive lens that brings into focus three assessments: that scholars do well to pay attention to the processes of children's theological meaning-making, not just products; that consideration must be given to the communal nature of children's theologies; and that culture needs to be critically studied at every step of research into children's spiritual and theological lives.

Product and Process

A significant amount of research into children's spirituality and theology involves a quest to learn about what children think – their theological and spiritual ideas about all sorts of topics – at the expense of learning about *how* children make theological meaning in the first place. Take, for example, Ubani and Tirri's study into how children in Finland understand religion and spirituality, or Moore, Talwar, and Bosacki's research into the perceptions of spirituality held by a relatively diverse cross-section of children in Canada. Another recent example is a study by Pamela Caudill Ovwigho and Arnold Cole, who explored the meaning children make of aspects of their spiritual lives – such as their family, peers who don't self-identify as people of faith, and experiences of Sunday school – and then used the children's meaning to generate recommendations for ministry leaders and congregations.[71] Studies such as these, which aim to generate insight into the content of children's theological and spiritual ideas, make up a significant portion of contemporary research in the field. Yet while they may open windows into *what* children think – their theological products – many of them overlook *how* children think, that is, the processes by which they generate their beliefs. For example, in her research into children's views of the Sacrament of Reconciliation, Jennifer Beste seems to gloss over the fact that her young participants may be actively making meaning through their interviews with her.[72] Although Beste's analysis can be seen as evidence for perceiving children as "active learners," to use her words, her focus on how children "express" themselves in interviews passes over the active learning they are engaging in as they *create* meaning before her very eyes.[73]

The children who participated in my research urge scholars to study how young people construct theological meaning by engaging in generative processes during research. As demonstrated in previous chapters, the children may have come to our interviews with pre-constructed and personalized theological ideas tucked under their arms, but they also generated theology right then and there through the interview process. Perhaps this was most evident among the children at Parkdale, who explored ideas and shared opinions as they created meaning in conversation with one another and with me and my assistant.

My discussions with children also allowed me to see ways that they processed and landed on ideas before setting foot in the interview. For example, in my conversations with Ally, Ethan, Melissa, and Laura, four young members of Colkirk, I noticed that they each possessed a narrative approach to theology, which I fleshed out in chapter 5. By hearing, reflecting on, and telling stories about their experiences at their congregation, they were able to play with and hold particular ideas that they may not have made sense of in other ways. Had I been focused solely on learning *what* these children believed, as is common among some contemporary scholars of children's spirituality and theology, I may have overlooked the fascinating ways that these young theologians had already processed and created the content of their theological ideas, as well as how they were doing so in that moment.

One of the most interesting dimensions of this critique is that the theological meaning that children make and the processes by which they make such meaning may yield very different insights into their inner lives. This was certainly the case among the children at Burke Street. During my first visit to this congregation, I noticed that both Stephen and Rebecca were Sunday school superstars: the children Denise could always count on to answer questions and, for the most part, offer the hoped-for responses. Both children were willing to talk about their congregation and their ideas, and Stephen in particular displayed both eloquence and a degree of complexity as he shared his theological ideas with me. Yet Stephen and Rebecca both struggled when pushed to go deeper in their thinking, with the former going silent and the latter repeating ideas she had already shared, sometimes word for word. While the *content* of their theological ideas seemed to showcase degrees of maturity and thoughtfulness, the *processes* for creating their own theology were weak and underdeveloped.

On the other hand, some children had a difficult time speaking about their theologies, but were engaged in rigorous processes of producing meaning – even if uncertain meaning. Nicholas was anything but a Sunday school superstar. He disliked going to Sunday school and at times it was challenging for me to get him to talk about his theological ideas at any length – the polar opposite of Stephen and Rebecca. Yet over halfway through our conversation, this boy began telling me about how he struggles to believe some of the things he hears about in Sunday school and worship services at Burke Street. As I asked him to tell me more about why he believes some things that he hears but not others, he made meaning in a way that demonstrated a desire to engage in deep theological thinking as he formed his own parameters for discerning the level of truth among biblical stories. The content of Nicholas's theological meaning-making may have been tenuous, but the means by which he generated meaning demonstrated a willingness to think deeply and wrestle with issues, like the Resurrection, that are inherently wrapped in uncertainty, mystery, and wonder.

Solo and Group Theology

A second critique raised by the participating children is that research into children's spirituality and theology needs to consider not just individual theology, but communal theology as well. Many of the studies mentioned earlier in this chapter – especially those in the second and third categories – rely on methods such as interviews, research activities, or surveys aimed at learning about the spiritual and theological lives of individual children. For example, in exploring perspectives of spirituality held among a diverse sample of Canadian children, Moore relied on brief interviews with children; although she does not explicitly state that she held interviews with individual children, her description of the study gives this impression.[74] Another example is Elena Savina's quest to learn about how Russian children give meaning to the concept of the soul. She conducted individual interviews with 148 randomly selected public school children, asking each child a series of seventeen questions.[75]

The young theologians I've introduced in the previous chapters demonstrate that theological meaning-making can be a highly collaborative and communal process. As mentioned in chapter 5, those children who met with me for interviews in pairs or small groups engaged in theological meaning-making through conversations with one another, challenging, affirming, and questioning each other's ideas and perspectives on issues such as God, sin, and creation. Yet I also demonstrated that even those children who were interviewed individually at times generated theology through dialogue with me and, when present, my research assistant. In fact, such a conversational approach to theology was the most frequent and obvious commonality among the variety of processes by which all children made theological meaning.

The collaborative and communal nature of the children's theologies was most clearly evident among the five young participants from Parkdale. Not only did they engage in conversation as a key process by which they each generated theological thinking – as exemplified in the exchange between Enoch and Jacob in chapter 1 – but at times I had a hunch that the meaning they generated was actually communal meaning, created collaboratively through discussion with one another. For example, during my conversation with Lizzy, Angela, and Grace, the three of them theologically riffed off each other, finishing one another's thoughts and responding to questions I posed to their peers. Such a communal theological process didn't simply involve the mining of past experiences and individual ideas; it was a shared and communal experience that unfolded in that very moment – and it must be interpreted as such.

These young theologians challenge scholars to study children's theological meaning-making as a communal endeavour. They can not only be seen as solo performances, but also as jazz improvisation, a highly relational enterprise.[76] Yes, each child brings her or his own particular ideas and questions and slants to the process of creating theology; but as they put their heads together new sounds are formed that cannot be heard fully apart from what their peers bring to the music. Theirs is a call for researchers to take seriously Nye's finding that children's spirituality is inherently relational.[77] To study it without taking this into account would be to impose a culturally particular set of epistemic norms onto children – such as prizing the individual over the community – even though their approaches for making theological meaning may not fully fit such norms and assumptions.

Considering Culture at Every Stage

This brings us to the final critique that the child participants pose to the field of children's spirituality and theology: culture needs to be critically attended to at every stage of research. As mentioned, Mercer's research, in building on Bourdieu's notion of habitus, stands as a rare example of scholarship that carefully considers the role of culture in the organization and method of research, as well as in the analysis of knowledge generated about the spiritual and theological lives of children. Yet many of the studies cited in the first three of the four categories I describe earlier in this chapter ignore how culture is bound up with children's meaning-making of theological and spiritual issues. For example, in bringing together independent studies in Canada and the United Kingdom, Sandra Bosacki and Cathy Ota wished to find answers to questions surrounding "the emotional, spiritual, and cultural aspects of preadolescent [nine to eleven years old] development."[78] After making a case for researching how culture influences children's perceptions of spirituality and their sense of self – which they name as a significant dimension of spirituality among older children – the authors interpret the findings of their respective qualitative studies. While their studies were organized and carried out in ways that considered the cultural contexts in which they were being conducted (for example, by using "self-esteem" in interviews with Canadian children, who were accustomed to this term by both middle-school teachers and social studies curricula[79]), the authors neglected to consider the cultural dynamics at play within the knowledge generated by their research studies.

If, as I have demonstrated, children's theologies are in many ways reflective of their broader cultural contexts (in the case of this book, their congregational culture), then researchers cannot afford to ignore this at any stage of study. In particular, scholars like those cited above must engage culture in the analysis and interpretation of knowledge generated through qualitative and ethnographic studies. To do otherwise is to risk missing crucial meaning embedded in children's theologies by relying on either a decontextualized analysis or one that is covertly freighted with the assumptions, norms, and epistemologies of the researcher.

This critique became especially clear through my interpretation of the interviews with the children from Colkirk and the narrative style of their theologies. As I reviewed transcripts of my conversations with these four children, I had the sense that the stories they were telling were more than just sources of generating and means for conveying theological insights. I wondered if perhaps the stories were the very stuff of their theology. Yet I struggled to make sense of this emerging interpretation, for my preexisting assumptions surrounding theology caused me to see theology as inherently factual, that is, as something best expressed through propositions and arguments. If, for instance, someone was to ask me about what I learned from my research, I might respond with, "The theological meaning-making that children generate seems to be related in many ways to their congregational cultures." This is a fact that can be proposed and debated based on the results of my ethnographic research.

The narrative nature of the theology of the children at Colkirk challenges this epistemological assumption. For these children, theology is inherently storied, and it needed to be interpreted in a manner that aligned with this reality. Thus, to more fully and accurately make sense of the theological meaning these children generated, I had to attempt to interpret them not through my own epistemological assumptions, but through the ones they were offering to me. In such a paradigm shift (which I am only partially able to make), my response to the question about my research might consist not in an argument or thesis statement, but in telling a story about my time among these children and their congregations. The story would not demand analysis or explanation, nor would it be a mere example or description of a particular idea. The story itself would be the response, one left open to those receiving it to do with it what they must.

Scholarship into children's spirituality and theology must attend to culture at every stage of research – from organizing a study to conducting it, interpreting knowledge and communicating it to audiences. To honour and more accurately hear the voices of the children who participated in this research, I had to keep culture in my sights as I pieced together interpretive lenses that reflected their broader cultural contexts – in the case of the children from Colkirk, a narrative epistemology characteristic of Aboriginal knowledge.[80] Yet such critical attention to culture is riddled with difficulties, for the field of children's spirituality and theology developed from and rests on research and assumptions within Western contexts. The theologies of these children are a call to action, an invitation to peer behind our embedded presuppositions and see the field through their eyes.

* * *

In this chapter, I have allowed the knowledge generated from my research and laid out in earlier chapters to shed new light on the field of children's spirituality and theology, an academic arena that tends to neglect issues of culture and cultural diversity. When interpreted in this way, three significant assessments emerge: a focus on the products of children's theologies rather than processes; an overlooking of communal theologies for the sake of individual meaning-making; and a lack of critical attention to culture at every stage of research, particularly analysis of findings. Clearly, the knowledge created through such a lens – which flips the common interpretive script of seeing children in light of academic research – has significant implications for children's spirituality and theology as an academic field of inquiry. But what implications does it hold for practitioners engaged in formation with children in congregations? And what questions for further study spring forth from this research? It is to these matters that I turn in the final chapter.

8 Waymarks for the Road Ahead

Future Directions for Research and Pastoral Practice

This concluding chapter examines the questions and implications that arise out of the research I have presented thus far. I begin by raising broad sets of questions that can be launched from this study, which surround different levels and experiences of congregational involvement among children, the effect of parents, the influences of multiple cultural contexts on children's lives, and how theological meaning-making shifts and changes in children over time. Following this, I move from avenues for research to those for pastoral practice as I offer three significant implications that this project raises for the practice of spiritual formation with children in congregations. These implications have to do with the importance of equipping children to engage in deep theological meaning-making, the need to assess congruence between broader congregational culture and pastoral practices with children, and the formative power of offering children opportunities to speak theologically.

I began this book by asking questions about how children generate theology in ways that reflect the particularities of their congregation's culture, and how they draw from other experiences and ideas as they make theology their own. My search for adequate answers to such questions led me to pursue exploratory research at congregations that self-identify culturally in styles and approaches that are distinct from one another.

This multi-year process of formulating the study, participating in the lives of the congregations, and interpreting the data generated has been a deeply personal journey, one marked by blessings and challenges, laughter and sorrow. It has been a sacramental sojourn, causing me to catch glimpses of God in the lives of the children and congregations that opened themselves to me. I resonate with Pierre Bourdieu's assertion that "the interview can be considered a sort of *spiritual exercise* that, through *forgetfulness of self*, aims at a true *conversion of the way we look at* other people in the ordinary circumstances of life."[1] These congregations have plunged me deep into the waters of their lives and I have arisen from them forever changed.

The places where I have lived during this journey have been intertwined with the research process. I began by dividing my time between a city of incredible cultural diversity and one that was becoming more pluralistic through a recent surge in immigration. Only weeks after completing my participation in the four congregations, I moved to Halifax, a small urban centre that is much more culturally homogenous than where I had been for the past four or five years – even though recent years have brought to it increasing levels of diversity. Living here, in the city that houses the Canadian Museum of Immigration at Pier 21, I am continually struck by the irony of writing a book about cultural diversity and difference in a milieu where such conversations are less common and given less priority. Without the obvious and everyday experiences of diversity that are impossible to escape in the cities from which I had moved, the culture of Halifax is one with deep historical roots embedded in a particular dominant culture. And as much as these roots are being questioned by those who wish to tell a more honest history and have more diverse voices represented, as I sit in my office at Atlantic School of Theology, nestled among the stately homes on the bank of the Northwest Arm, I am reminded of the cultures that are swept under the rug by British-Canadian hegemony: the Mi'kmaq people who signed treaties of friendship and peace with the British, only to have their land exploited and their culture undermined in the centuries that followed; the Acadians who were exiled by the British in the Great Expulsion in the middle of the eighteenth century; the ongoing struggles of Black Nova Scotians who keep their stories of hope and survival alive against continued racism; the thousands of international students who make their temporary homes in Halifax to study at one of the city's six universities; and the generation of young adults who leave the province because of a lack of adequate employment opportunities.

By placing cultural diversity at the centre of my vision, I have been able to demonstrate that the content, sources, and methods of children's theological meaning-making are in many ways reflective of the broader cultures of their congregations. Even so, they are not mirror images of their congregations, for they put their own unique touches on theology by generating it in ways that are particular to their experiences, perceptions, and the additional cultures in which they participate. This knowledge presents challenges to the United Church's vision for becoming intercultural as well as to the field of children's spirituality and theology. But the influence does not end here. This research is filled with questions for further study and implications for pastoral practice with children.

Questions for Further Study

Although I began this research seeking answers to a particular set of questions, it has also generated even more questions that identify pathways for further study. In this section I will discuss four sets of questions that serve as avenues for further inquiry.

Congregational Involvement

A first set of questions involves exploration into the effects of children's involvement in congregations on their theological meaning-making. In chapter 3, I posited that the different congregational experiences that children at Burke Street engaged in – such as children who attend with great frequency and those who attend on occasion, or the older children who participate in Sunday school and the younger ones who are part of Godly Play – were related to the ways they reflect the theological ethos of their congregation. I am curious, however, as to what could be learned about children's theologies by placing this phenomenon at the centre of study. Thus, some fascinating questions raised by this book surround how congregational involvement affects the degree to which children reflect the theological ethos of their broader congregation, and the manner in which they reflect it.

While each of the children involved in this research was a participant in her or his congregation's life, they were all involved with great degrees of variance. While this was most clear at Burke Street, it was evident at each site. The children at Messiah, for example, ranged from lifetime members to those who made the change to Messiah from a Roman Catholic parish only a few months earlier. And while, as I demonstrated, it is possible to interpret the theologies of all the children to find reflections of their congregation's theology, had I framed this research differently, I could have generated interesting insights about how congregational involvement affects parallels between the theologies of children and their congregations. Such research could examine correlations between children's theologies and not only the level of participation (such as the frequency with which children participate in their congregations), but also the type of involvement (such as worship services, Sunday school, service projects, vacation Bible school, or intergenerational activities). The knowledge generated by such research would offer fascinating insights into whether or not congregational involvement matters to the development of children's theologies, and how. It would also reveal implications for how leaders can invite children to participate in the life of congregations to foster the generation of theological insight.

The Parent Factor

Second, this research raises interesting questions about the influence of parents on the production of theological knowledge in children. In summarizing the findings of the National Study of Youth and Religion, Smith and Denton argue that "the single most important social influence on the religious and spiritual lives of adolescents is their parents ... [W]hen it comes to the religious outcomes of youth, parents and adults 'will get what they are.'"[2] They also posit that a similar assertion can be made for religious communities, meaning that the more a congregation or another faith community invests in the lives of their teens, the more likely their teens are to make an investment in their faith. As is evidenced in this book, children are indeed capable of reflecting – and in many ways do reflect – the faith espoused and practised by their broader congregation. But if what Smith and Denton argue about teenagers in the United States is at least partially true for children in Canada,[3] then another set of questions arising from this research revolves around parental influence in the lives of children's faith: How do the theologies of parents – espoused and implied – influence those of their children? Does parental involvement in congregations (i.e., if one or both parents do not participate in a congregation) affect the degree to which children reflect their congregational theologies? What about when the theologies of parents and those of the congregation conflict with one another – how would this phenomenon be reflected in children's theologies?

The central question of this study concerned children in relation to congressional cultures, not families. As familial influence made itself clear throughout the book, I considered how parents and the family at large might be having an influence on the theology of a particular child. Yet if one were to foreground parental involvement and familial practice alongside congregational culture in relation to how children generate theological meaning, a number of new avenues for research open. For example, one could conduct a similar qualitative study and additionally hold interviews with parents of the child participants, as well as talk with the children about their perceptions of the faith lives of their parents and families. This would add a further layer of complexity and insight into the theologies of children, which could lead to knowledge about how the family acts as a cultural context in which children's theological ideas and practices take shape.

Multiple Cultures

A third set of questions revolves around the fact that children live and participate in multiple cultural contexts. Throughout the research process, I held to the broad and multifaceted view of culture that I outlined in the introduction to this book, one that acknowledges that children exist and participate in multiple cultures that intermingle and even compete for formative influence.[4] Using the knowledge generated in this research, further study could expand such knowledge by considering the multiple cultural contexts in which children exist. Such research could go far in answering questions such as: How do children draw not only from congregations, but also from the culture of social media, the broader cultures of their neighbourhoods and cities, and even other faith communities as they generate theology? To what degree do varying levels of involvement in multiple cultural contexts shape children's theological meaning-making? What subtle theological messages are embedded in non-congregational cultural contexts that are reflected in children's theologies?

Further studies could explore children from one congregation who participate in multiple additional cultural contexts. A series of interviews with children could be arranged, with each focused on a particular cultural context under investigation. Another avenue for further research could be to explore the phenomenon considered in chapter 2, in which children from a congregation belonging to one Christian tradition attend a school of another Christian tradition. Juxtaposing multiple cultural contexts in this way would surely lead to new learnings about the cultural nature of children's theological meaning-making, which would in turn shed even greater light on the United Church's prospects for becoming truly intercultural, and on research within the field of children's spirituality and theology.

The Long View

I stated in the introduction to this book that, while they are not the central focus of this study, the developmental capacities of children matter. Throughout the book I have drawn attention to developmental issues – especially those related to faith development – as they intersect with children's theological meaning-making within their congregational contexts. Yet further research could more closely consider developmental factors alongside cultural considerations that influence how children produce theological knowledge in order to add further layers of meaning to the cultural nature of children's theologies and to speak back to and critique developmental theories in light of such meaning.

Further research could engage in longitudinal studies that explore how children's theological meaning-making changes as they grow older and progress along developmental trajectories. The interpretations I offer in this book rely on research that was conducted over a relatively abbreviated period of time. Depending on the requests of the various congregations and my relationships with them, my time within these communities varied from site to site. With this in mind, a final series of further questions centre on a shift toward longitudinal research: How do children's theologies change over time? Do the ways that they reflect and depart from the theological ethos of their congregation (i.e., in the content, sources, and methods of theological meaning-making) shift as they pass through childhood and move into adolescence? Are there particular features of their theologies that are more salient at particular stages of development? Do important life events – both planned and unexpected, joyful and sorrowful – impact the ways their theologies change over time? And what of congregational cultures? As they shift and adapt, what impact do they have on children's theologies?

The quest for answers to these sorts of questions requires research conducted over several years. One possible research design would be to select a number of questions and/or exercises (such as drawing) meant to investigate the theological lives of children that could then be utilized in a series of interviews with a set of children who meet for interviews at various points in childhood (for example, when they are six, nine, and twelve years old). Alternatively, a small group of children could participate in a study that has a researcher meeting with them every year from the ages of six to thirteen. Such longitudinal studies certainly give rise to a number of challenges (such as relocation of the children, financial viability, shifts in congregational involvement, etc.), but when organized with these challenges in mind, they could lead to ground-breaking insights into how children do theology in light of congregational culture as they and their congregations both change over the years.

Implications for Pastoral Practice

In these final pages, I propose three broad implications for pastoral practice with children in congregations. Chapters 6 and 7 have already raised implications for two fields of inquiry that have influenced this research. But what about practitioners involved in spiritual formation and religious education with children? What insights does this research offer for congregations, clergy, and practitioners who are seeking to better engage and form children in communities of faith? There are at least three implications that arise from this research: helping children develop capacities for engaging in theological meaning-making; examining consistency between congregational culture and formational practices with children; and giving children opportunities to speak openly about their theologies.

Equipping for Theological Meaning-Making

First, congregations and pastoral practitioners do well to put primary emphasis on equipping children to make their own theological meaning. In the world of children's ministry, there is a tendency for resources, programs, and curricula to focus on giving children particular nuggets of theological content. For example, Group Publishing's VBS curriculum, which is incredibly popular among evangelical congregations but also used in mainline Protestant congregations and Catholic parishes, seeks to use games, crafts, and skits to impart a particular "Bible point" to the children each day, such as "God has the power to provide" and "God has the power to forgive." Programs such as this are designed to help children learn a predetermined point or fact.

The interpretations of children's theologies that I offered in the preceding chapters challenge this instructional style of children's ministry. Each of the participating children demonstrated that theology is not simply something that children learn through what Paulo Freire names as a "banking" approach to education.[5] Rather, theology is produced as they engage in and reflect on their congregations, life experiences, and theological ideas shared by others in their lives. Yet at some congregations, children's ministry seemed to focus on imparting specific points or facts to children, and within these congregations children struggled to engage in their own processes of generating theology. Pastoral ministry with children can move away from attempts to teach children particular facts or points and toward approaches that provide children with tools for and practice in active theological reflection. Such resources can include a wide variety of sources for theology (such as films, music, stories, etc.) and a number of different approaches (such as storytelling and conversation) for creating theology.

Congregational Congruency

Second, this research calls practitioners to more closely examine their curricula and models for children's ministry – whether Sunday school, VBS, or other initiatives – in light of their broader congregational culture. There were moments during the research process when I perceived congregations to be engaging in children's formation in a way that contradicted – or even undermined – the broader cultural ethos of their community. This was most clearly evident at Burke Street, where their model of Sunday school promoted a style of theology that was different from that which the leaders espoused as vital to the wider congregation. Perhaps this phenomenon is intertwined with Burke Street's identity as a "mainstream" (read: White) United Church congregation. Since they struggled to articulate what makes their congregational culture distinct, maybe these leaders are like fish in water whose surrounding culture and theological ethos are implicit and unchecked. Contrasting this situation is Messiah, a congregation keenly aware of its position as a Ghanaian community on Canadian soil. With a clearer vision for how their culture guides their community, Messiah's leaders devote a great deal of energy to adapting programs and curricula to fit their unique context.

It is incumbent on pastoral practitioners, especially among congregations that self-identify as part of the dominant surrounding culture, to become researchers in their own communities and study the multifaceted and complex culture of the entire congregation. Inconsistencies between children's ministry and the wider congregation do not create a terribly hospitable environment in which children can flourish as young theologians. Armed with a thick description of their congregation, practitioners can become better equipped to examine their existing and proposed ministries with children and adapt them to better reflect their wider community. Such examinations need to consider not only the explicit curriculum, that is, the overt and clearly stated ideas and practices, but also the covert, often unintentional messages of the implicit curriculum, and even the null curriculum, which is the information conveyed through what is not taught or practised.[6] This can go a long way in helping practitioners adapt their initiatives to better align with those of the whole congregation. This is not to say, of course, that this is a one-way street. The broader congregation can – and I believe should – be changed by the presence of children as well. But no party – children's ministry or the wider faith community – can shift in light of the other unless there is clarity as to the culture of both.

Something to Talk About

Finally, since I have shown that a primary means through which these nineteen children engaged in theological meaning-making was conversation, congregations should provide children with opportunities to talk about their views. Whether with one another or with me, being able to discuss their views and experiences gave the children who participated in this research space to reflect on and build theology for themselves. Unfortunately, as I mentioned in chapter 5, several of the young participants expressed that they do not often speak about their deep theological ideas and experiences with others. And even among those who have shared with others, some, such as Dawn, told me that their thoughts were not always taken seriously. Again, this finding aligns with those of Smith and Denton. Writing about teens in the US, they stated that "it was our distinct sense that for many of the teens we interviewed, *our interview was the first time that any adult had ever asked them what they believed and how it mattered in their life.*"[7] If children generate theology by talking it through with trusted companions, then congregations ought to be placing primary emphasis on providing opportunities for them to do just this.

There are countless possibilities that could be unleashed if congregational leaders encouraged children not only to learn stories and hear theology, but to tell their own stories and talk about their beliefs together.

At times, this could mean that adults model processes of generating theology by talking about their own ideas and experiences, while in other instances they could make space for children to talk with one another about their theological presuppositions. Further still, adults can do what I did in this study: simply meet with children to ask their opinions about what matters to them.

As adults engage in such conversational practices with children, they would do well to remember a few ground rules that emerge from this research. First, we must take children's thoughts seriously and be careful not to judge their theologies as more or less correct; Dawn's experience of feeling unheard and disbelieved caused her to keep subsequent faith experiences to herself. Second, it is incumbent on us to trust that, even if it is difficult to perceive, children will make their own theological connections and insights, so we should not push our own tendencies and assumptions onto them. Third, sometimes children need a bit of encouragement to engage in a conversational approach to the production of theology. The fact that Laura and Melissa were very quiet at the outset of our interview yet afterward asked to talk with me more is a reminder that children may not dive right into the process of doing theology and they may simply need some time to become comfortable with it. Children's ministry leaders – and parents! – do not need graduate degrees or the best curriculum to help children make theological meaning. All we need is a listening ear … and maybe a few questions to get things rolling.

Notes

INTRODUCTION

1 The use of the mosaic as a metaphor for Canadian diversity is often first credited as the idea of Victoria Hayward in her 1922 book *Romantic Canada*. Hayward, *Romantic Canada*, 187.

2 United Church of Canada, "A Transformative Vision."

3 Ammerman et al., "Introduction," 9.

4 See Lawrence-Lightfoot and Davis, *The Art and Science of Portraiture.*

5 See Hennink, "Language and Communication."

6 This finding was particularly true for teens who self-identified as belonging to mainline Protestant Christian traditions. Smith with Denton, *Soul Searching*, 131–3, 267–8.

7 Greene and Hill, "Researching Children's Experience," 10.

8 Hood, "Six Children Seeking God," 245. See also Clark, *In a Younger Voice.*

9 Brown and Strega, "Transgressive Possibilities," 10.

10 Hill, "Ethical Considerations," 63.

11 Merriam et al., "Power and Positionality," 409.

12 Garbarino, Stott, and Faculty of the Erickson Institute, *What Children Can Tell Us*, 80.

13 Pranee Liamputtong writes about the importance of building trust, saying that it may take a considerable amount of time to build trust among research participants. She states that accepting invitations to share meals with participants is important to the building of trust, a statement that certainly rings true from my experience. Liamputtong, "Doing Research."

14 After completing the research and moving to Halifax, I received a handmade card from Rev. Martha, Arlene, and the children, that said in huge letters, "Thank you for everything." A few months later I visited the congregation for Sunday worship on a trip from Halifax and was warmly greeted by the community. One elder even acknowledged my special relationship with the congregation by looking me in the eye and saying "Welcome home."
15 Wilson, *Research is Ceremony*, 101.
16 Coles, *The Spiritual Life of Children*, 308.
17 Browning, *A Fundamental Practical Theology*, 15, 44, 46.
18 van der Ven, *Practical Theology*.
19 Ibid., 101.
20 Ibid., 93–101.
21 Osmer, *Practical Theology*.
22 Ibid., 4.
23 Ibid., 37–9, 47–64.
24 Ibid., 4.
25 Ibid.
26 Ibid., 176.
27 Mager, "Do We Learn," 193, 198.
28 Moschella, *Ethnography*, 4.
29 Wigg-Stevenson, *Ethnographic Theology*.
30 Moschella, *Ethnography*, 4.
31 Wigg-Stevenson, "Faith in My Bones."
32 Moschella, *Ethnography*, 9.
33 "Spiritual Direction," IgnatianSpirituality.com, accessed 9 January 2020, http://www.ignatianspirituality.com/making-good-decisions/spiritual-direction.
34 Moschella, *Ethnography*, 13.
35 Wigg-Stevenson, *Ethnographic Theology*, 2.
36 Moschella, *Ethnography*, 11.
37 Ibid., 11–12.
38 Ibid., 13.
39 Ibid., 40.
40 Psalm 8:2.
41 Hay with Nye, *The Spirit of the Child*, 109.
42 See Yust, *Real Kids, Real Faith*, 6.
43 There is disagreement and inconsistency within journalistic and academic formatting guidelines as to whether or not "black" should be

capitalized. I capitalize Black to indicate that I am using this term to speak of a socially constructed racial-ethnic marker that is infused with meaning beyond a simple adjective that denotes a particular colour or shade. See L.D. Burnett, "To 'B' or Not to 'B': On Capitalizing the Word 'Black.'" See also Merrill Perlman, "Black and White: Why Capitalization Matters."

44 Csinos, *Children's Ministry That Fits.*

45 Csinos, "Yours, Mine, and Ours." Csinos, "Jesus Loves Which Little Children?"

46 My understandings of modernist and postmodern views of culture are based on Tanner, *Theories of Culture.*

47 My view of culture is in part influenced by that of Carl James, who writes that "culture is a concept that refers to the way in which a given society, community, or group organizes and conducts itself as distinguished from that of other societies, communities, or groups. Culture consists of a dynamic and complex set of values, beliefs, norms, patterns of thinking, styles of communication, linguistic expressions, and ways of interpreting and interacting with the world that help people understand and thus survive their varied circumstances." James, *Seeing Ourselves*, 26.

48 Ammerman, "Culture and Identity in the Congregation," 78.

49 Ibid.

50 Ryan, *Multicultiphobia*, 12.

51 See Wilson, *Research Is Ceremony.*

52 See Ammerman, "Culture and Identity in the Congregation."

53 Kluckhohn and Murray, "Personality Formation."

54 Lartey, *In Living Color*, 34.

CHAPTER ONE

1 I visited Parkdale four times during the autumn and winter of 2013–14. In November, I participated in a worship service; in January, I visited twice to interview the children; and in early February, I returned to participate in worship again, following which I conducted a focus group interview with adults.

2 Ronald Nydam has stated this shift in influence clearly by writing, "at approximately age eleven, peers become more powerful than parents in terms of influence. That is to say, having friends become a priority, and listening to them, going along with the peer crowd, becomes a powerful tug." Nydam, "Early Adolescence," 208.

3 Fowler, *Stages of Faith*, 153.

4 Balswick, King, and Reimer, *The Reciprocating Self*, 158–9.

5 In his explanation of Intuitive-Projective faith (about two to six or seven years old), Fowler writes that "the child's thinking is fluid and magical. It lacks deductive and inductive logic; it has an episodic flavor in which associations follow one another to imaginative processes not yet constrained by stable logical operations." Fowler, *Stages of Faith*, 123.

6 Throughout this book I will use male pronouns for God only when speaking of children's views that perceive God to be male. I employ this to be consistent with the male God some of the children imagine.

CHAPTER TWO

1 My involvement at Messiah spanned a period of six months in 2014. During my first visit, which was in February, I joined the congregation for worship and went with the children to Sunday school for the latter half of the service. Upon realizing that Jemina and Emmanuel were struggling with a lack of teachers on this day, I offered to assist in any way I could, and Jemina asked me to lead the youngest class (about age four to five) in another classroom so that she could continue her lesson with the grade-school children. During two Sunday services in March and April, I conducted interviews with children from the congregation. Because the adult leaders at Messiah were not able to find a time when I could conduct one focus group with them, in late July and early August I held three meetings with adults (one with Emmanuel and Sophia, another with Jemina, and a third Rev. Ayensu). I attended another worship service on the first Sunday in August.

2 Westerhoff, *Will Our Children Have Faith?* Rev. ed.

3 In arguing for the consideration of culture and ethnicity in research surrounding children's spirituality, Mattis et al. state that institutions such as congregations can play a role in socializing in-group members about what it means to be a member of the ethnic community. Mattis et al., "Ethnicity, Culture, and Spiritual Development," 290. Messiah certainly exemplifies this as it teaches and passes on aspects of Ghanaian culture to its children, most of whom were born in Canada.

4 The Indigenous authors in *Crisp Blue Edges* address the topic of creative non-fiction in a way that alludes to the fact that the need to define and categorize is part of a Westernized understanding of the world, and is neither inherent nor important to all cultures. Indigenous Creative Non-Fiction Forum, "Speaking in the Round," 34–5.

5 See Airhart, *A Church with the Soul of a Nation*.

6 Acolatse, *For Freedom or Bondage?*, 27–8.
7 Kaitlyn used the term "communion" when referring to participating in Eucharistic services with her school.
8 During my first visit to Messiah, I helped lead Sunday school with the youngest group of children (about four to five years old), an experience that I describe at the beginning of this chapter. At the end of the class, a young girl who volunteered to offer a closing prayer led the group in praying the Hail Mary and many of the children knew the prayer and joined in. After the prayer, the girl made the sign of the cross – while saying it – alongside many of her peers in the room.
9 Luke's faith exhibits many of the characteristics of the Synthetic-Conventional stage. See Folwer, *Stages of Faith*, and Fowler and Dell, "Stages of Faith from Infancy."
10 Acolatse, *For Freedom or Bondage?*, 66.
11 See, for example, Smith with Denton, *Soul Searching*, 261–2.
12 Boyatzis, Dollahite, and Marks, "The Family as a Context."
13 Although the term *Nazarite* can be used to refer to men and women who consecrate themselves to God by taking special vows (see Numbers 6:1–21), Jemina is speaking about the fact that Jesus was born in Nazareth and, as such, he was part of a racial lineage with particular physical attributes.
14 Lartey, *Pastoral Counselling in Inter-Cultural Perspective*, 56.
15 Ibid., 55.
16 Lartey, *Postcolonializing God*, 112–13. See also Ephirim-Donker, *African Religion Defined.*
17 Ephirim-Donker, *African Religion Defined*, vii–viii.

CHAPTER THREE

1 John 4:5–42.
2 Airhart, *A Church with the Soul of a Nation*, 257.
3 Other spaces in the church include a youth room, a nursery, offices, storage closets, and a parlour decorated with antique furniture.
4 Created by Jerome Berryman, Godly Play is an approach to religious education for children. Based on pedagogical assumptions and practices similar to those typical in Montessori education, Godly Play introduces children to Christian stories, language, and liturgy in ways that seek to enliven their imaginations and help them make their own meaning as they open themselves to God. For more information, see http://godly play.ca/about-godly-play/.

5 I visited Burke Street throughout the spring of 2014. I began by participating in a worship service and Sunday school, where I led a lesson, in late March. I then held all children's interviews and the focus group with adults on weeknights and weekends throughout April. Following these interviews, I attended worship and assisted with Sunday school once more in early May.

6 Berryman, *Godly Play*.

7 Urban T. Holmes identified speculative spirituality in his phenomenology of prayer, briefly explaining it as a spiritual method that "emphasizes the illumination of the mind" rather than the heart. Holmes, *A History of Christian Spirituality*, 4.

8 Ibid.

9 See Berryman, *Godly Play*.

10 Berryman, *Teaching Godly Play*, 47, 50.

11 See Westerhoff, "Formation, Education, Instruction," and Westerhoff, *Will Our Children Have Faith?*

12 I.e., Denise. Most of the Sunday school teachers and leaders at Burke Street have the children call them by their first names, but Denise prefers "Mrs Hill" because she is a teacher at a local public school.

13 Like many other children of her age, Rebecca is at a stage of faith in which she is able to engage in more complex thought processes, narrate her own experiences, and start seeing things from the perspectives of others; but these abilities are not pronounced when she speaks of theological matters. While she demonstrates that she is certainly taking the stories and symbols of her faith community and making them her own (a core trait of the faith development of school-age children), she does not yet possess the ability to perceive of God in abstract terms. One of the characteristics of Mythic-Literal faith is concrete operational thinking that departs from the boundless imagination of preschool children and moves toward the realm of reality (Fowler, *Stages of Faith*, 135–6, 149–50). Rebecca exemplifies such as shift in her proclivity to speak about memorized facts related to an abstract God that she has learned from her congregation, but which remain concrete, one-dimensional, and literal. Still, while the developmental capacities of this child – normal and healthy for her age – prohibit her from grasping the full sense of the theological ideas she shared with me, she certainly speaks of her faith in a way that made her a clear example of the information-based and cognitive approach to theology shared among some of her peers and manifested in Burke Street's approach to Sunday school.

14 I describe a cognitive approach to experiencing God as one of four spiritual styles in Csinos, *Children's Ministry That Fits*. While some people are apt to sense God's presence first-hand through gaining knowledge and insight, Stephen's discussion of the importance of learning about God does not appear to be directly tied to a felt sense of experiencing the divine, as evidenced by his struggle to pinpoint a moment that stands out as one in which he experienced God.

15 Throughout this portion of my conversation with Nicholas and Theo, the younger of these brothers interrupted and moved the discussion to topics such as the 2014 Winter Games and movies. The excerpt I include here has been edited to remove the extraneous bits of our conversation about God.

16 In naming Nicholas as a skeptic, I do not wish to convey that he has no faith, but rather that a tendency to question, doubt, and be curious is central to his faith.

17 Perhaps Jeremy's tendency to express uncertainty is related to that fact that his mother, who spoke with me while Jeremy was taking a washroom break, told him before our interview that I was not looking for right answers from him, and I just wanted to know what Jeremy thought about things.

18 Jeremy's uninhibited imagination aligns squarely with the Intuitive-Projective faith of the first stage of Fowler's faith development theory. Fowler, *Stages of Faith*, 133.

19 One could argue that the fact that Jeremy expressed a theology that was creative and imaginative is related to the "fantasy-filled" Intuitive-Projective stage of faith and cognitive abilities firmly resting within the preoperational ways of thinking common among younger children (Fowler, *Stages of Faith*, 133). Conversely, Rebecca's more concrete approach to acquiring knowledge is likely intertwined with the forms of faith and reasoning common to children her age. Yet such an interpretation of the differences in theological meaning among these children remains limited because we cannot fully place children in one camp or the other (having a more cognitive, information-acquisition approach to faith or one that relies on the imagination) based solely on their age. Nicholas, for example, is almost the same age as Rebecca. Yet he seems to express a way of generating theology that is wholly different from hers in his willingness to question, doubt, and reconstruct ideas he has learned yet does not understand.

20 In making this statement, I do not assume that the children at Parkdale,

Messiah, and Colkirk had experiences or ways of thinking that were identical to their congregational peers. I am simply highlighting that the correlation between congregational experience and theological thinking was so evident among the children at Burke Street that it warrants closer interpretation as a theme in and of itself.

21 Fowler, *Stages of Faith*, 149–50.

CHAPTER FOUR

1 My relationship with Colkirk began in the winter of 2013, when I met with Rev. Martha and Arlene to talk about my research and how I hoped their congregation could participate in it. Over the next several months, we continued to meet together and discuss how I could give back to the community without creating additional work for them, and to find a way to reciprocate their assistance to my studies. We agreed that I would help them with some VBS programs they hoped to run during 2014, but for which they struggled to find enough leaders. Rev. Martha invited me to attend worship with them in November 2013, and then again in February to help the children and me get to know one another before the two VBS programs that I assisted with in February and March of 2014. After helping with another VBS in July, at which I conducted the interviews with children, I participated in worship in August, following which I held the focus group conversation with Arlene and Rev. Martha. Since moving to Halifax shortly after this visit, I have continued to maintain a relationship with Colkirk through occasional letters, emails, and even a few visits when I am back in their area.

2 According to Health Canada, the suicide rate for First Nations youth in Canada is five to six times higher than that for non-Aboriginal youth (Advisory Group on Suicide Prevention, "Acting on What We Know"). Some Aboriginal communities have experienced so much suicide among their youth that they have declared states of emergency. CBC News, "Aboriginal Suicide Rate Rising in Ontario, New Report Says," *CBC Thunder Bay*, last modified 9 July 2015, http://www.cbc.ca/news/canada/thunder-bay/aboriginal-suicide-rate-rising-in-ontario-new-report-says-1.3141939.

3 Over the course of the many months that I spent getting to know Colkirk, I had many informal conversations with the children in this congregation. However, based on our mutual understanding, I am relying on the more formal interviews, which happened at the end of this time.

4 Castellano, "Updating Aboriginal Traditions of Knowledge."
5 While Melissa, Laura, and Ally all attend school on the reserve, Ethan attends a Catholic school in a nearby city.
6 Fowler and Dell, "Stages of Faith from Infancy," 38–9.

CHAPTER FIVE

1 Lartey, *In Living Color*, 34.
2 Merriam et al., "Power and Positionality," 414.
3 Liamputtong, *Performing Qualitative Cross-Cultural Research*, 20.
4 Lartey, *In Living Color*, 32.
5 Kluckhohn and Murray, "Personality Formation."
6 Lartey, *In Living Color*, 34. Lartey is certainly not the first or only practical theologian to draw from Kluckhohn and Murray's threefold understanding of personhood in order to understand culture. See, for example, Tisdale, *Preaching as Local Theology*, 11–12; Popock and Henriques, *Cultural Change and Your Church*, 102; Cooper-White, *Many Voices*.
7 This description of the three spheres of human life is drawn from Lartey, *In Living Color*, 34–5.
8 Lartey, *In Living Color*, 35.
9 See Rizzuto, *The Birth of the Living God*, and Bellous, de Roos, and Summey, "The Child's Concept of God."
10 See Fowler, *Stages of Faith*, 122–34.
11 Westcott and Littleton, "Exploring Meaning in Interviews with Children," 153.
12 Fowler, *Stages of Faith*, 135.
13 Sasso, *Cain and Abel*.
14 Both Ally and Ethan were around the age at which children tend to use stories to give meaning to their experiences. See Fowler, *Stages of Faith*, 136.
15 Castellano, "Updating Aboriginal Traditions of Knowledge," 31.
16 King, *The Truth about Stories*, 2.
17 Lartey, *Pastoral Counselling in Inter-Cultural Perspective*, 53. Mbiti, *African Religions and Philosophy*, 229.
18 In their study of dreams among children in South Africa, Potgieter, van der Walt, and Wolhuter also found that children were not prone to share their divine dreams with others, particularly their parents. Potgieter, van der Walt, and Wolhuter, "The Divine Dreams," 41.

CHAPTER SIX

1 Day, *Multiculturalism*, 6.

2 Ibid., 20. Day notes that while conversations about multiculturalism are new, diversity in this land is not. His broad arguments and sweeping interpretation of the history of diversity in Canada demonstrate that throughout the post-European contact history of Canada, the presence of diverse "others" has always existed and has always sparked official and non-official government bureaucratic "solutions" in order to manage, control, and even exterminate these "others."

3 Galabuzi, "Hegemonies, Continuities, and Discontinuities," 68.

4 Walcott, "Disgraceful," 18, 25.

5 Chazan et al., "Introduction," 1. Richard Day distinguishes between *multiculturalism* as a word used to "prescribe a social idea" and one that describes an "already achieved ideal." Day, *Multiculturalism*, 6.

6 Galabuzi, "Hegemonies," 67–8.

7 For one thing, Chazan et al. note that such policies are actually a fluid set of policies that the government adapts as the "multicultural consensus" and the reality of diversity changes over time. For another thing, multicultural policies do not always meet their self-proclaimed mark and remain nominal and marginal to federal initiatives. Chazan et al., "Introduction," 1.

8 Leman, "Canadian Multiculturalism."

9 Day, *Multiculturalism*, 157, 178.

10 Ibid., 178.

11 Ibid., 165, 171.

12 Ibid., 195.

13 Unless stated otherwise, I use *multiculturalism* and *multicultural* to refer to both the ideology of multiculturalism in Canada and multicultural policies.

14 Jansen, "Canadian Multiculturalism," 25. Day, *Multiculturalism*, 180. Chazan et al., "Introduction," 2.

15 Day, *Multiculturalism*, 187. Chazan et al., "Introduction," 2.

16 Jansen, "Canadian Multiculturalism," 25.

17 Jansen, "Canadian Multiculturalism," 21, 25. Day, *Multiculturalism*, 184–5.

18 Clarke, "For a Multicultural, Multi-Faith, Multiracial Canada," 51.

19 Elabor-Idemudia, "Immigrant Integration in Canada," 58.

20 Day, *Multiculturalism*, 199.

21 Galabuzi, "Hegemonies," 70.
22 Chazan et al., "Introduction," 4.
23 Walcott, "Disgraceful," 15. Chazan et al., "Introduction," 5.
24 Adams, *Unlikely Utopia*, 86.
25 Hill, *Black Berry*.
26 Bissoondath, *Selling Illusions*.
27 Bannerji, "Geography Lessons."
28 See Hill, *Black Berry*, 104–14, 173–80.
29 Ibid., 75.
30 Ibid., 155.
31 Bissoondath, *Selling Illusions*, 7.
32 Ibid., 76–7.
33 Ibid., 77, 222–3.
34 Ibid., 81.
35 Ibid., 75.
36 Ibid., 77.
37 Ibid., 81.
38 Ibid., 80.
39 Bannerji, "Geography Lessons," 65–6.
40 Ibid., 66.
41 Ibid., 73.
42 Ibid., 65.
43 Ibid., 67.
44 Ibid., 65. When arguing that members of non-dominant racial groups are not "Canadians," Bannerji is referring to a perception among dominant (White/male) Canadians and not a status of legal citizenship.
45 Bissoondath, *Selling Illusions*, 108.
46 Bannerji, "Geography Lessons," 78.
47 Ibid., 79.
48 Ibid., 77.
49 Ng, "The United Church of Canada," 204.
50 Ibid.
51 For an overview of the history of the United Church of Canada's response to Canadian multicultural and immigration policies during this time, see Cho, "'We Are Not Alone.'"
52 Ng, "The United Church of Canada," 206, 208.
53 Cho, "'We Are Not Alone,'" 53.
54 Ibid., 56–7.

55 Ng, "The United Church of Canada," 209–10.

56 Ibid., 210.

57 United Church of Canada, "A Transformative Vision," 579.

58 Resources include: Ng, ed., *Our Roots, Our Lives*; Ng, ed., *That All May Be One*; United Church of Canada, ed., *A Healing Journey*; United Church of Canada, *Circle and Cross*; Schmidt, *Ending Racial Harassment*; and Fennell, ed., *Intercultural Visions*. In addition to these print resources, the United Church has hosted a number of conferences to address interculturalism, including Behold! One Another: An Intercultural Conference (Toronto, 2008); River Running: An Intercultural Conference (Winnipeg, 2009); Behold! We Are Many, We Are One (Vancouver, 2011); Prairie Mosaic (Saskatoon, 2012); Behold! Many Circles, One Sacred Hoop (Halifax, 2013); Prairie Paths (Regina, 2014); and Prairie Horizons: Unfolding Church (Saskatoon, 2014). The United Church distributes many highlights from these events through the "Intercultural Ministries" playlist on its YouTube channel. The denomination has also set up a Facebook group for sharing ideas and resources for intercultural ministry, called "Behold! An Intercultural Community."

59 Halliday, "Introduction," x.

60 In Quebec, interculturalism has a particular definition, since multicultural policies in this province are perceived as dangerous to the maintenance of Quebec's distinct culture and its relatively homogenous national identity. Susan Judith Ship argues that scholars and policy-makers in the province see the threat of multiculturalism as "an attempt to deny the cultural integrity of *la belle provence*, and as a policy that, by relativizing culture, occludes the issue of the national question that has otherwise dominated federal politics." *Interculturalisme* in Quebec is a way of managing diversity in ways that preserve the province's national and cultural identity. It rests on the idea of "cultural convergence," of a society arranged by peripheral ethnic groups and the dominant Quebec nation. But, unlike the way I use *interculturalism* in this book, *interculturalisme* is based on a hierarchical notion of the Québécois nation standing above minority groups and it does not include any element of reciprocity. Ship, "Citizens of the State," 86–7.

61 Hutchinson, *Ethical Choices*, 11.

62 United Church of Canada, "A Transformative Vision," 580.

63 Ibid., 582. Ng, "United Church of Canada," 218.

64 Hutchinson, *Ethical Choices*, 5.

65 United Church of Canada, "A Transformative Vision," 583.
66 United Church of Canada, "Intercultural Ministries."
67 Ito, "Race, Culture, and Interculturality,"
68 United Church of Canada, "A Transformative Vision," 580.
69 Ibid., 585.
70 Ibid., 588.
71 Bannerji, "Geography Lessons," 78.
72 United Church of Canada, "A Transformative Vision," 580. See also ibid., 586.
73 Ng, ed., *That All May Be One.*
74 Ibid., 80.
75 Ng, "The United Church of Canada," 206, 208.
76 United Church of Canada, "A Transformative Vision," 580.
77 Ibid., 587.
78 Ibid., 581–2.
79 Ibid.
80 Ibid., 590.
81 See, for example: Allen and Ross, *Intergenerational Christian Formation*; Beckwith, *Formational Children's Ministry*, 91–102; Csinos, "A Little Child Shall Lead Them": 26–9; Csinos and Beckwith, *Children's Ministry in the Way of Jesus*, 110–25; Keeley, *Helping Our Children*, 97–114; May et al., *Children Matter*, 215–45; Ng and Thomas, *Children in the Worshipping Community.*
82 Lartey, *Pastoral Counselling in Inter-Cultural Perspective*, 53. Mbiti, *African Religions and Philosophy*, 229.
83 United Church of Canada, "A Transformative Vision," 579.
84 Ibid., 582.
85 Ibid., 585.
86 Tanner, *Theories of Culture*, 57.

CHAPTER SEVEN

1 Coles, *The Spiritual Life of Children.*
2 Hay with Nye, *The Spirit of the Child.*
3 Priestly, "A Brief Introduction."
4 Ibid.
5 Mountain, "Four Links," 263.
6 In Nye's words, the spirituality of children in her research "was recognized by a distinctive property of mental activity, profound and intricate

enough to be termed 'consciousness', and remarkable for its confinement to a broadly relational, inter- and intra-personal domain." Hay with Nye, *The Spirit of the Child*, 109.

7 Lawson, "Introduction," xii.

8 Two scholars who have been most influential in scholarship around theologies of childhood throughout the history of Christianity are Marcia Bunge and Jerome Berryman. See Bunge, ed., *The Child in Christian Thought*; Bunge with Fretheim and Gaventa, eds., *The Child in the Bible*; Berryman, *Children and the Theologians*.

9 See, for example, Miller-McLemore, *Let the Children Come*.

10 Mountain, "Four Links," 263.

11 Hay with Nye, *The Spirit of the Child*.

12 Westerhoff, *Will Our Children Have Faith?*, rev. ed.

13 Coles, *The Spiritual Life of Children*, xvii.

14 Hay with Nye, *The Spirit of the Child*, 9.

15 Ibid., 22–4, 108–9.

16 Ibid., 170.

17 Ibid., 51, 138.

18 Ibid., 18.

19 Ibid., 165.

20 Ibid., 170.

21 Ibid., 137.

22 Ibid., 86.

23 Ibid., 87.

24 Ibid.

25 Ibid., 109.

26 Westerhoff, *Will Our Children Have Faith?* rev. ed., 80.

27 Ibid., 52.

28 Ibid., 132–3.

29 Ibid., 133.

30 Ibid., 10.

31 Ibid., 12.

32 Ibid., 133.

33 One can argue that all qualitative research is attuned to a specific cultural context. In the category I am proposing here, I am paying particular attention to scholarship that is not only carried out within a particular context, but also names and considers that cultural context in the design, implementation, and/or analysis of such research. See, for example, Dei, "Spirituality in African Education"; Funnell-Kononuk,

Young, and Michaelson, "Adolescent Perceptions and Experiences of the Hijab"; Humphrey, Hughes, and Holmes, "Understanding of Prayer"; Hwang, "Understanding Korean-American Children's God-Concept"; Junker, "Resistance and Resilience"; Kay and Ziebertz, "A Nine-Country Survey of Youth"; Keränen-Pantsu and Ubani, "The Holistic and Spiritual Relevance of Bible Stories"; Mason, Singleton, and Webber, "The Spirituality of Young Australians"; Michaelson, "Like a Bicycle Tire"; Potgieter, van der Walt, and Wolhuter, "The Divine Dreams"; Savina, "Soul"; Stockinger, *Dealing with Religious Difference in Kindergarten*; Tolbert and Brownlee, "The African American Church"; Ubani, "What Makes Students Feel Authentic."

34 Ubani and Tirri, "Finnish Pre-Adolescents."

35 Ibid., 357.

36 Ibid., 358, 361.

37 Ibid., 357.

38 Hammond et al., *New Methods in Religious Education Teaching.*

39 Ubani and Tirri, "Finnish Pre-Adolescents," 358.

40 Ibid., 360.

41 Ibid., 367, 368.

42 Ibid., 368.

43 Ibid.

44 Ibid., 363.

45 See, for example, Bosacki and Ota, "Preadolescents' Voices"; Keller, Camardese, and Abbas, "'We Don't Talk about That Here'"; Moore, Talwar, and Bosacki, "Canadian Children's Perceptions"; Nazar and Kouzekanani, "A Cross-Cultural Study"; Search Institute, *With Their Own Voices*. Additionally, Peter Hemming's study of spaces within children's school environments exemplifies a broad view of culture in its consideration of both a Community primary school and a Voluntary Aided Roman Catholic primary school in England as two distinct contexts for children's spiritual experiences. See Hemming, "Spaces of Spiritual Citizenship."

46 Moore, Talwar, and Bosacki, "Canadian Children's Perceptions."

47 Ibid., 217, 221.

48 Ibid., 222.

49 Ibid., 217.

50 Ibid., 218, 219.

51 Ibid., 222.

52 Ibid., 225–7.

53 Ibid., 232.
54 Ibid., 219.
55 See, for example, Couture, *Child Poverty*; Couture, *Seeing Children, Seeing God*; Mattis et al., "Ethnicity, Culture, and Spiritual Development."
56 Mercer, Matthews, and Walz, "Children in Congregations"; Mercer, *Welcoming Children.*
57 Mercer, *Welcoming Children,* 29.
58 Ibid. *Habitus* are complex milieu made up of elements from multiple cultures, communities, and social groups whose interactions form a way of life into which people are socialized.
59 Mercer, *Welcoming Children*, 31–2.
60 Ibid., 32–6.
61 Ibid., 29.
62 Ibid., 174.
63 Ibid., 98.
64 Mercer, Matthews, and Walz, "Children in Congregations."
65 Ibid., 250.
66 Ibid., 249.
67 Ibid., 252.
68 Ibid., 250.
69 Ibid., 251.
70 Ibid.
71 Ovwigho and Cole, "Making Faith Their Own."
72 Beste, "Second Graders' Spirituality," 285, 303.
73 Ibid.
74 Moore, Talwar, and Bosacki, "Canadian Children's Perceptions," 224.
75 Savina, "Soul," 56–7.
76 Thomas Reynolds explores the dynamic and relational nature of jazz performance as a lens for understanding Christian solidarity and hospitality in Reynolds, "Improvising Together."
77 Hay with Nye, *The Spirit of the Child*, 109.
78 Bosacki and Ota, "Preadolescents' Voices," 204.
79 Ibid., 213.
80 Castellano, "Updating Aboriginal Traditions of Knowledge."

CHAPTER EIGHT

1 Bourdieu, "Understanding," 614. Emphasis original.
2 Smith with Denton, *Soul Searching*, 261–2.
3 Reginald Bibby's research into adolescents in Canada demonstrates that

shifts in religious affiliation and participation among teenagers are related to and not unlike those of their parents' generation. One can surmise, then, that the religious and spiritual lives of Canadian adolescents, like those of their counterparts to the south, are influenced by their parents, even if young people seek greater freedom and choice in how they practise their faith. See Bibby with Russell and Rolheiser, *The Emerging Millennials*, and Bibby, Thiessen, and Bailey, *The Millennial Mosaic*.

4 See also Mercer, *Welcoming Children*, 174.

5 Freire, *Pedagogy of the Oppressed*, 72.

6 See Eisner, *The Educational Imagination*, 87–107.

7 Smith with Denton, *Soul Searching*, 133. Emphasis original.

Bibliography

Acolatse, Esther E. *For Freedom or Bondage? A Critique of African Pastoral Practices*. Grand Rapids, MI: Eerdmans, 2014.

Adams, Michael. *Unlikely Utopia: The Surprising Triumph of Canadian Multiculturalism*. Toronto: Penguin, 2008.

Advisory Group On Suicide Prevention. "Acting on What We Know: Preventing Youth Suicide in First Nations." Accessed 9 January 2020. http://www.hc-sc.gc.ca/fniah-spnia/alt_formats/fnihb-dgspni/pdf/pubs/suicide/prev_youth-jeunes-eng.pdf.

Airhart, Phyllis D. *A Church with the Soul of a Nation: Making and Remaking the United Church of Canada*. Montreal and Kingston: McGill-Queen's University Press, 2014.

Allen, Holly Catterton, and Christine Lawton Ross. *Intergenerational Christian Formation: Bringing the Whole Church Together in Ministry, Community and Worship*. Downers Grove, IL: InterVarsity, 2012.

Ammerman, Nancy T. "Culture and Identity in the Congregation." In *Studying Congregations: A New Handbook*, edited by Nancy T. Ammerman, Jackson W. Carroll, Carl S. Dudley, and William McKinney, 78–104. Nashville: Abingdon, 1998.

Ammerman, Nancy T., Jackson W. Carroll, Carl S. Dudley, and William McKinney. "Introduction." In *Studying Congregations: A New Handbook*, edited by Nancy T. Ammerman, Jackson W. Carroll, Carl S. Dudley, and William McKinney, 7–21. Nashville: Abingdon, 1998.

Balswick, Jack O., Pamela Ebstyne King, and Kevin S. Reimer. *The Reciprocating Self: Human Development in Theological Perspective*, 2nd ed. Downers Grove, IL: IVP Academic, 2016.

Bannerji, Himani. "Geography Lessons: On Being an Insider/Outsider to the

Canadian Nation." In *The Dark Side of the Nation: Essays on Multiculturalism, Nationalism, and Gender*, 63–86. Toronto: Canadian Scholars' Press, 2000.

Beckwith, Ivy. *Formational Children's Ministry: Shaping Children Using Story, Ritual, and Relationship*. Grand Rapids, MI: Baker, 2010.

Bellous, Joyce E., Simone de Roos, and William Summey. "The Child's Concept of God." In *Children's Spirituality: Christian Perspectives, Research, and Applications*, edited by Donald Ratcliff, 201–18. Eugene, OR: Cascade, 2004.

Berryman, Jerome W. *Children and the Theologians: Clearing the Way for Grace*. Harrisburg, PA: Morehouse, 2009.

– *Godly Play: An Imaginative Approach to Religious Education*. Minneapolis: Augsburg, 1991.

– *Teaching Godly Play: How to Mentor the Spiritual Development of Children*. Denver: Morehouse, 2009.

Beste, Jennifer. "Second Graders' Spirituality in the Context of the Sacrament of Reconciliation." In *Understanding Children's Spirituality: Theology, Research, and Practice*, edited by Kevin E. Lawson, 283–306. Eugene, OR: Cascade, 2012.

Bibby, Reginald W., with Sarah Russell and Ron Rolheiser. *The Emerging Millennials: How Canada's Newest Generation Is Responding to Change and Choice*. Lethbridge, AB: Project Canada, 2009.

Bibby, Reginald W., Joel Thiessen, and Monetta Bailey. *The Millennial Mosaic: How Pluralism and Choice Are Shaping Canadian Youth and the Future of Canada*. Toronto: Dundurn, 2019.

Bissoondath, Neil. *Selling Illusions: The Cult of Multiculturalism in Canada*. Rev. ed. Toronto: Penguin, 1994/2002.

Bosacki, Sandra, and Cathy Ota. "Preadolescents' Voices: A Consideration of British and Canadian Children's Reflections on Religion, Spirituality, and Their Sense of Self." *International Journal of Children's Spirituality* 5, no. 2 (2000): 203–19.

Bourdieu, Pierre. "Understanding." In *The Weight of the World: Social Suffering in Contemporary Society*. Translated by Priscilla Pankhurst Ferguson, 607–26. Stanford: Stanford University Press, 1999.

Boyatzis, Chris J., David C. Dollahite, and Loren D. Marks. "The Family as a Context for Religious and Spiritual Development in Children and Youth." In *The Handbook of Spiritual Development in Childhood and Adolescence*, edited by Eugene C. Roehlkepartain, Pamela Ebstyne King, Linda Wagener, and Peter L. Benson, 297–309. Thousand Oaks, CA: Sage, 2006.

Brown, Leslie, and Susan Strega. "Transgressive Possibilities." In *Research as Resistance: Critical, Indigenous, and Anti-Oppressive Approaches*, edited by Leslie Brown and Susan Strega, 1–17. Toronto: Canadian Scholars' Press, 2005.

Browning, Don S. *A Fundamental Practical Theology*. Minneapolis: Fortress, 1991.

Bunge, Marcia J., ed. *The Child in Christian Thought*. Grand Rapids, MI: Eerdmans, 2001.

Bunge, Marcia J., with Terence E. Fretheim and Beverly Roberts Gaventa, eds. *The Child in the Bible*. Grand Rapids, MI: Eerdmans, 2008.

Burnett, L.D. "To 'B' or Not to 'B': On Capitalizing the Word 'Black.'" *U.S. Intellectual History Blog*. 23 April 2016. Accessed 9 January, 2020. https://s-usih.org/2016/04/to-b-or-not-to-b-on-capitalizing-the-word-black/.

Castellano, Marlene Brant. "Updating Aboriginal Traditions of Knowledge." In *Indigenous Knowledges in Global Contexts: Multiple Readings of Our World*, edited by George J. Sefa Dei, Budd L. Hall, and Dorothy Goldin Rosenberg, 21–36. Toronto: University of Toronto Press, 2000.

Chazan, May, Lisa Helps, Anna Stanley, and Sonali Thakkar. "Introduction: Labours, Lands, Bodies." In *Home and Native Land: Unsettling Multiculturalism in Canada*, edited by May Chazan, Lisa Helps, Anna Stanley, and Sonali Thakkar, 1–11. Toronto: Between the Lines, 2011.

Cho, Hyuk. "'We Are Not Alone': Historical Journey of the United Church of Canada's Response to Becoming an Intercultural Church." *International Review of Mission* 100, no. 1 (2011): 48–61.

Clark, Cindy Dell. *In a Younger Voice: Doing Child-Centered Qualitative Research*. Oxford: Oxford University Press, 2011.

Clarke, George Elliott. "For a Multicultural, Multi-Faith, Multiracial Canada: A Manifesto." In *Home and Native Land: Unsettling Multiculturalism in Canada*, edited by May Chazan, Lisa Helps, Anna Stanley, and Sonali Thakkar, 51–7. Toronto: Between the Lines, 2011.

Coles, Robert. *The Spiritual Life of Children*. Boston: Houghton Mifflin, 1990.

Cooper-White, Pamela. *Many Voices: Pastoral Psychotherapy in Relational and Theological Perspective*. Minneapolis: Fortress, 2007.

Couture, Pamela. *Child Poverty: Love, Justice, and Social Responsibility*. St Louis: Chalice, 2007.

– *Seeing Children, Seeing God: A Practical Theology of Children and Poverty*. Nashville: Abingdon, 2000.

Csinos, David M. *Children's Ministry That Fits: Beyond One-Size-Fits-All*

Approaches to Nurturing Children's Spirituality. Eugene, OR: Wipf and Stock, 2011.

– "Jesus Loves Which Little Children? A (Canadian) Proposal for Nurturing Children's Spirituality in Intercultural Contexts." In *Exploring and Engaging Spirituality for Today's Children: A Holistic Approach*, edited by La Verne Tolbert, 307–19. Eugene, OR: Wipf and Stock, 2014.

– "A Little Child Shall Lead Them." *Sojourners* 45, no. 5 (2016): 26–9.

– "Yours, Mine, and Ours." In *Faith Forward: A Dialogue on Children, Youth, and a New Kind of Christianity*, edited by David M. Csinos and Melvin Bray, 229–40. Kelowna, BC: CopperHouse, 2013.

Csinos, David M., and Ivy Beckwith. *Children's Ministry in the Way of Jesus.* Downers Grove, IL: InterVarsity, 2013.

Day, Richard J.F. *Multiculturalism and the History of Canadian Diversity.* Toronto: University of Toronto Press, 2000.

Dei, George J. Sefa. "Spirituality in African Education: Issues, Contentions, and Contestations from a Ghanaian Case Study." *International Journal of Children's Spirituality* 7, no. 1 (2002): 37–56.

Eisner, Elliot W. *The Educational Imagination: On the Design and Evaluation of School Programs.* 3rd ed. Upper Saddle River, NJ: Merrill Prentice Hall, 2001.

Elabor-Idemudia, Patience. "Immigrant Integration in Canada: Policies, Programs and Challenges." In *Possibilities and Limitations: Multicultural Policies and Programs in Canada*, edited by Carl E. James, 58–75. Halifax: Fernwood, 2005.

Ephirim-Donker, Anthony. *African Religion Defined: A Systematic Study of Ancestor Worship among the Akan.* Lanham, MD: University Press of America, 2010.

Fennell, Rob, ed. *Intercultural Visions: Called to Be the Church.* Toronto: United Church Publishing House, 2012.

Fowler, James W. *Stages of Faith: The Psychology of Human Development and the Quest for Meaning.* San Francisco: Harper and Row, 1981.

Fowler, James W., and Mary Lynn Dell. "Stages of Faith from Infancy through Adolescence: Reflections on Three Decades of Faith Development Theories." In *The Handbook of Spiritual Development in Childhood and Adolescence*, edited by Eugene C. Roehlkepartain, Pamela Ebstyne King, Linda Wagener, and Peter L. Benson, 34–45. Thousand Oaks, CA: Sage, 2006.

Freire, Paulo. *Pedagogy of the Oppressed.* 30th anniversary ed. Translated by Myra Bergman Ramos. New York: Continuum, 2007.

Funnell-Kononuk, Emma, Pamela Dickey Young, and Valerie Michaelson.

"Adolescent Perceptions and Experiences of the Hijab – A Qualitative Canadian Study." *Journal of Childhood and Religion* 7 (2017): 1–27.

Galabuzi, Grace-Edward. "Hegemonies, Continuities, and Discontinuities of Multiculturalism and the Anglo-Franco Conformity Order." In *Home and Native Land: Unsettling Multiculturalism in Canada*, edited by May Chazan, Lisa Helps, Anna Stanley, and Sonali Thakkar, 58–82. Toronto: Between the Lines, 2011.

Garbarino, James, Frances M. Stott, and Faculty of the Erickson Institute. *What Children Can Tell Us: Eliciting, Interpreting, and Evaluating Critical Information from Children*. San Francisco: Jossey-Bass, 1992.

Greene, Sheila, and Malcolm Hill. "Researching Children's Experience: Methods and Methodological Issues." In *Researching Children's Experience: Approaches and Methods*, edited by Sheila Greene and Diane Hogan, 1–21. London: Sage, 2005.

Halliday, Adele. "Introduction: A Transformative Vision." In *Intercultural Visions: Called to Be the Church*, edited by Rob Fennell, ix–xii. Toronto: United Church Publishing House, 2012.

Hammond, J., David Hay, Jo Moxon, Brian Netto, Kathy Robson, and Ginny Staughier. *New Methods in Religious Education Teaching: An Experimental Approach*. London: Oliver and Boyd, 1990.

Hay, David with Rebecca Nye. *The Spirit of the Child*. Rev. ed. London: Jessica Kingsley, 2006.

Hayward, Victoria. *Romantic Canada*. Toronto: Macmillan, 1922.

Hemming, Peter J. "Spaces of Spiritual Citizenship: Children's Relational and Emotional Encounters with the Everyday School Environment." *International Journal of Children's Spirituality* 18, no. 1 (2013): 74–91.

Hennink, Monique M. "Language and Communication in Cross-Cultural Qualitative Research." In *Doing Cross-Cultural Research: Ethical and Methodological Perspectives*, edited by Pranee Liamputtong, 21–33. Netherlands: Springer, 2008.

Hill, Lawrence. *Black Berry, Sweet Juice: On Being Black and White in Canada*. Toronto: HarperCollins, 2001.

Hill, Malcolm. "Ethical Considerations in Researching Children's Experiences." In *Researching Children's Experience: Approaches and Methods*, edited by Sheila Greene and Diane Hogan, 61–86. London: Sage, 2005.

Holmes, Urban T., III. *A History of Christian Spirituality: An Analytical Introduction*. Harrisburg, PA: Morehouse, 2002.

Hood, Dana Kennamar. "Six Children Seeking God: Exploring Childhood Spiritual Development in Context." In *Children's Spirituality: Christian*

Perspectives, Research, and Applications, edited by Donald Ratcliff, 233–48. Eugene, OR: Cascade, 2004.

Humphrey, Natalie, Honore Hughes, and Deserie Holmes. "Understanding of Prayer among African American Children: Preliminary Themes." *Journal of Black Psychology* 34, no. 3 (2008): 309–30.

Hutchinson, Roger C. *Ethical Choices in a Pluralistic World.* Camrose, AB: The Chester Ronning Centre for the Study of Religion and Public Life, 2009.

Hwang, Mariana. "Understanding Korean-American Children's God-Concept in Relation to their Self-Concept Development." *Christian Education Journal* 2, no. 2 (2005): 282–301.

Indigenous Creative Non-Fiction Forum. "Speaking in the Round: Transcript of the Indigenous Creative Non-Fiction Forum." In *Crisp Blue Edges: Indigenous Creative Non-Fiction*, edited by Rasunah Marsden, 25–37. Penticton, BC: Theytus, 2000.

Ito, Ren. "Race, Culture, and Interculturality: A Critique of the United Church of Canada's 'Transformative Vision.'" Presentation. Toronto School of Theology Graduate Students' Association Conference, 8 March 2013.

James, Carl E. *Seeing Ourselves: Exploring Race, Ethnicity, and Culture.* 4th ed. Toronto: Thompson Educational, 2010.

Jansen, Clifford J. "Canadian Multiculturalism." In *Possibilities and Limitations: Multicultural Policies and Programs in Canada*, edited by Carl E. James, 21–33. Halifax: Fernwood, 2005.

Junker, Débora Barbosa Agra. "Resistance and Resilience: Cultivating Christian Spiritual Practices among Brazilian Children and Youth." In *Nurturing Child and Adolescent Spirituality: Perspectives from the World's Religious Traditions*, edited by Karen Marie Yust, Aostre N. Johnson, Sandy Eisenberg Sasso, and Eugene C. Roehlkepartain, 449–75. Lanham, MA: Rowman and Littlefield, 2006.

Kay, William K., and Hans-Georg Ziebertz. "A Nine-Country Survey of Youth in Europe: Selected Findings and Issues." *British Journal of Religious Education* 28, no. 2 (2006): 119–29.

Keeley, Robert J. *Helping Our Children Grow in Faith: How the Church Can Nurture the Spiritual Development of Kids.* Grand Rapids, MI: Baker, 2008.

Keller, Tina, Amy Camardese, and Randa Abbas. "'We Don't Talk about That Here': Teachers, Religion, Public Elementary Schools and the Embodiment of Silence: A Binational United States and Israel Study." *Journal of Childhood and Religion* 7 (2017): 1–42.

Keränen-Pantsu, Raili and Martin Ubani. "The Holistic and Spiritual Relevance of Bible Stories among Finnish 10-Year-Old Pupils: A Classroom Case Study." *International Journal of Children's Spirituality* 23, no. 2 (2018): 136–51.

King, Thomas. *The Truth about Stories: A Native Narrative*. Toronto: Anansi, 2003.

Kluckhohn, Clyde, and Henry A. Murray. "Personality Formation: The Detriments." In *Personality in Nature, Society, and Culture*, edited by Clyde Kluckhohn and Henry A. Murray, 35–48. New York: Knopf, 1949.

Lartey, Emmanuel Y. *In Living Color: An Intercultural Approach to Pastoral Care and Counselling*. 2nd ed. London: Jessica Kingsley, 2003.

– *Pastoral Counselling in Inter-Cultural Perspective: A Study of Some African (Ghanaian) and Anglo-American Views of Human Existence and Counselling*. Frankfurt am Maim: Peter Lang, 1987.

– *Postcolonializing God: New Perspectives of Pastoral and Practical Theology*. London: SCM, 2013.

Lawrence-Lightfoot, Sara, and Jessica Hoffmann Davis. *The Art and Science of Portraiture*. San Francisco: Jossey-Bass, 1997.

Leman, Mark. "Canadian Multiculturalism." Political and Social Affairs Division. Last modified 15 February 1999. Accessed 9 January 2020. http://publications.gc.ca/Collection-R/LoPBdP/CIR/936-e.htm#A.

Liamputtong, Pranee. "Doing Research in a Cross-Cultural Context: Methodological and Ethical Challenges." In *Doing Cross-Cultural Research: Ethical and Methodological Perspectives*, edited by Pranee Liamputtong, 3–20. Netherlands: Springer, 2008.

– *Performing Qualitative Cross-Cultural Research*. Cambridge: Cambridge University Press, 2010.

Mager, Robert. "Do We Learn to Know God from What We Do? A Plea for a Relational Concept of Action." In *Pathways to the Public Square: Practical Theology in an Age of Pluralism*, edited by Elaine Grahame and Anna Rowlands, 191–201. Münster: LIT, 2005.

Mason, Michael, Andrew Singleton, and Ruth Webber. "The Spirituality of Young Australians." *International Journal of Children's Spirituality* 12, no. 2 (2007): 149–63.

Mattis, Jacqueline S., Muninder K. Ahluwalia, Sheri-Ann E. Cowie, and Aria M. Kirkland-Harris. "Ethnicity, Culture, and Spiritual Development." In *The Handbook of Spiritual Development in Childhood and Adolescence*, edited by Eugene C. Roehlkepartain, Pamela Ebstyne King, Linda Wagener, and Peter L. Benson, 283–96. Thousand Oaks, CA: Sage, 2006.

May, Scottie, Beth Posterski, Catherine Stonehouse, and Linda Cannell.

Children Matter: Celebrating Their Place in the Church, Family, and Community. Grand Rapids, MI: Eerdmans, 2005.

Mbiti, John S. *African Religions and Philosophy.* 2nd ed. Oxford: Heinemann, 1989.

Mercer, Joyce Ann. *Welcoming Children: A Practical Theology of Childhood.* St Louis: Chalice, 2005.

Mercer, Joyce Ann, Deborah L. Matthews, and Scott Walz. "Children in Congregations: Congregations as Contexts for Children's Spiritual Growth." In *Children's Spirituality: Christian Perspectives, Research, and Applications*, edited by Donald Ratcliff, 249–65. Eugene, OR: Cascade, 2004.

Merriam, Sharan B., Juanita Johnson-Bailey, Ming-Yeh Lee, Youngwha Kee, Gabo Ntseane, and Mazanah Muhammad. "Power and Positionality: Negotiating Insider/Outsider Status within and across Cultures." *International Journal of Lifelong Education* 20, no. 5 (2001): 405–16.

Michaelson, Valerie. "Like a Bicycle Tire: Lived Experiences of the Spiritual Worlds of Canadian Adolescents." Paper presented at the Childhood Studies and Religion Unit of the American Academy of Religion, Denver, CO, 19 November 2018.

Miller-McLemore, Bonnie J. *Let the Children Come: Reimagining Childhood from a Christian Perspective.* San Francisco: Jossey-Bass, 2003.

Moore, Kelsey, Victoria Talwar, and Sandra Bosacki. "Canadian Children's Perceptions of Spirituality: Diverse Voices." *International Journal of Children's Spirituality* 17, no. 3 (2012): 217–34.

Moschella, Mary Clark. *Ethnography as a Pastoral Practice: An Introduction.* Cleveland: Pilgrim, 2008.

Mountain, Vivienne. "Four Links between Child Theology and Children's Spirituality." *International Journal of Children's Spirituality* 16, no. 3 (2011): 291–305.

Nazar, Fatima, and Kamiar Kouzekanani. "A Cross-Cultural Study of Children's Perceptions of Selected Religious Concepts (Kuwait, the United States, and India)." *Alberta Journal of Education* 49, no. 2 (2003).

Ng, David, and Virginia Thomas. *Children in the Worshipping Community.* Atlanta: John Knox, 1981.

Ng, Greer Anne Wenh-In. "The United Church of Canada: A Church Fittingly National." In *Christianity and Ethnicity in Canada*, edited by Paul Bramadat and David Seljak, 204–46. Toronto: University of Toronto Press, 2008.

Ng, Greer Anne Wenh-In., ed. *Our Roots, Our Lives: Glimpses of Faith and Life from Black and Asian Canadian Women.* Toronto: United Church Publishing House, 2003.

– *That All May Be One: A Resource for Educating toward Racial Justice.* Toronto: United Church of Canada, 2004.

Nydam, Ronald. "Early Adolescence: Venturing toward a Different World." In *Human Development and Faith: Life-Cycle Stages of Body, Mind, and Soul*, edited by Felicity B. Kelcourse, 205–22. St Louis: Chalice, 2004.

Osmer, Richard R. *Practical Theology: An Introduction.* Grand Rapids, MI: Eerdmans, 2008.

Ovwigho, Pamela Caudill, and Arnold Cole. "Making Faith Their Own: Lessons for Children's Ministry from Kids' Reflections on Their Spiritual Lives." In *Exploring and Engaging Spirituality for Today's Children: A Holistic Approach*, edited by La Verne Tolbert, 158–69. Eugene, OR: Wipf and Stock, 2014.

Perlman, Merrill. "Black and White: Why Capitalization Matters." *Columbia Journalism Review.* 23 June 2015. Accessed 9 January, 2020. http://www.cjr.org/analysis/language_corner_1.php.

Popock, Michael, and Joseph Henriques. *Cultural Change and Your Church: Helping Your Church Thrive in a Diverse Society*. Eugene, OR: Wipf and Stock, 2002.

Potgieter, Ferdinand J., Johannes L. van der Walt, and Charl C. Wolhuter. "The Divine Dreams of a Sample of South African Children: The Gateway to their Spirituality." *International Journal of Children's Spirituality* 14, no. 1 (2009): 31–46.

Priestly, Jack. "A Brief Introduction to the Notion of the Spiritual." International Association for Children's Spirituality. Accessed 1 June 2016. http://www.childrenspirituality.org/documents/notionOfTheSpiritual.pdf.

Reynolds, Thomas E. "Improvising Together: Christian Solidarity and Hospitality as Jazz Performance." *Journal of Ecumenical Studies* 43, no. 1 (2008): 45–66.

Rizzuto, Ana-Maria. *The Birth of the Living God: A Psychoanalytic Study.* Chicago: University of Chicago Press, 1979.

Ryan, Phil. *Multicultiphobia.* Toronto: University of Toronto Press, 2010.

Sasso, Sandy Eisenberg. *Cain and Abel: Finding the Fruits of Peace.* Woodstock, VT: Jewish Lights, 2001.

Savina, Elena. "Soul: What Does It Mean for Russian Children?" *International Journal of Children's Spirituality* 6, no. 1 (2001): 55–65.

Schmidt, Susannah. *Ending Racial Harassment: Creating Healthy Congregations.* Toronto: United Church of Canada, 2008.

Search Institute. *With Their Own Voices: A Global Exploration of How Today's Young People Experience and Think about Spiritual Development.*

Minneapolis: Center for Spiritual Development in Childhood and Adolescence, 2008.

Ship, Susan Judith. "Citizens of the State but not Members of the Nation: The Politics of Language and Culture in the Construction of Minorities." In *Possibilities and Limitations: Multicultural Policies and Programs in Canada*, edited by Carl E. James, 76–90. Halifax: Fernwood, 2005.

Smith, Christian, with Melinda Lundquist Denton. *Soul Searching: The Religious and Spiritual Lives of American Teenagers*. Oxford: Oxford University Press, 2005.

Stockinger, Helena. *Dealing with Religious Difference in Kindergarten: An Ethnographic Study in Religiously Affiliated Institutions*. Münster: Waxmann, 2018.

Tanner, Kathryn. *Theories of Culture: A New Agenda for Theology*. Minneapolis: Augsburg Fortress, 1997.

Tisdale, Leonora Tubbs. *Preaching as Local Theology and Folk Art*. Minneapolis: Fortress, 1997.

Tolbert, La Verne, and Marilyn Brownlee. "The African American Church and Its Role in Nurturing the Spiritual Development of Children." In *Nurturing Children's Spirituality: Christian Perspectives and Best Practices*, edited by Holly Catterton Allen, 320–38. Eugene, OR: Cascade, 2008.

Ubani, Martin. "What Makes Students Feel Authentic in an Integrated RE Classroom?" *Journal of Beliefs and Values* 39, no. 2 (2018): 169–81.

Ubani, Martin, and Kirsi Tirri. "How Do Finnish Pre-Adolescents Perceive Religion and Spirituality?" *International Journal of Children's Spirituality* 11, no. 3 (2006): 357–70.

United Church of Canada. *Circle and Cross: Dialogue Planning Tool*. Toronto: United Church of Canada, 2008.

– "Intercultural Ministries: A Process of Church-Wide Transformation (Interim Report)." Report to the 40th General Council of The United Church of Canada. 2009. *Record of Proceedings*. Kelowna, BC: The United Church of Canada, 2009.

– "A Transformative Vision for the United Church of Canada." Report to the 39th General Council of The United Church of Canada. 2006. *Record of Proceedings*. Thunder Bay: The United Church of Canada, 2006.

United Church of Canada, ed. *A Healing Journey for Us All: Uncovering the Wounds of Empire*. Toronto: United Church of Canada, 2006.

van der Ven, Johannes A. *Practical Theology: An Empirical Approach*. Kampen: Pharos, 1993.

Walcott, Rinaldo. "Disgraceful: Intellectual Dishonesty, White Anxieties, and Multicultural Critique Thirty-Six Years Later." In *Home and Native Land: Unsettling Multiculturalism in Canada*, edited by May Chazan, Lisa Helps, Anna Stanley, and Sonali Thakkar, 15–30. Toronto: Between the Lines, 2011.

Westcott, Helen L., and Karen S. Littleton. "Exploring Meaning in Interviews with Children." In *Researching Children's Experience: Approaches and Methods*, edited by Sheila Greene and Diane Hogan, 141–57. London: Sage, 2005.

Westerhoff, John H., III. "Formation, Education, Instruction." *Religious Education* 82, no. 4 (1987): 579–91.

– *Will Our Children Have Faith?* Rev. ed. Harrisburg, PA: Morehouse, 2000.

Wigg-Stevenson, Natalie. *Ethnographic Theology: An Inquiry into the Production of Theological Knowledge*. New York: Palgrave Macmillan, 2014.

– "Faith in My Bones: An Exercise in Ethnographic Theology." PhD diss., Vanderbilt University, 2011. https://etd.library.vanderbilt.edu//available/etd-07212011-110912/unrestricted/Dissertation.pdf.

Wilson, Shawn. *Research is Ceremony: Indigenous Research Methods*. Halifax: Fernwood, 2008.

Yust, Karen Marie. *Real Kids, Real Faith: Practices for Nurturing Children's Spiritual Lives*. San Francisco: Jossey-Bass, 2004.

Index

www.ingramcontent.com/pod-product-compliance
Lightning Source LLC
LaVergne TN
LVHW092152181025
823752LV00005BA/21